Erhard Meyer-Galow
Business Ethics 3.0

Erhard Meyer-Galow

Business Ethics 3.0

The New Integral Ethics from the Perspective
of a CEO

DE GRUYTER
OLDENBOURG

Erhard Meyer-Galow
www.business-ethics-3.com

ISBN 978-3-11-057228-5
e-ISBN (PDF) 978-3-11-057229-2
e-ISBN (EPUB) 978-3-11-057242-1

Library of Congress Control Number: 2018934554

Bibliographic information published by the Deutsche Nationalbibliothek
The Deutsche Nationalbibliothek lists this publication in the Deutsche Nationalbibliografie;
detailed bibliographic data are available on the Internet at http://dnb.dnb.de.

© 2018 Walter de Gruyter GmbH, Berlin/Boston
Cover illustration: Erhard Meyer-Galow
Typestting: Integra Software Services Pvt. Ltd.
Assistant Editor: Richard Warrington
Printing and binding: CPI books GmbH, Leck

www.degruyter.com

Business Ethics 3.0, by Erhard Meyer-Galow provides a much needed beacon of light to a segment of our society that seem to be sinking deeper and deeper into darkness. The term "business ethics", once an important topic within the business community, has slowly descended through the fog of profitable ends justifying unprincipled means to become nothing more than a self-contradictory oxymoron – especially among large international corporations. In *Business Ethics 3.0*, Erhard Meyer-Galow has taken a fresh approach that appeals to individual personal growth rather than the usual proffering of academic arguments that are not implementable in the real world of relentless Machiavellian competition. Only through raising and improving individual awareness and responsibility can real long-term change have a chance of developing. *Business Ethics 3.0* is on the right track with a positive and compelling message...may it succeed where the academics have failed.

— Thomas Campbell, physicist, consciousness researcher, author of My big TOE

Acknowledgments

I gratefully acknowledge the considerable historical work of C.G. Jung and Erich Neumann and the ongoing efforts of the HH The Dalai Lama, who have contributed immensely to increasing our understanding and raising our consciousness to the importance of moral decisions and ethical practices in our personal and professional lives.

> In 1948, C.G. *Jung* wrote the following to Erich *Neumann* in a letter. "I have read your book *Depth Psychology and a New Ethic* once more. Again it made a very strong impression on me and with that gave me the certainty that its effect would be like a bomb. Your formulations are brilliant and of piercing precision; they are challenging and aggressive, an *avant-garde* in open country where, alas, nothing was visible before ... Already your title *New Ethic* is a fanfare: '*aux armes citoyens!*' ... Your book will be a *petra scandali*, but also the most powerful impulse for future developments ..." (Neumann 1990, p. 9).

> C.G. Jung stated that the "psychology of the unconscious leads to an esoteric form of ethics" (Jung 1959).

> Young people today have many more opportunities to get to know each other globally – and they would be wise to take advantage of them, working to improve the world. Compassion and love have been neglected far too much in education. We can and must change that *now* (Paraphrased from the Dalai Lama and Alt 2016, p. 20).

> The most important question we can ask in order to improve the world is "How can we serve each other?" "To make that shift, we need to sharpen our awareness ... Meditation is more important than ritualized prayer. Children must learn the importance of morals and ethics, that learning being more important than any religion" (Edited from the Dalai Lama and Alt 2016, p. 25).

I sincerely thank Dr. Michaela Haase of The Freie Universität Marketing Department, Berlin, Germany, along with Professor Dr. Claus Dierksmeier, Academic Director, and Katharina Hoegl of the Global Ethics Institute at the University of Tübingen, Germany, for the inspiration to write this book.

Heartfelt thanks go to my teachers: Karlfried Graf Dürckheim for the initial encouragement to strive for inner wisdom, Willigis Jäger for my extensive Zen-instruction, Walter Schwery for my tuition in Depth Psychology, and Lance Owens, Henning Weyerstrass and Dr. Thomas Arzt for the inspiration arising from their introduction to the *Red Book* of Carl Gustaf Jung. I am also grateful to Thomas Campbell for facilitating powerful, personal experiences based upon the Natural Sciences.

I am indebted to Dr. Andreas Bell, Armin Peter Bode, Inge Brose-Müller, Dr. Klaus Engel, Professor Dr. Friedrich Gaede, Dr. Inge Kader, Professor Dr. Peter Knauer SJ and Dr. Barbara Schmidt for their important contributions. Judi Neal's exchange of thoughts and personal experiences on transformation along with her invitation to author a chapter in her *Handbook of Personal and Organizational Transformation* were tremendously helpful and appreciated. Dr. Günter Stahl made an invaluable contribution by generously sharing his considerable knowledge of relevant literature.

https://doi.org/10.1515/9783110572292-201

I extend personal appreciation to my sons and my daughter: Patrick, who created the great title, Philipp, who contributed an important perspective from the experience of a young professional, with his essay "The CEO of the Future," and Kathrin for sharing and discussing with me her experience and wisdom gained from Karlfried Graf Dürckheim's collected works.

Profound thanks and appreciation to my wife Nora for her support and patience when I was so often absorbed in the writing this book.

Finally, Richard Warrington, editor of this book, who not only improved my English and my presentation style but also supported me tremendously through the contribution of his knowledge, experience and insights into subtleties contained within the content.

Erhard Meyer-Galow
January 2018

Foreword

Capital knows no morality. This was never more clearly demonstrated than by the financial crisis of 2007–08, which illustrated that trust placed in the invisible hand of the market is misplaced. For 30 years, the economic consensus has been that the free market system is intrinsically reliable and stable. The theory has been that if each individual acts rationally and follows his own economic aims, then under ideal market conditions opportunities will be created which will be of benefit to everyone. However, people do not always behave rationally, intelligently or wisely. Adam Smith's theory overlooked the fact that people are often driven by noneconomic motivations, are prone to irrational behavior and can embrace a destructive dream. In short, as well as being rational beings, people also follow their "animal spirits," often resulting in contradictions, ambiguity and uncertainty (Akerlof and Shiller 2009).

Following the financial crisis, many governments attempted to control the financial markets through additional regulations. It was assumed to be self-evident that this was necessary. New rules were deemed to be essential in order to force the markets to behave more responsibly in order to win back trust in the economic system; a trust which had been shattered.

Rules, and regulations regarding their application, are as essential within large corporations as they are within society at large. With compliance guidelines, corruption and lack of transparency can be minimized, monopoly laws can prevent consumers and competitors from being disadvantaged by price fixing, while environmental protection laws safeguard the future of our planet. Companies are bound by many rules intended to establish the framework within which they work. In our social market economy, this constitutes the basis for our economic success.

As important as laws, legislation and regulations are, not every action can be controlled by establishing new rules. Too much bureaucracy stifles creativity and motivation. It is therefore important that we encourage personal responsibility and emphasize the importance of those ethical principles which form the very heart of the spirit of entrepreneurship. While a lack of trust as a result of the financial crisis lingers, the self-regulating systems in the free markets are still operational. As business leaders, we must begin to listen to our inner voice and be guided by our ethical compass; that sense of justice which arises from the intuitive aspect of our mind.

In this book, Professor Dr. Meyer-Galow has compiled an impressive compendium, drawing upon a comprehensive range of sources which affect our personal decisions and behavior. He shows, most convincingly, that in addition to laws and guidelines there are other powerful resources: from religion and philosophy to psychoanalysis and spirituality, all of which inspire integrated and ethical practices in business. From Aristotle to the Dalai Lama, from Pope Francis to the psychologist C.G.

https://doi.org/10.1515/9783110572292-202

Jung, the author takes us on a journey which reveals a rich panorama of the sources of our ethical decisions. This book shares a treasure chest of experience from which students and managers can take daily inspiration on their way to facing, accepting and taming their hidden "animal spirits."

Dr. Klaus Engel, Ex-CEO Evonik Industries AG, Essen, Germany

Contents

1 Introduction

None of us has unfailingly applied the highest ethical practices in either our personal or our professional lives. We are all guilty of lapses in morality, be they deliberate or unintentional. Sometimes our thoughts, words or actions have contributed to others taking upon themselves the experiences of disappointment and anger. In hindsight, we often deeply regret those occasions, realizing that greater empathy and compassion would have better served all of us, along with our common goals. We are fortunate that maturation is generally accompanied by an increase in mindfulness, a quality which allows us insight into ourselves, helping us to thwart inappropriate thoughts, words or actions in time to avoid behaviors which our seductive dark side, our ego's ally, informs us will massage our ego and further our personal agenda. Mindfulness encourages us to choose actions which are in accord with our *actual self*, that intuition within all of us which encourages more empathetic behavior. Thoughts, words and actions arising from our *actual self* are the antithesis of those encouraged by our ego, which is formed by an accumulation of our superficially pleasurable experiences.

This book makes no pretense of being a comprehensive study of the benefits of moral decisions or ethical practices. The wish is simply to encourage personal psychological and spiritual evolution with the confidence that it will lead to a reevaluation of ethical business practices, something which will benefit both employers and employees. *A New Ethic*, such as that espoused by Erich Neumann (Neumann 1990) is well established and defended in the literature, but not yet so well understood or established in our personal consciousness. Despite the profusion of books, articles, seminars and forums on ethics, with new keywords and pervasive ethical guidelines presented as *Corporate Social Responsibility*, *Shared Value* practices and *Governance Ethics* becoming fashionable, we continue to hear, almost daily, reports of unethical practices, many of which appear to be stretching the boundaries of insensitivity, actions almost completely devoid of compassion and common sense. Ruthlessness in business has increased dramatically during the past 20 years. Globalization and digitization allow for far greater damage to be unleashed far more quickly than ever before. We must conclude that current policies aimed at turning around this rush toward destructive, self-centered practices are insufficient. Attempts at remedial approaches are diluted due to a lack of recognition of personal responsibility, of insufficient attention to spiritual maturity. It is far simpler to acquire ego-centered knowledge, of which much is available, than to embrace intuitive knowing and acting, of which little is in evidence. As a result, societal credibility in the area of ethical business practices, in spite of well-meaning interventionist efforts, is on the decline.

An academic understanding of ethical business practices without actually applying them is not going to pay dividends. One must transcend ego-centered *knowledge* with intuitive, spiritual-centered *knowing*. Then, and only then will ethical practices become manifest in our personal and professional life and begin to catapult, each

https://doi.org/10.1515/9783110572292-001

step building upon the one before, each success multiplying the following, resulting in a degree of satisfaction which will make it difficult to believe that we procrastinated implementing something so obviously beneficial, for so long.

What criteria may best establish our decisions around behaving responsibly in economic endeavors? Many criteria from the past are no longer morally acceptable, economical or defensible in the present. The paradigm shift initiated and fueled by the globalization of information available from the internet promises even further quantum shifts in the evolution of managing both responsibly and economically. This shift necessitates not merely *tinkering with the existing machine*, but rather completely re-thinking, reevaluating and re-defining that which is of fundamental importance to us. Consideration of the human factor leads us to morally defensible practices; those which value and promote individual growth and contributions. This in turn encourages us to tap into far-too-long ignored ideas, support and excitement from those who were previously often viewed simply as impractical economic philosophers. How will we decide to proceed? Profit at any cost, or ethical, efficient, economical business practices which result in even greater profitability? We need to find a way to win back our credibility and trust as managers and entrepreneurs. Perhaps C. G. Jung's and Erich Neumann's new ethics approach (Neumann 1990) can help us to better understand the causes of individual immoral decisions and unethical behavior, and to propose practical approaches which will lead us to beneficial changes.

This book is intended to create a desire for change in both our conception and our application of ethical business practices.

2 The Problem

2.1 The Burden of an Anachronistic Economic System

In my early professional life practices which are unthinkable today were common. When our work environment condones, or even encourages questionable practices, it is difficult, as a young professional, to stand against the accepted norm. While my personal and professional conduct may not have always been impeccable, I have not intentionally betrayed others for personal gain. It is fortunate that moral and ethical awareness evolves over time, both within us as individuals, and within society at large. Unfortunately, in spite of greater personal and societal awareness, immoral decisions and unethical practices remain entrenched in many workplaces. **Making them especially dangerous is that like an iceberg only about one-sixth of them are readily evident.**

Behind all immorality in the economy lies the irrational fear that our business opportunities, the performance of our employees or some other *uncontrolled* factor will cause our profits to decline. This fear breeds greed! Those managers who suffer from low self-esteem are seeking greater recognition through implementing greater controls, and those managers who possess an exaggerated self-worth are fearful of failure as their ego wishes to demonstrate it is infallible. In either case, bolstered by their deluded belief that they are acting in the best interests of the company, there is often no sense of injustice with the immoral policies and unethical practices being regarded as trivial. But failure is immanent, as are the resulting burn out, depression and debilitating anxiety.

Meanwhile, if a manager's unethical behavior becomes public knowledge and the media find a story they can sell, there is a short period of turmoil, but it is short lived. Time heals all wounds and the consumers are soon once again lining up to buy the offending companies' products or services.

2.1.1 Falsifying Balance Sheets

Balance sheet fraud is a form of economic crime. What is a balance sheet? Ideally a balance sheet itemizes the complete assets and liabilities of a company. As the legal requirements differ from country to country, it is difficult to accurately compare balance sheets internationally, or to determine how well they comply with the appropriate legal requirements. This makes it tempting to "fudge" valuation approaches, resulting in the raising or lowering of individual balance sheet items in order to overestimate the particular company's worth.

The internationalization of German companies has been growing, and as a result German companies are increasingly being evaluated according to the Anglo-Saxon accounting rules which have been adopted in Germany in recent years. This makes it increasingly difficult to compare international balance sheets with German balance

https://doi.org/10.1515/9783110572292-002

sheets in accordance with the German Stock Corporation Act, that dictates of which are now often not taken into account. However, not every aspect of the Anglo-Saxon accounting rules is acceptable in Germany; it is a legal obligation for German companies to be evaluated and accounted for under the German Stock Corporation Act. In Germany, creditor protection is the first priority, followed closely by the tax assessment of the value of the company. In Anglo-Saxon countries shareholder interest has first priority. International accounting can only be recognized in Germany if it does not run counter to the dictates and intentions of the German Stock Corporation Act. Two examples of where the differences come under careful scrutiny are accounting practices which affect pension provisions, and how the actual value of assets is determined. In the USA the current value of assets is recorded, while in Germany the acquisition cost of assets is determined and then corrected by amortization.

In general, the greater a company's assets are the greater the profit is and the higher the taxes assessed. If a company owns assets which it fails to list on the asset side of its annual balance sheet the result will be a tax saving.

Because creditor balances are regularly confirmed by auditors the opportunity for falsifying records is less on the debt side of the balance sheet. But never underestimate the creative ways in which balance sheets can be manipulated! Companies sometimes transfer assets to holding companies, with the parent company retaining only up to 49% of the shares. The parent company is only obligated to consolidate on their balance sheets holding companies in which they own more than 50% of the shares, effectively allowing them to shelter numerous valuable assets from taxation. Operating losses can also be manipulated by "selling" assets to an unconsolidated holding company at a higher than market price.

Ultimately the economic foundation of a society is undermined by the balance sheet fraud.

2.1.2 Bank Account Manipulation

Traditionally, auditors examined a company's bank statements, then the company's commercial banks were asked to confirm the company's balance at the end of the year. In this way the validity of a company's bookkeeping practices could be determined. But a company could have bank accounts "off-shore" which are known only to the Executive Board. In these cases even auditors are powerless to detect such fraudulent practices. Fortunately, this loop hole has recently been largely closed.

2.1.3 Inventory

All companies must create an annual inventory. This allows for an annual determination of assets. Fixed assets must then be reevaluated every five years. But how are they evaluated? Therein lies the possibility for manipulation and deception. If acquisition value is used as a basis, how is the actual acquisition value of thousands, or tens of thousands of products purchased each year determined? Sometime the LIFO (last in first out) procedure is used and sometimes the FIFO (first in first out) procedure is applied.

There are numerous opportunities for manipulation of the net worth of a company's assets. Auditors can only confirm what they can see. It is relatively easy to withhold essential information from them. There may be inventory which is not obvious, or a shortage of inventory in a company with both retail and consignment outlets. The greater the declared inventory the healthier the company appears to currently be, but what if prices fall? Then the following year the company appears to have suffered greater losses than it actually did. It is highly unlikely, in spite of industry guidelines, that most inventories are an accurate reflection of assets. It is entirely possible, given today's general acceptance of profit at any cost to society, that company directors do not even believe their actions are unethical. But any intention to deceive, no matter how universally "acceptable" it may have become, is immoral.

Even with diligent and meticulous reporting a company can become bankrupt if revenues do not cover expenses. But if the assets are over evaluated insolvency proceedings may be delayed. This is a common occurrence. The delay may be deliberate, for example when the Board of Directors are hoping for a rise in prices or for sales to improve so that the company can recover. It is also often the case that underwriting banks don't call in debts until the company is in dire straits, with insufficient inventory to make sufficient sales to remain solvent.

2.1.4 Illegal Price Fixing

When I began my career as sales representative in the 1970s, the director of sales routinely informed us about his price agreements with competitors, further telling us to which customers we should offer special prices, and to which we should not. We did not consider this behavior to be unethical. Now, almost 50 years later no one can argue ignorance of the price fixing laws. In spite of this, illegal price fixing remains pervasive.

The following is a list of some of the largest cartel antitrust penalties in the EU: Truck cartel, Google cartel preference, Libor cartel, TV tube cartel, car glass cartel, gas market sharing, Intel discounts, elevator and escalator cartel, rolling bearings cartel, vitamin cartel, airfreight cartel, cartel for gas insulated switch gear, wax cartel, butadiene rubber cartel, flat glass cartel, pre-stressing steel cartel, gypsum board cartel, sanitary cartel, bleaching agents cartel, sausage cartel, beer cartel, cement cartel, detergent cartel, zipper cartel, high-voltage cable cartel, sugar cartel, carbon fiber cartel, chloroprene rubber cartel, liquid gas cartel, food retailers and brand

manufacturers cartel, acrylic glass cartel, rail cartel, graphite cartel, graphite elec-
trode cartel and carbon brush cartel.

Many of the best known and respected companies dealing in the above products
and services have been involved in price fixing.

2.1.5 Bribes

In many countries and numerous businesses payment of a bribe is commonly necessary in order to close a sale or purchase. It can be difficult to differentiate between a
commission payment and a bribe. Commissions as a compensation for reliable and
acceptable services in connection with a deal are normally in the range of 1–5%.
Bribes are generally much higher, and reflect a personal relationship between a supplier and a consumer with the intention of excluding competitors. This is immoral.
If the supplier is overpricing the product and then paying a bribe out of the excess,
the customer is ultimately disadvantaged. Since competitors are excluded, they are
also disadvantaged.

In Germany, up until the middle of the 1990s bribes could be listed as expenses
in a company's *Profit and Loss Statement*. Beginning in the latter half of the 1990s,
companies were compelled to disclose the recipients of bribes, which remained legal
until January of 2002, when they became illegal. Regardless, there can be no doubt
that bribes continue to play an active role in the business world in the closing of deals
with targeted, preferred buyers.

Not all bribes are paid in cash. There are also numerous non-cash benefits which
are offered to selectively secure business deals.

2.2 Existing Conceptualizations of Ethics Are Insufficient

Business Ethics 1.0 (Gill 2010) was largely practiced as damage control. It considered
the criteria which must constitute an ethics agenda and encouraged us to direct our
attention and energy toward the management of specific crises, dilemmas and related
ethical misdemeanors.

Business Ethics 2.0 (Gill 2010) was more proactive, prompting us toward a clar-
ification of the vision and the mission around a more philosophically based set of
ethical guidelines and ethics training.

A lack of ethical practices in the marketplace, even with Corporate Social
Responsibility (CSR 2.0) embedded as a part of Business Ethics 2.0, leads us to the
observation that we have made, at best, only marginal advances toward a New Ethic,
one which encompasses sustainable moral decisions and subsequent ethical business practices. Clearly something vital is still missing.

There are currently many initiatives which embrace spirituality as the missing link, which if adopted would allow us to conceptualize a more holistic model for the governance of ethics in the economy. This movement is referred to as "Spiritual Based Ethics," and is a welcome step in a positive direction. But reflecting upon my business life of almost 40 years, 20 of which were spent as a senior manager, I doubt that the people in positions of authority in our business enterprises are willing or capable of quickly initiating the necessary personal transformation which would encourage the embracing of ethical business practices by simply being asked to explore and accept spirituality as a directing force in their lives. Until we have welcomed spirituality into our *being*, into our *essential self*, we cannot experience its benefits, and thus cannot understand the need for it, the desirability of embracing it, or the advantages which inevitably arise from it. There are those who have intellectually explored spiritual practices, but this too often results in an ongoing "spiritual flight." The practice of spiritual exercises which simply involve our rational ego mind does not protect us from the temptations arising from our "dark side" when we are stressed by the competitive demands of managing our niche in the marketplace. Spirituality *per se* is not *the* missing link, but rather *a* missing link.

What else is missing then?

First, it is necessary that those of us working in the economic sector of society understand that practices built upon immoral foundations or unethical practices can never result in lasting personal or professional success or satisfaction.

Second, we must realize that it is not possible to live and manage in a morally and ethically defensible fashion by simply following an externally imposed set of rules.

Third, it is essential that we recognize that a sustainable morality resulting in ethical practices can never be realized while we remain obsessed with our energy-draining focus upon striving for success and wealth at any cost. It is only the inner peace, stability and balance in our life, which arises from the awakening of our awareness of our inner dimension, which can lead us toward unfailingly ethical practices. Once we begin to tap into this inner resource we are able to establish a satisfying, peaceful work/life balance, one which leads to lasting inner peace and freedom. This personal inner satisfaction in turn allows us to find the resilience to withstand the temptations of the outer world, by buffering us against acting in a self-serving fashion which ultimately leads to anxiety, stress and suffering.

We must also consider the fascinating discoveries resulting from research in quantum physics. Almost one hundred years after Werner Heisenberg's theory and its experimental validation we are becoming increasingly aware of how the holistic nature of reality, something previously espoused by only a few mystics, has now become mainstream, with significant implications for our personal lives; specifically with how we now regard our spiritual interconnectedness with all of creation. Quantum physics focus is on interconnectedness, creativity, nonduality and nonlinearity. This recognition of a functioning, practical reality, which was previously largely unrecognized, has a major impact upon ethical considerations.

Finally, and perhaps the catalyst which will energetically unite the previous considerations allowing us to understand the individual who desires to be good but all of a sudden acts in an unexpectedly immoral fashion is C.G. Jung's and Erich Neumann's Depth Psychology (Neumann 1990). Our individual, suppressed and repressed dark side is blocking our good and bright side from manifesting. As much as we may wish to live only in the light, we encompass both light and dark. The integration of our dark side is fundamental to the development of the "*SELF*," as Jung calls it. Our bright side and inner growth must be encouraged and strengthened so as to be able to encompass, accommodate and integrate our dark side. In the absence of inner growth we become victims of intrinsic attacks by our own "Dark Brother/Sister" aspect, in addition to extrinsic attacks by other individuals.

Our ego mind has become so dominant that we have separated ourselves from our inner sources, our most important roots, especially our intuition. We must heal ourselves in order to be able to embrace ethical practices in a sustainable fashion. **An essential step toward this healing is reestablishing the connection to our soul and to our spirit.**

This book will help us to understand why an ethical approach based upon moral reason, rather than upon the ego-based rational mind, or upon any of the many various philosophical approaches advanced since Aristotle's time, or upon any given theology which embraces a particular religion, or upon spirituality *per se* has been unable to substantially alter the ethical behavior of either the individual or the collective.

The generalized immoral decisions resulting in the unethical behavior currently rampant in society is evidence that all of the books, numerous appeals, guidelines and serious protestations for a sustainable ethical approach which is directed by moral decisions have had no discernable effect upon individuals or the economy. If my teacher Karlfried Graf Dürckheim were still alive he would make the following observation:

> It helps little to constantly preach about collective ethics and morality, when the individuals that make up this collective are stuck in their rational one-sided egocentricity which constantly blocks our actual purpose in life, our individuation, and our balance of body, ego mind, soul and spirit necessary to become a completely holistic person. The human in the Anthropocene has no consciousness of this aberration. He has completed the separation from the numinous. Therefore, as we do not know why we are suffering, we cannot build the bridges to our soul that could lead us to the unconscious wherein lies the huge energy and creative potential which could expand our severely restricted consciousness. We have destabilized and weakened ourselves and now we are asked to entertain the upholding of morality and ethics. It is even all the more difficult when we are also suppressing our dark side, repressing it into the shadow out of which it then again and again bursts forth, expressing itself societally in an immoral, unethical fashion.

Only when we painfully experience this failure in a serious life crisis can we make our way back, reestablishing the connection to our psychic and spiritual dimension.

But this turning point in our life presupposes an initiation in the form of a personal insight. Only then can our inner growth develop, integrating our dark side into our SELF and by so doing bring it under our control. To accomplish this may well necessitate daily meditative exercises over many years. But it is *only* when this integration has occurred that we will increasingly embrace a sustainable ethic based upon morally defensible decisions. Not simply because we wish to, but because we cannot do otherwise!

There is a sincere desire that this book will act as a catalyst to those who are suffering, encouraging them to begin the initiation process through meetings with other like-minded individuals, or through the searching out of those who are already more developed within their inner dimension in order to receive guidance. Only then the collective will begin to slowly change, because the change can only be exemplified by mature individuals. Wherever we work in our society and whatever responsibility we take upon ourselves, the blessing of our work depends upon our personal depth and maturity.

2.3 Morality Cannot Be Legislated

We often hear, sometimes even espousing it ourselves, that if existing rules and regulations are being followed then our practices must be ethically sound. We know, intuitively, that this is not the case. If our intentions are immoral then our practices which flow from them are unethical.

"Society Is Always Present in Board Meetings" was the headline in Germany's most important newspaper *FAZ* (*Frankfurter Allgemeine Zeitung*), which was exploring this concept.

> Even legally sound decisions can become a scandal. Society expects moral integrity from managers. Scandal, scandal we read! Yet the actions fall within the framework of all legal requirements. We read on. Can Fiat be exonerated because its cars can demonstrate the required low exhaust emissions during a stationery test, or is Fiat being deceptive because car drivers believed that the exhaust emissions would remain low while the cars were being driven? Fiat is not an individual case in which corporate decisions are leading to public disputes about how morally a company is expected to behave. Is the planned takeover ... Monsanto by Bayer ... due to Monsanto's bad reputation an expression of unscrupulousness and greed? Are banks allowed to shirk their responsibility for the global financial crises by referring to common practice or human error? ...
>
> The over-riding question is: What responsibility do business people have in the economy beyond their direct duty to comply with applicable laws ... (Edited from *FAZ* May 28, 2016).

I suggest the answer to the question is: Every individual is obliged, in both intention and action, to be morally and ethically faultless, so as not to harm either other individuals or the environment.

2.4 Individuals as Instruments of Societal Change

When I met my first teacher, Karlfried Graf Dürckheim, he stated:

> Wherever you work in our society and whatever responsibility you assume the blessing of your work depends upon the depth and the maturity of your own person. It is crucial to witness the other world within. Only the individual can witness the other world, not a group, not an institution, not a society.

In his commentary on the Aeon Lectures, Jungian author Edward Edinger writes:

> If my reading of the symbolism of [Jung's] *Aion* is correct, the aeon of Aquarius will generate individual water carriers. This will mean that the psyche will no longer be carried by religious communities but instead it will be carried by individuals with expanded consciousness. This is the idea C.G. Jung puts forward in his notion of a continuing incarnation, the idea that individuals are to become the incarnating vessels of the Holy Spirit on an ongoing basis. (Edinger 1996)

Pope Francis expressed certain doubts about self-improvement *per se* in his latest Encyclical Letter *Laudato Si'*:

> Self-improvement on the part of individuals will not by itself remedy the extremely complex situation facing our world today. Isolated individuals can lose their ability and freedom to escape the utilitarian mindset, and end up prey to an unethical consumerism which is bereft of social or ecological awareness. (Francis, Pope 2015)

Self-improvement is slowly gaining momentum on a universal scale.

C.G. Jung in a radio interview remarked:

> It starts with a few people with the vision for the new Age. They will be the light in the darkness; Guides and Hope; And a blessing for the future generations. Destiny depends on the consciousness of these few who will become more and more. A new religion is arising. You must not deny the call from the depth. What a great honor to live now and be one of the new guides. The treasury is in your depth. (Owens 2012).

Dr. Owens MD, Ph.D. has devoted the past 30 or more years of his life to the study and application of Jung's Depth Psychology.

The First Great Vow of Buddhism is: "The number of beings is infinite; I vow to save them all!" How is that possible? The answer is found in the following caption of a Zen painting in the home of my friend Peter Zürn: "If you change, the whole world will change" (Zen).

2.5 Synchronicity

It is no coincidence that during the writing of this book the Dalai Lama sent an appeal around the world, an appeal in the form of a revolutionary pronouncement. He stated:

2.5.1 "ETHICS ARE MORE IMPORTANT THAN RELIGION"

The Dalai Lama's (Dalai Lama and Alt 2016) appeal is a powerful impulse for a new secular ethics. Following are excerpts from his appeal:

> Ethics are more important than religion. We are not members of a particular religion by birth. But ethics is innate. (Dalai Lama and Alt 2016, p. 5–6)

> The Dalai Lama's secular ethics transcend national, religious and cultural boundaries, defining values that are innate in all people and apply to everyone alike. Rather than superficial, material values, these are inner values like mindfulness, compassion, training of the mind and the pursuit of happiness. (Franz Alt in Dalai Lama and Alt 2016, p. 6)

> Religion is often abused or exploited, even by religious leaders, in order to further political and economic interests. For that reason I say that in the twenty first century we need a new form of ethics beyond religion. That is why I am speaking of a secular ethics that can be helpful and useful for a billion atheists and an increasing number of agnostics. More *integral* than religion is our fundamental human spirituality. That is the affinity we humans have for love, benevolence, and affection – no matter what religion we belong to. (Dalai Lama and Alt 2016, p. 15)

> I believe that humans can get by without religion, but not without inner values, not without ethics. The difference between ethics and religion is like the difference between water and tea. Religion based ethics and inner values are more like tea. The tea that we drink is made mostly of water, but it contains other ingredients as well – tea leaves, spices, perhaps a little sugar, and, at least in Tibet, a pinch of salt – and that makes it more substantial, more lasting, something we want to drink every day. Yet no matter how tea is prepared, its main ingredient is always water. We can live without tea, but not without water. Likewise, we are born without religion, but not without the basic need for compassion – and not without the fundamental need for water. (Dalai Lama and Alt 2016, p. 16)

> Franz Alt: "What are the core tenets of secular ethics?"

> But I see with even greater clarity that our spiritual well-being depends not on religion but on our innate human nature, our natural affinity for goodness, compassion and caring for others. Regardless of whether or not we belong to a religion, we all have a fundamental wellspring of ethics within ourselves. We need to nurture that shared ethical basis. Ethics, as opposed to religion, are grounded in human nature. And that is how we can work on preserving the environment. That is religion and ethics put into practice. Empathy is the basis of human coexistence. I believe human development relies upon *cooperation and not competition*. That is scientifically proven ... (Dalai Lama and Alt 2016, pp. 19–20)

> Mindfulness, education, respect, tolerance, caring and nonviolence. We have achieved great material advances over the past century. That was generally positive. But those material advances are also what has led to environmental destruction. Now, in the twenty first century, we need to learn, cultivate, and apply more inner values on all levels ... The principle of global responsibility is a key element of my secular ethics ... (Dalai Lama and Alt 2016, pp. 18–19)

> There are two viewpoints of human nature. One believes that humans are naturally violent, reckless and aggressive. The other believes that we have a natural tendency towards benevolence, harmony and a peaceful life. I subscribe to the second viewpoint. That is why, in my opinion,

ethics are not a collection of commandments and prohibitions to abide by, but a natural inner offering that can bring happiness and satisfaction to ourselves and others ... (Dalai Lama and Alt 2016, p. 20)

To be sure, secular ethics requires training of the heart, plenty of patience and persistent effort. It is also clear that for secular ethics to be truly helpful, we need not only knowledge, but action ... (Dalai Lama and Alt 2016, p. 23)

How does the Dalai Lama view the current reality? "Unfortunately, the six billion believers in the world include many corrupt people who only pursue their own interests" (Dalai Lama and Alt 2016, p. 22).

As this book may be prescribed as a reference for students and young professionals, the Dalai Lama's following appeal to the younger generation is pertinent:

The young people of today have many more opportunities to get to know each other globally – and they should take advantage of them to work on improving the world. Compassion and love have been neglected far too much in education. We can and must change that now ... Ethical education starting around the age of fourteen is more important than religion. Education changes everything ... (Dalai Lama and Alt 2016, pp. 20–21)

The most important question we can ask for a better world is 'How can we serve each other? *To make that shift we need to sharpen our awareness* ... Meditation is more important than ritualized prayer. Children should learn morals and ethics. That's more important than any religion. (Dalai Lama and Alt 2016, p. 25)

The above is not only an appeal. With his wording the Dalai Lama is giving us the recipe for inner growth; growth which will lead to more ethical and moral behavior in the outside world. It consists of training of the heart, plenty of patience and persistent effort. *We know it as meditation.*

Far too much stock is placed on material values. They are important, but they will not solve our stress, anxiety, fear, anger or frustration. We must still overcome these mental burdens. That's why we need a deeper level of thinking. That's what I call mindfulness ... (Dalai Lama and Alt 2016, p. 31).

A meeting in Zurich in 2010 in the Kongresshaus on the theme *Altruism and Compassion in Economic Systems* was attended by neuroscientists, psychologists, economists, financial investors and the Dalai Lama (Tibet Office 2010). He sat cross-legged on a chair, wearing a red baseball cap in the spotlight. In front of the white armchair are his shoes. Behind him were flowering cherry branches. He begins by stating the following, and then laughs his throaty laugh:

"My business knowledge is zero."

There is no need for his Holiness to have a deeper business knowledge.

There can be no question that the Dalai Lama's opinion that we urgently need a New Ethic in our society is accurate. This is also true for ethics in the economy. As this book is focused on business ethics it accommodates the Dalai Lama's vision, especially the spiritual content, of a secular ethics as a beginning point in the development of a Business Ethics 3.0 concept, by adding the dimensions and impacts of Depth Psychology and quantum physics.

During the last few decades neoliberalism has developed as a replacement for religion or as a substitute religion. It may be argued that this neoliberalism was directly responsible for the financial crisis of 2007–08. If ethics is more important than religion, then ethics is *by far* much more important than this substitute religion. Unfortunately, there is an intense resistance to change the *status quo* even when it is clearly failing. Those who try are often attacked, belittled and misrepresented.

2.5.2 Laudato Si: On Care for Our Common Home

In yet another synchronistic event, in June, 2015, *The Holy Father Francis*, the religious leader of the Catholic Church published the Encyclical Letter *LAUDATO SI: ON CARE FOR OUR COMMON HOME* (Francis, Pope 2015). The letter is a strong critique of technology and a warning against blind belief in progress, but rather than being an anti-market approach or an anti-technology position, it is one in which Pope Francis encourages a holistic view of the economy.

As a former manager and entrepreneur in the economy I know that there are many responsible managers, particularly on environmental issues. Hans-Peter Dürr often quotes the following Tibetan wisdom. "The tree that falls makes more noise than a forest that is growing!" And he continues,

> Yes, it is normal that our perception is dominated by falling trees, of that which is violent, massive, happens quickly, threatens us or at least appears as a threat. Our whole history is full of falling trees ... But then we wonder how, despite all of this destruction we are still living on Earth. We recognize the fact that it is the growing forest that matters ultimately. It is the growing forest which allows for the continuation of life. But who notices? The forest and its trees change slowly and quietly, but consistently, only becoming apparent when we choose to focus our attention in that direction. Growth always proceeds more slowly and quietly than all of the destructive forces in the world, which today can unleash their fury in a matter of hours. To establish real, solid values requires time and patience, as they are being built up beyond our normal perceptions ... (Dürr 2012)

Of course there are the black sheep. In every situation there is a Gaussian distribution: a few are doing everything right, there are plenty doing some things right and some things wrong, and a few doing everything wrong. We have a long way to go to reach the ideal, a goal which I hope this book will assist us to achieve. We must all be open minded, avoid making judgments without sufficient information and work on improving that with which we are entrusted, including ourselves!

The Pope's statement represents the old ethic, which does not serve us well in the new economy. Later in this book the ideas put forth by Erich Neumann (Neumann 1990) will elaborate upon why this is the case. Concerning the old ethic he states,

> The Old Ethic has many sources, Judaea Christian beliefs and Greek philosophy being the most influential among them. The ideal prototype at the center of the Old Ethic may be the figure of a Saint or a Wise Man, the Noble or the Good, the Devout or the Orthodox Fulfiller of the Law, the Hero or the Man of Self-control ...

Pope Francis promotes this prototype of "only be good" as a way to cure the ailing economy, but this only ensures that mankind continues to suppress and repress his dark side, something which has been promoted for centuries without success. While his appeal to the masses may have honorable intentions the possibility of this tired, failed approach toward improving the economy is destined to fail.

2.6 Why We Urgently Need a Business Ethics 3.0

The question which remains, one to which we *must* find a solution, is why time and time again we fail to follow an ethical approach which promotes sustainability. Pete Geissler and Bill O'Rourke explain that the science of morality in human conduct is limited to moral principles and rules of conduct, such as medical ethics where one is taught "first, do no harm," and political or societal ethics where one is admonished to "act for the greater good." Ethics however, extends beyond the law (Geissler and O'Rourke 2015).

David W. Gill (Gill 2010) writes about Business Ethics 2.0, asserting that it must promote more than simply damage control.

> "Do we have an 'ethics problem' in business today? I think so. Most people I hear from think so. Businesses and their leaders are too often doing the wrong thing, not the right thing. Something is 'wrong' when it results in physical, financial, relational or environmental harm as a result of irresponsible actions. In business something is 'right' if it protects people from harm and empowers them by providing goods and services which will enable them to create and live the lives that they, and their God choose.
>
> When people are harmed by banking practices, insurance policies, pharmaceutical products, defective automobiles or unhealthy food, even if these things are legal and almost universally practiced, these things are unethical. Regardless of whether bad things happen because of greed and malice or as a result of personal irresponsibility and willful ignorance, they are wrong. Reports of unethical business activity are a frequent, daily occurrence. We have a serious problem! Ironically, business ethics courses, publications, organizations and company training programs have proliferated over the past thirty or so years. I wouldn't be surprised if a graph of the growth of the emphasis on such ethics resources didn't correlate pretty closely with a graph of the rise in number of business ethics scandals and crises. Correlation is certainly not causation, but one lesson is clear: *the way we are confronting and implementing business ethics is not getting rid of the problem.*"

Paul Gorrell (Gorrell 2010) wrote,

> Business ethics inside organizations is typically focused on legal concerns in an attempt to lower a company's potential exposure. In business schools, case studies such as the Johnson

& Johnson Tylenol scare in the 1980s are used to explore the principles behind an organization's mission statement, business policies and leadership decisions. It is time for a larger, more purposeful business ethics discussion focused on values based leadership, a business ethics 2.0 approach that goes beyond compliance.

2.7 What Was Business Ethics 1.0

David Gill (Gill 2010) writes:

The basic problem is that business ethics is largely practiced as damage control. What sets the ethics agenda, what draws our energy and attention are specific crises, dilemmas, or problem cases. The Exxon Valdez oil tanker runs aground ... the Union Carbide chemical plant explodes in Bhopal, India ... Google accepts government censorship as a condition of doing business in China ... Vice President Joe sexually harasses employee Jane.

What are the facts in each case? What are the ethical values and principles at stake? How can Kant or Mill or Rawls help us reason our way to a conclusion about who is at fault and what to do with the culprit? It is not so much that we actually care about Alaskan shore birds, or Indian peasants, or Chinese students or Jane. What counts is that litigation, fines, or a big brand tarnishing scandal is about to occur. Can we stop it and contain the damage? This approach is too reactive, negative and narrow to do much good. It does little to ensure the problems don't occur in the first place. It simply mops up the blood after the crash. And yet, how many business ethics courses endlessly focus on case discussions and analyses pointing toward a "decision" at the end? How many training programs focus on cases and multiple choice options?

Health care provides an analogy of this practice. For many individuals, health care is little more than "disease control" or "injury control." Until I get deathly ill or badly injured I don't care or even think about health care. This is a terribly short-sighted and ultimately self-defeating approach to health. A much better approach to our health is to ask, "What is my ideal health vision and goal?" Perhaps I'd like to be able to dance with my wife or husband, tramp around old cities and museums, eat and drink a range of good food, hike up moderate hills, play golf with my grandchildren and have my clothes still fit well when I'm in my eighties! And now that I'm clear on the vision, the question is: "What do I need to do to get there?" Or perhaps better stated: "What do I need to do to optimize my possibilities of getting there?"

This strategy then will lead us to identify the systems and processes that affect our personal health, such as nutrition, resistance training, cardiovascular training, stretching, rest, and stress management. Let's be sure to think rigorously and holistically about what it takes to achieve the vision, let's be proactive, positive, and holistic.

Paul Gorrell (Gorrell 2010) comments on Business Ethics 1.0:

A similar trend provides us with a glimmer of the future of business ethics. Given the early 2000's scandals of Enron, Tyco and WorldCom, businesses were placed in a defensive position where they were forced to comply with new expectations focused upon protecting shareholders. The Sarbanes-Oxley Act of 2002 created standards for accounting and reporting, which enforced and inscribed new levels of transparency. Because of this legislation, organizations focused carefully on compliance to ensure they were managing risk exposure and the potential penalties involved. This was a reactionary and protective approach to be above board as an organization. This approach does not build public trust in brands, or raise stock price or customer loyalty, because the ethics focus has been more about limiting bad behavior than promoting good behavior.

2.8 What Is Business Ethics 2.0

David Gill (Gill 2010) writes the following on Business Ethics 2.0, which has a focus upon Mission, Vision and Culture Control:

> Of course, companies (and MBA programs) must have effective, best practice problem, trouble shooting, crisis management and dilemma resolution processes in place. Damage happens even in the best of companies. We need to approach this part of ethics better than ever. But if that's all we do we are doomed to face an unending stream of problems. Business Ethics 2.0, however, will take proactive steps to clarify the mission and vision. Why have we formed this company? Why don't we all just stay home and work on our own interests? What is the product or service that we work together to deliver at such an extraordinary level of excellence that our customers can't wait to pay us for more? What is the positive change we make in the lives of our customers?
>
> Then, having sharpened up the mission and vision, making sure that it self-consciously taps into the basic human drives to innovate and to help others, the next question becomes, "What kind of culture and corporate character do we need to create and nurture to best empower our company toward the achievement of its mission and vision?" And then, "What kind of action-guidelines shall we articulate so that we all do our work in the most effective, most excellent way?" To get its employees to own and espouse its ethical guidelines and core values a company must mobilize its entire workforce, from top to bottom, to figure out those ethics and values which are in alignment with the mission and vision. Business Ethics 2.0 also involves ensuring that communication is constant, clear, and compelling, and that training is collaborative and practical.
>
> Of course, even a super fit physical specimen can get hit by a runaway bus or virus coming out of nowhere. There are no guarantees! And so too, a company could do everything in alignment with Ethics 2.0 and still be brought down by a greedy rogue leader or a crash in the market. Ethically healthy 2.0 companies are not guaranteed business success or ethical immunity. It still takes a brilliant product, a timely market and other factors to succeed. Great ethics and values will not mitigate inept management. But sound 2.0 ethics do increase and optimize a company's chance of quickly recovering from, if not altogether avoiding, serious ethical problems, which allows it to focus on business process execution and excellence.
>
> Mission and culture controlled ethics is the classical way to manage a company. It dates back to Aristotle, it is the Decalogue; it is the traditional communities and organizations everywhere, throughout time. Companies must move past the abstraction and dry impracticality of modernity's approach to ethics, as well as postmodernity's chaotic and disconnected focus on dealing with first this problem, then that one. We need Business Ethics 2.0.

Paul Gorrell (Gorrell 2010) comments on Business Ethics 2.0:

> Despite the perceived ethical lapses of particular companies or industries, there are many indicators that ethics is evolving to provide exciting opportunities for organizations, leaders and talent managers. We are shifting to a stage where ethics is understood in a more holistic framework with an intersecting connection between the employee and consumer. This connection happens at the brand level; how that brand is perceived by those who purchase products and services and by those who make up the organization's workforce.
>
> We are moving toward a new age of ethics in the way we do business and encourage behavior from our leaders. This is not because we want to be do-gooders, but because doing "good" is good business. Consider the following:

- Ethical organizations build marketplace loyalty. Consumers are more likely to buy products and services if they are provided by companies that also promote and commit to the social good; improving the circumstances of people, the Earth and its resources.
- Ethical organizations attract talent. We may be in a state of high unemployment, but organizations still want the best of the best. The best employees are still valuable in the marketplace. Social conscience acts as a magnet for many stars and emerging leaders from younger generations.
- Ethical organizations engage employees, promoting retention and higher levels of productivity. People feel proud when their brand stands for something beyond traditional ideas of profit and sales volume.

Two pieces of evidence which are indicative of the move toward a commitment to ethics in the workplace are the increasing numbers of companies that have both corporate social responsibility programs, and sustainability programs. Corporate social responsibility efforts incorporate ethics within organizations to create alignment between the public good and business operations. This often includes demonstrated commitment to social causes, whereby the organization provides resources for specific events or opportunities. But true corporate social responsibility involves a more integrated effort where business operations, employee decisions and causes endorsed by the organization are part of an effort to achieve a cultural vision. Sustainability is similar in that it attempts to bring together an *integrated* focus on planet, profit and performance. Here, organizations commit to green ways of working that are measured, rewarded and proven to drive profit.

2.8.1 Ethics and Talent Management

In the new age of ethics, talented managers can provide significant value, deepening an organization's capability to commit to social responsibility and to practice what it preaches. Some ideas include:
- Incorporating ethics based and values based leadership qualities within competency models. We must be careful as many ethical notions, such as courage and integrity, are difficult to measure and validate. Competency models that include notions linked to social responsibility can provide significant value to every aspect of leadership and more effective teamwork.
- Creating development experiences that are embedded within the current work that leaders and employees undertake. Ethics is typically taught through case studies, but employees' current working challenges provide incredible scenarios with which to learn how to operate in line with one's values while leveraging capabilities. While action learning can be effective for leadership development when offered in a programmatic manner, such as high potential development, it is even more effective if presented within intact teams so they can wrestle with real challenges together in light of competing values, ideas and strategies.
- Integrating social causes within the learning and development space. We can teach great leadership behavior and commitment to values by using extra work related activities as fodder for learning.

Building ethical organizations involves specific work with the leaders who represent the firm and act as champions of its culture. (Swailes 2013, pp. 32ff.)

CSR has been moved up in the meantime from a status of 1.0 to 2.0. Wayne Visser (Visser 2010) writes about the birth of CSR 2.0:

By May 2008, it was clear to me that this evolutionary concept of Web 2.0 held many lessons for CSR. I published my initial thoughts in a short article online entitled *CSR 2.0: The New Era of Corporate Sustainability and Responsibility* (Visser 2008), in which I said: "The field of what is variously known as CSR, sustainability, corporate citizenship and business ethics is ushering in a new era in the relationship between business and society. Simply put, we are shifting from the old concept of CSR – the classic notion of 'Corporate Social Responsibility', which I call CSR 1.0 – to a new, integrated conception – CSR 2.0, which can be more accurately labelled 'Corporate Sustainability and Responsibility'. The allusion to Web 1.0 and Web 2.0 is no coincidence. The transformation of the internet through the emergence of social media networks, user generated content and open source approaches is a fitting metaphor for the changes business is experiencing as it begins to re-define the role in society".

When we observe the current situation, even Business Ethics 2.0 with CSR 2.0 has not resulted in significantly moving the economy toward a New Ethical approach which incorporates sustainable moral attitudes which result in ethical behavior. Something is clearly still missing!

Luk Bouckaert (Bouckaert 2015, p. 16) calls it *"Spirituality: The Missing Link in Business Ethics."* There is a lot of material published about spirituality in business but I believe Bouckaert says it best:

By linking the notion of spirituality to leadership, social responsibility and sustainability I hope to demonstrate that spirituality is not just an individual matter but a public good that is necessary for leveraging change in institutions. … Of course, we can explain the ethical deficit as a *lack* of business ethics and see the remedy in more business ethics and more CSR programs. I am afraid that this strategy of *"more of the same"* will fail if the efforts made in business ethics are not supported by critical reflection about the mechanisms of selective blindness in business ethics.

2.9 What Is Business Ethics 3.0

Business Ethics 3.0 is the further development and advancement of Business Ethics 2.0. It is not only holistic, but it is an Integral Business Ethics. It is integral to all that we have learned and experienced thus far. It incorporates objective REASON, numerous philosophical directions following upon the Aristotelian approach, theological considerations of many different religions, and the depth psychology and spirituality of the Doctrines of Wisdom instead of simply the ego mind. All of these influences are the foundation upon which the first and second iterations of ethics was built, leading to the third iteration which is Business Ethics 3.0. The weaknesses of these previous stages are recognized and will be remedied by the new framework. For an individual to successfully apply the essential wisdom contained within Integral Ethics to Business Ethics 3.0, a pre-condition is an excellent education and years of experience in business management. Without practical experience people working in the economic sector may become enamored by theoretical statements but lack the necessary judgment to apply them appropriately, increasing the risk of compensating with self-serving, unethical behavior. Thanks to the internet we have unprecedented access to an understanding of all of the aspects which constitute Business Ethics 3.0. It is the ideal new ethical approach for todays digitalized and globalized economy.

2.10 Our Ego-Dominated Mind

Our ego-dominated mind is so dominant that we have separated ourselves from our sources. From our most important roots.
- We have separated our *Ego* from our *Self*.
- We have separated our *Mind* from our *Soul*.
- Men have separated their *Masculinity* from their *Femininity*.
- Women have separated their *Femininity* from their *Masculinity*.
- We have buried *Sophia*, the divine *Wisdom*, under layers of materialism.
- We wish to embrace *Good*, but having suppressed and repressed our *Dark* side, we render that impossible.
- We have separated our *Spirit* from our *Mind* and *Soul*, denying the possibility of a united *Body/Mind-Soul-Spirit*.
- We have cut our connection to the *Mystical*.

The above is a summary of the reasons why so many attempts to develop a new ethical approach have failed. In order to be successful we must bridge the gap to our soul and our spirit. This can be achieved by developing a new *integral* ethics approach.

2.11 Integrative Business Ethics

Integral business ethics has a crucial, active and deliberate "integrative" approach. This ethical approach does not separate, but integrates and merges. It is inclusive of light and dark, good and evil, subject and object, masculine and feminine, young and old, ego and self, ego mind and reason, suppliers and customers, companies and shareholders, and managers and employees. All of these apparent opposites are merely polarities of a *single reality* which cannot be described, only experienced. The experience of inter-connectedness, advanced and enhanced by both modern quantum physics and mystics for thousands of years, integrates the apparent opposites into a single unity. This uniting process is what Jung refers to as Individuation and the "*Coincidentia Oppositorum*" which lead naturally and seamlessly to moral and ethical decisions and practices.

In order to effect a change in the attitude and decisions of the entrepreneurs and managers in the business world we must first speak their language, and demonstrate empathy toward their various conflicting demands. We must also present business cases to clearly illustrate what we mean. The author has drawn upon his extensive success in the business world to explain how the tenets of Business Ethics 3.0 can be applied in specific areas of the economy, facilitating an understanding and appreciation of the approach.

This book is not a treatise on theological, philosophical or spiritual teachings. Depth Psychology is a far more understandable "landing slot" in the economy than is spirituality. Many managers either have or are well on their way to having severe psychological challenges, only continuing to be competitive in their positons by resorting to compensations and projections. They suffer in a world where volatility, uncertainty, complexity and ambiguity (VUCA) has never been so rampant, and where disruptive innovations destroy old technologies in the process of creating new ones. We are ourselves more and more volatile, uncertain, complex and ambiguous, and as individuals we project these qualities onto the collective. We are the reason for this dilemma but for the large part we neither realize nor accept this reality. Our comfortable worldview is that it is always "others" who are responsible, but it is our responsibility as individuals to change and improve the world in which we live. This change will necessitate growth through our own psychological "individuation" which will lead to either concurrent or subsequent spiritual enlightenment.

Individuation, encouraged by Depth Psychology, is a process of transformation whereby the personal and collective unconscious are brought into consciousness, often by dreams or active imagination practices, to be assimilated into the whole personality. It is a necessary process for the integration of the psyche. It supports inner peace and an improved work/life balance which result in greater serenity, humor, harmony, compassion, charity and love; all of which encourage the individual to embrace a New Ethic. Mere appeals to do what is "right" do not help a lot. "Ethics does not only denote moral appeals but moral action" (Hans Küng). This book contains concrete recommendations for the individuation and spiritualization of individuals.

If we can get the attention of business people by a consideration of Depth Psychology, then even without yet knowing what spirit really means, they may become more receptive to the building of bridges to their soul. Yes, it may take years of practicing meditation to experience substantial inner growth, and no, many professionals are not likely to make the time in their rush for performance and success to make this self-improvement effort. Many distractions await them daily. But if they feel psychologically distressed and their performance is at stake, then and maybe only then will they listen, practice and change. If not, it is only a question of time until they are out of balance and out of business. Depth Psychology which encourages individuation can be the preparation for initiating spiritual training, or the necessary support for embarking upon meditative practices. At the very least it supports our efforts to explore a spiritual pathway when the ego mind is exercising its "dark side" influence. It assists in the effort to remain on track. Inner peace and a satisfying work/life balance resulting in greater serenity, humor, harmony and love will be the reward, encouraging us all to embrace the New Ethic through moral decisions.

Business Ethics 3.0 is more than ego mind and moral reasoning, more than philosophy and religion, more than psychology and spirituality, more than laws and guidelines. It is the New Integral and Integrative Ethics, which contains and combines all these sources which are within us, and which desire to manifest in our life and in the economy. The current wave of "disruptive innovations" which lead to "disruptive ethical behavior" combines to create an urgent need for an understanding and adoption of Integral Ethics.

The new Integral Business Ethics 3.0 emerges from an Integral Consciousness which takes into account the old ethic based upon mental consciousness, with all its successes, while also attending to the damage resulting from the suppression and repression of the dark side, along with the psychological and spiritual immaturity of the vast portion of humanity. What once was unified in the mythical consciousness was separated in the advancement of mental consciousness, and must now, with difficulty, be reunited in Integral Consciousness.

Ethics can be a very powerful factor in the economy. Ethical actions can result in a strong competitive advantage. Why then do so few people understand this and apply it? Pete Geissler and Bill O'Rourke, the authors of *The Power of Ethics: The Thoughtful Leader's Model for Sustainable Competitive Advantage*, answer as follows:

> Ethics, or its lack, sticks its multi-faceted nose into just about every inter-personal activity, or it could and should. But unfortunately not everyone understands and practices this truism, and all too few of the folks who lead our institutions are aware of the need for ethics and have made ethical practices an integral part of their everyday activities, although we dare say that most or all say that they do, which of course is lying and, obviously, unethical ...
>
> So if ethical behavior is widely thought to be needed and is beneficial to individuals and institutions, why doesn't everyone practice it all the time? The answer is deceptively simple: too many people, unfortunately and to their own detriment, are unaware, ignorant of the need for or positive consequences of ethical behavior. On the other side of the same coin, too many people, unfortunately and to their own detriment, are blissfully unaware of the negative consequences of unethical behavior, blinded as they are by selfishness, greed, and the need for control over others ... We live in a clamorous world, a blatant and relentless cacophony and constant time pressures force us to make, literally *force us to make* decisions without serious consideration of doing what is "right" ... (Geissler and O'Rourke 2015)

The old dualistic ethic has contributed to an unconscionable number of immoral decisions and unethical practices in the economy. Suppression and repression are the reasons, and projections are the result. Due to growing egocentric behavior people are more and more destabilized. We no longer have the wise and experienced elite to counsel both the individual and the collective to behave wisely. Religion and philosophy are no longer the solution. Globalization and digitalization exacerbate the problems exponentially. *We have lost the connection to our soul, which is the guide to our unconscious.* Neumann (Neumann 1990) advocates for a *New Ethic,* one where the dark side is accepted, integrated and controlled in the consciousness and behavior of the individual.

2.12 Being Responsible Is Profitable

It has been one hundred years since the publication of John Maurice Clark's article, *The Changing Basis of Economic Responsibility* in the *Journal of Political Economy* (Clark 1916, pp. 209–229). Yet there is no overwhelming evidence of widespread adoption and subsequent application of his thesis that *responsible business practices result in greater profitability.* A search of the relevant literature reveals that there are indeed a few examples of businesses which have seen the light and are successfully factoring ethically responsible behavior into their business decision-making process. Where this attitude shift has occurred it has inevitably resulted in the generation of greater profits. Sadly, the lessons learned by these forward-looking organizations which have adopted a twenty-first century moral consciousness; one recognized as the *only* viable model which will allow us to advance as a world society have been largely ignored by most politicians, religious leaders and leaders in the business sector. It is time to reconsider the unsustainable and immoral proposition that being reckless and irresponsible toward others in the quest for greater profitability is an acceptable business model, even to reevaluate *whether this approach does in fact result in increasing profitability.*

It is time for the economics of business to embark upon the high road, to assume responsibility not only for the bottom line, but also for the morality of applying the methodologies embraced in generating a profit. Individuals with authority over others must also assume responsibility for those over whom their decisions, or lack of decisions have an impact, whether they be employees or customers. Without excuse! This responsibility implies engaging in humanistic, morally defensible decisions. There can be no excuse in today's interconnected world to continue to subscribe to anachronistic business practices which don't embrace the now universally evident direct connection between a respected and valued workforce and an increase in productivity, employee satisfaction and retention. In today's world, managers and employees share responsibility for the financial viability of any business enterprise. However, this is possible only to the degree that employees have a responsible and realistic voice in business decisions which concern their well-being and their expertise. Senior managers, as their position dictates, manage a greater diversity of responsibilities than do individual employees. Thus the impact of those in the top echelons of a company is most often greater than those of an employee who answers to those entrusted with the ultimate success of a business endeavor.

While managing employees in a responsible fashion has become a more recognizable priority and reality than it was for centuries past, ironically, irresponsible behavior on the part of senior managers has recently created some of the greatest damage ever experienced both inside corporations, and collaterally, upon investors and customers.

In spite of selfish practices which too often fail to recognize and reward the true value of employees, we must not fail to recognize advances that have been made in ethical management and the resulting benefits enjoyed by individuals, enterprises, countries and, to a limited extent, the world economy. There has never been a time in recorded history during which material wealth has been as readily available to as many as it is today.

Perhaps it is time to readdress the meaning of economic responsibility. Clark's article has not received much attention in terms of practical decisions concerning the economy, but many of the arguments that he raises are still relevant today. It may be prudent to address them when formulating a future concept of ethics in the economy.

I began writing this book in response to a Springer Book Series initiative, *Studies in Economic Ethics and Philosophy,* which I recognized as an important opportunity to compare a discussion about the basis and meaning of the concept of economic responsibility from today's perspective with Clark's thesis. The *Freie Universität Berlin*, Germany and the *Global Ethics Institute at the University of Tübingen*, Germany led the Springer initiative. Meanwhile, *Economic Responsibility: John Maurice Clark – A Classic on Economic Responsibility* was published (Haase 2017).

This book is intended to support the academic material which the Springer initiative considered. It is a welcome and exciting opportunity to present the personal perspective I have gained during 40 years of business experience, 30 years of Zen meditation and the knowledge and experience of Depth Psychology achieved during the last 15 years under the tutorship of Jungian Walter Schwery, in Bremgarten, Bern, Switzerland.

This age of VUCA, in which we find ourselves, is ripe for a reconsideration of ethics and morality in the business world.

2.13 Depth Psychology Creates New Directions

During the one hundred years since C.G. Jung wrote his *Red Book* we have had ample opportunity to understand why previous ethical standards, which were based upon Judea-Christian and Greek sources, have failed to provide guidance to managers who wish act responsibly to ensure morally justifiable and sustainable economic decisions. A materialistic, mechanistic approach, whenever it involves people's lives and efforts is a dead-end street doomed to fail. What will become of us when our most admirable human qualities, including our ability to think, to reason, to analyze, to synthesize and to manipulate information and systems are perceived as precursors of failure? As we can be certain that they will if the human element is ignored. Empathy, compassion, equality of opportunity and appreciation are all economically sound parameters which need to be plugged into any economic equation. We urgently need to change both our attitude and our approach. There is an immediate and urgent need for a new ethical approach.

I believe it can be demonstrated that the Depth Psychology of C.G. Jung and Erich Neumann, which illustrates and explains the reasons underlying the egocentric behavior of individuals, is better suited as a foundation upon which to develop a new approach to ethics than are Social Psychology, the Analytical Psychology of S. Freud, the Gestalt Therapy of Fritz Perls, Behaviorism, Humanistic Psychology, Cognitive Psychology or any form of Bio-Psychology.

Depth Psychology refers to the ongoing development of theories and therapies pioneered by Pierre Janet, William James and Carl Gustav Jung along with Freud; methodologies which explore the relationship between the conscious and the unconscious, and thus include both psychoanalysis and Jungian psychology. The psychoanalytical approach can lead us to an awareness of the need and appreciation for, along with a possible approach toward the development of holistic, ethically sound management of business enterprises which, at the same time, are economically sound and defensible.

2.14 Clark's Analysis and Proposals for the Twentieth Century

John Maurice Clark (1884–1963) was an American economist whose work combined the rigor of traditional economic analysis with an institutionalists' attitude. Clark was a pioneer in developing the theoretical basis of modern Keynesian economics, including the concept of the economic multiplier.

From Clark's point of view we inherited an economics of *irresponsibility* at the beginning of the twentieth century. In response, he postulates an economics of responsibility which allows for a dynamic interaction with working business ethics. He proposes that it is time for the pendulum to swing from narrow individualism to solidarity and social mindedness, from *personal* responsibility *to social* responsibility. This is *not* meant to imply that individual responsibility is of lesser importance and collective responsibility of greater. But rather that the scope of individual responsibility must become broader than ever before. Business managers must be free to act in a morally acceptable fashion, with courage, self-reliance and generosity. Their decisions will consequently have more far-reaching effects than ever, affecting the entire system either positively or negatively. Morality in business practices does not result from simply following binding laws. It is far more dynamically interactive than that. Clark critically observes that Liberal Economics too often lends itself to denying responsibility. He cautions against acting in a Darwinian fashion where there is always a winner at the expense of a loser. We do not need strength so much in the modern world, as wisdom. Clark foresaw individuals in modern society becoming increasingly interdependent in new and as yet unforeseen ways. He was a proponent of benefits like minimum wage, unemployment insurance, pension plans and a mother's pension, all of which remain topical today. He recognized that unemployment is a disease of our economic system, while many still misrepresent it as a matter of personal fitness and/or unwillingness to work.

Clark addressed crucial environmental failures and challenged business managers to assume more responsibility for environmental issues. He was ahead of his time in discussing pending climate changes and the urgent need to be proactive. Clark also explained what may happen if the balance of supply and demand is not maintained, and how this would result in chaos in the banking system. He even foresaw how this breakdown in the stability of the banks would likely lead to a worldwide panic in financial systems. There is no shortage of social and environmental causes which have become evident and urgent due to advances in science and industry. It was long thought that it would be easier to change people's attitudes than to change the environment, but Clark makes a case for changes in the environment predicating changes in people. He also has major concerns about the short-sighted way the least qualified employees are laid off, or dismissed outright, when a company wishes to improve its profits. He suggests that offering training to improve their skills would be more beneficial to both employees and employers.

Clark does not advocate that there should be no controls in place to ensure that greed does not rein freely. Both workers and employers must assume personal responsibility for making moral decisions and following ethical practices. What he does advocate is that both free exchange and social reform need to be governed by one consistent set of rules and regulations. He is keenly aware of the difficulties inherent in any system of public control. Any regulation of private industry must be well considered, well developed and widely and thoroughly agreed upon if the system is to have any hope of succeeding. If people distrust the leaders of industry, and in turn the leaders distrust the people, the result will be the loss of good will followed quickly by financial losses. All perceived failures on the part of leaders lead to hostile public opinion. All *right* or *wrong* actions have numerous effects upon others. But, when there are no laws which are agreed upon and equitably applied, individuals must decide, based upon their own moral code, how best to assume responsibility for society and the environment. It is not sufficient that our guideline will be to simply not hurt others and to leave the world just as we found it. From today's perspective, that is no longer sufficient. Sustainable management includes the premise that it must *improve* the world for future generations. We will revisit this theme later in this book.

Clark discusses the relative merits of socialism and capitalism. The socialists believe that under capitalism much of the good is offset by its harmful aspects, that the strain resulting from conflicting selfish interests will ultimately destroy a capitalist society. On the other hand Clark points out that an objection to socialism is that it relies on altruism. However, the pros and cons of any two conflicting systems are always a matter of degree. The real question to be addressed is what intrinsic responsibility, that not explicitly covered by laws and legislation, does business have? We have a tremendous potential for improving society through responsible economic decisions.

Clark concludes with a serious concern; that of an ever-increasing concentration of wealth controlled by a few capitalists. He believes that the world is quite familiar with the concept of *social* responsibility in its many and varied forms in differing societies, but that the perhaps equally important concept of responsible business practices has not been subjected to nearly the same considerations. It is for this reason that such a powerful sense of injustice is rapidly increasing amongst the disenfranchised. This movement has the potential to radically destabilize *both* societal institutions *and* business enterprises, unless we seize the present opportunity to address global inequality of opportunity.

Upon reflection and close analysis, one hundred years after Clark's work on Keynesian economics his concerns and conclusions remain as valid now as then. Why have we apparently made so little progress? Is ethical management of business enterprises more difficult today? Perhaps. Advances in electronic access to, and manipulation of, all aspects of business management potentially separate management from those producing the products or services. This globalization enabled by the internet is a paradigm shift, the magnitude of which has never before been experienced. It potentially changes the basis of economic responsibility. John Maurice Clark's promotion of a balance between *economic responsibility* and *being profitable* in his article, *The Changing Basis of Economic Responsibility* seems no closer to acceptance than when he promoted it one hundred years ago. While it is true that there are a few examples from the business world where profits are being generated through the employment of ethical attitudes and decisions, more often it is the case that those enterprises which are ruthless and reckless when it comes to their employees are accumulating the greatest wealth.

There is hope. In 2017 a "Corporate Excellence Award" was initiated by the consulting company Ceams in conjunction with professors from the Universities of Zurich/Switzerland and Eichstätt/Germany. The CEOs of the companies receiving the award exemplified excellence in managing enterprises which demonstrated successful, sustainable growth while following ethically sound business practices (*FAZ* May 18, 2017).

Also, following a history of corruption, including falsifying data about the safety of drugs and displaying a lack of transparency, GlaxoSmithKline has begun to focus upon transparency and ethical practices, breaking ranks with some other companies in the pharmaceutical industry (*CHEManager* 8/2017).

Finally, according to a study of PWC there is also an encouraging trend to dismiss CEOs who are involved in fraud, corruption, insider trading, causing environmental damage, falsifying CVs and engaging in sexual harassment (*FAZ* May 15, 2017).

It always comes down to the individual level. We are all responsible for our practices. At the personal level there is no excuse for unethical behavior. Within the framework of our authority we are accountable for the results of our decisions. Of course top management decisions generally have a much higher impact than those of a worker on the lowest level. Management has a top-down responsibility, and on the other side all employees have a bottom-up responsibility for the company. *Responsible Care* has achieved a lot of success during the last few decades, but on the other side continuing irresponsibility evidenced largely by those at the top has created immense corporate, societal and personal damage.

Despite the reality of inequality, immoral attitudes and unethical behavior in the workplace, we must not forget the good things that the economy has delivered. It is prudent to recognize that most of what is reported in worldwide media are failures, not successes. Public interest appears to be more on the *fallen trees*, than the *growing forest* (Hans-Peter Dürr). Nevertheless, it remains a fact that in the court of public opinion ethical business decisions are sadly lacking.

2.15 Managing Ourselves

There is no doubt that managers in the economy must generate an increase in the value of the company in which they have been entrusted with a leadership role. But the question is, what pathway will they follow in doing so? What will be the peripheral costs associated with the increase in the value of the company's stock? Managers have the responsibility to fulfill the expectations of *all* stakeholders, including employees, customers, suppliers, stockholders and the community at large, in an ethically acceptable manner. It is important to note that there are no universally identified ethical guidelines, morality laws or other externally defined regulations. Rather, the extent to which managers accept responsibility for ethical behavior is dependent upon their inner growth and the subsequent individual personal values which arise from this growth.

Since René Descartes's "*Cogito, ergo sum*" (I think, therefore I am), we have achieved incredible advances in science, technology, medicine and economics by narrowly focusing upon fulfillment of the ego, adopting an "I-centered" worldview. What is perhaps not universally recognized is that this has been at the expense of progress on equally important humanistic, personal, intrinsic values.

Personal wholeness, which results from an individual's entire life's activities, contemplations and introspective insights, is generally considered to be the unity of body, soul and *mind*. The emphasis upon *mind* in contemporary society is a fatal error. The whole person consists of a balanced unity of body, soul and *spirit*. (Latin: corpus, anima and *spiritus*; Greek: soma, psyche and *pneuma*). As a result of this misconception, the spiritual dimension of human life is not afforded its rightful place in our thoughts and actions. When our spiritual nature is not given its due recognition the wounds inflicted upon society are predictable. They result from an imbalance between our ego-centered interests and desires, and those considerations which embrace all of humanity. The only way forward which has any possibility of bringing about unity, consensus and equality in the workplace, indeed in the world at large, is through the application of both our psychological individuation and our spiritual dimension.

> **The world hangs on a thin thread, and that is the psyche of man.** Nowadays we are not threatened by elementary catastrophes. There is no such thing in nature as an H-bomb; that is all man's doing. *We are the great danger.* The psyche is the great danger. What if something goes wrong with our collective psyche? In these times we realize the power of our psyche and how important it is to know something about it. But we know nothing about it. Nobody would give credit to the idea that the psychical processes of the ordinary man have any importance whatever. Rather, we think 'Oh, he is only what is in his head. He is comprised of what he receives from his surroundings; he is taught such and such a thing, believes such and such a thing, and particularly if he is well housed and well fed, then he has no ideas at all.' And that's the great mistake because we are as we are born, and we are not born as *tabula rasa*, but as a reality (Edited from C.G. Jung, *A Matter of Heart*).

As a consequence Business Ethics in the economy hangs on a thin thread, and that thread is the psyche of managers.

Our materialistic world is in a dead-end street. Self-centered isolationism is destined to be no more than a footnote in the history of the development of humanity. There is an urgent need for change. The following quote from John Steinbeck is as relevant today as when it was first uttered:

> It has always seemed strange to me ... the things we admire in men, kindness and generosity, openness, honesty, understanding and feeling, are the concomitants of failure in our system. And those traits we detest: sharpness, greed, acquisitiveness, meanness, egoism and self-interest are the traits of success. And while men admire the quality of the first they love the product of the second.

The Depth Psychology of Jung and Neumann can explain the reasons for the egocentric behavior of the individual, and this understanding can lead us toward a more holistic approach to a *New Ethic*.

The quantum physicist Hans-Peter Dürr in his book, *Warum es ums Ganze geht* ("Why is it do or die?") promotes a win/win situation for everyone involved in the economy. He believes that if we really wanted to promote people who are peaceful, cooperative, empathetic and loving we could easily do so. Of course, this would not be possible in every individual, because opposing, competing forces are always present and can be expected to manifest over and over again in tense situations.

Dürr wisely points out that our competitive economy would be highly dissatisfied with such a friendly type of person. The economy rewards aggressive people, those who prevail at the expense of morality, people who promote new societal desires necessitating greater and greater consumption. Thus, successful economists are those who are trained from childhood to value speed, assertiveness and recklessness, opportunistically maximizing the system to their own advantage. Those who act thoughtfully, cooperatively and considerately, with a sense of community, are disadvantaged. Darwinism, in the primal sense, would act in our economy with the stronger overwhelming the weaker.

One hundred years following the publication of Heisenberg's *Quantum Theory* we are beginning to comprehend the reality of its ramifications for *all* aspects of our lives. A quantum field, an invisible, energetic force which connects all of humanity, indeed all of creation in the *cosmos*, is evidenced from our enhanced observations of the identifiable, quantifiable particles and waves which constitute all matter and energy of which the cosmos consists. According to Dürr this may be conceived of as a *Permanent Acting Process,* a cooperative background field with a high degree of potentiality, out of which all reality is created in each and every moment. The field is empty, but has the potential to manifest permanently as reality, a reality shaped and continuously *modified* by our *thoughts* and *actions*. In this way everything is interconnected. Each one of us, acting individually, influences the quantum field and thus simultaneously all other individuals. Since individuals have an effect upon the economy, a redirection of their intentions and focus will have a concomitant effect upon the economy. All of us, and especially those entrusted with corporate responsibility for others, must recognize this and accordingly act in a responsible fashion. If not, our irresponsible actions will lead to both personal failure and the failure of those under our guidance. Rather than a game in which there must be losers in order for there to be winners, Hans-Peter Dürr advocates a game more suited to higher life forms. Rather than accepting that one must always gain at the expense of others, he would have us play a win/win game, where *all advantages gained are for the benefit of everyone.*

In times of excessive economic growth most of us are focused upon our external, materialistic well-being, which diminishes our possibility of internal growth through the nourishment of our spiritual center. We increasingly need to explore new opportunities for real meaning in our lives; a meaning which is independent of the state of the economy. This quest, undertaken in a contemplative, receptive and self-reflective manner will lead us to the realization that any and all efforts which enhance our inner, spiritual growth, those based upon love and justice for ourselves and for all living creatures, are intrinsically rewarding, and all other efforts lead ultimately only to an empty, unfulfilled life. Being receptive to learning lessons from both the external world and our personal intuitions will lead to self-improvement resulting in both personal and societal gain. It is the only reasonable, ultimate goal of our lives. But we are stubborn! It too often takes a major personal or societal crisis, one which robs us of our external "security blanket," before our attention is directed toward examining the validity of our obsession with materialistic excesses at the expense of our mental, emotional and spiritual well-being. It is difficult to convince people that extrinsic rewards cannot represent the meaning of life, that the quest for material excesses can never represent our purpose. Our ego ensures that extrinsic rewards remain first and foremost for us. The harm resulting from this one-sided development of the mind is largely ignored, but the consequences are real and dramatic. They include loneliness, depression, anxiety, selfishness and suicide to name but a few.

We face double digit growth of burnout, depression and the use of psycho-pharmaceutical drugs. According to a report sponsored by a German health insurance company, workplace absenteeism due to depression increased by 70% between 2000 and 2013. Soren Gordhamer (Gordhamer 2013, p. 146) reports that Americans spend more than 23 billion dollars each year to battle insomnia and other sleep disorders (LaRosa 2008).

"The number of patients with psychological illness is increasing, with mental illness now one of the most common clinical conditions. We are almost dealing with a widespread disease of our entire population" (KBV Kassenärztliche Vereinigung- German Association of Health Insurances – in *Die Welt* December 8, 2017).

It is important, even crucial and urgent, that we explore new opportunities, find new directions and work on a new mindset, one which will serve us better for the rest of our lives, one which is more accepted by, and acceptable to, the world society. *Recognition of the importance of inner growth is that important opportunity*. But because of our reticence to change it will take a negative wave of huge dimension for us to finally question the validity of our obsession with external values at the expense of our mental, emotional and spiritual well-being.

2.16 Global Economic Ethics Manifesto

When looking for a strong impetus for a new business ethic, one which avoids the disadvantages of our current one-sided ego-minded orientation and which is able to identify consequences for the global economy, it is important to consider the *Global Economic Ethics Manifesto* (Küng, Leisinger, Wieland 2010). Following the recent financial crisis people expressed extreme disillusionment. But the resulting anger has too often been without focus, most of us being unaware that it was the lack of clear ethical standards that govern business practices which largely contributed to the crisis. This manifesto, as presented on October 6, 2009 under the *UN Global Compact* at the UN headquarters in New York, is intended as a working document, a proposal for discussion which will evolve over time. The first signatories of the manifesto were leaders from business, politics and religion. It is significant that of the eighteen signatories only two represented the economic community. The manifesto itself was authored by ten highly recognized people, including my dear friend Hans Küng of the Global Ethic Foundation. Four of the authors were economists.

At its core the Manifesto promotes humanity from which values such as nonviolence, respect for life, justice, solidarity, honesty and tolerance are derived. It is recognized that the management elite of all institutions have a special responsibility, both within their companies and within society. The goal is the pursuit of integrity in business, the foundation of which is moral education, moral leadership, ethically driven performance criteria and ethical business practices.

The signatories make the following declaration before explaining the individual articles of the manifesto (Küng et al. 2010, p. 154):

> In this declaration, the fundamental principles and values of a global economy are set forth, according to the *Declaration toward a Global Ethic* issued by the *Parliament of World Religions* in Chicago in 1993. The principles in this manifesto can be endorsed by all men and women with ethical convictions, whether these be religiously grounded or not. The signatories of this declaration commit themselves to being led by this letter and its spirit in their day to day economic decisions, actions, and general behavior. This *Manifesto for a Global Economic Ethic* takes seriously the rules of the market and of competition; it intends to put these rules on a solid ethical basis for the welfare of all. Nothing less than the experience of the current crisis affecting the whole economy sphere underlines the need for those internationally accepted ethical principles and moral standards which we all need to breathe life into in our day to day business practices.

In the preamble, the authors point out that globally accepted norms for economic actions and decisions exist on an ethos of economic activity which is still in its infancy. This economic ethos is based on moral values and principles that are already shared by all cultures and supported by common practical experience.

They point out that we all share in common, in our diverse roles as investors, entrepreneurs, lenders, employees and consumers in all countries of the world, the desire for the implementation of global economic ethical responsibility.

Hans Küng comments (Küng et al. 2010, p. 167):

> A couple of years ago, when I would speak on ethical aspects in economies, I felt often like a voice calling in the desert. With the present global economic crisis, however, it has become much easier for me to address this issue. More and more people realize that this crisis has also to do with common ethical values and standards. One might argue, do we not have laws which just need to be enforced? Sure, solutions to the crisis require all provisions of the law. But laws are not enough. As you know, the political will to fight greed, fraud, corruption and self-aggrandizement is often weak, because it is not supported by an *ethical* will. Laws without morality cannot endure, and no legal provision can be implemented without moral consciousness based on some elementary ethical standards. But is this not just an issue of individual morality? Not at all, it is also an issue of corporate morality and concerns the global market economy as a whole.

From Küng's point of view ethics does not only denote moral appeals but also "moral action." He reminds all stakeholders in global businesses of their individual responsibility for humanizing the functioning of the global economy.

2.17 People in Companies: The Essential Moral Factor

Klaus M. Leisinger declares (Küng et al. 2010, p. 185) that no company acts only as an abstract legal institution, but rather through, and in accordance with the many different levels of its hierarchy. This is the reason why social systems such as companies per se can only be moral to a limited extent. Morality, or the lack of morality, is introduced into a social system by people, their values and their levels of integrity.

The Manifesto was an honorable and dignified undertaking. It requested of people that they endeavor to consistently act in an ethically and morally defensible manner. Now, 8 years later we must confess that immorality in the economy has not diminished in spite of new laws and serious appeals. Hans Küng recognized that all appeals are of little use, and therefore rightly calls for moral action. It does not answer however, why man is not always capable of moral action. We often endeavor to take the moral high road, but then when life gets difficult and stressors increase, or enticing opportunities arise which act to obstruct our moral vision, we fail.

When those who have no experience in business preach morality and ethical behavior to business managers no one really listens. The manifesto was given credibility in so far as it was signed by business representatives. The promoters of ethics in business are the entrepreneurs and managers who for whatever reason are sufficiently spiritually developed that they behave in a morally exemplary fashion.

Individuals are the key to change. But why are there so few individuals in the business world who have accomplished a truly sustainable improvement in ethical practices? That there are not more enlightened individuals acting in the economic sector is not due to a lack of guidelines. The crux of the problem is the lack of human maturity and a subsequent lack of soul and spirit. An immature individual cannot detect this deficiency. Why and how have we failed?

Jung believes that our failure is at least partly due to having left behind our *inner instance*, our SELF, our divine aspect. Dürckheim calls this inner instance *essence* (Dürckheim 1986, p. 39): "The essence is the manner in which the trans-space and trans-time *Being* wants to manifest in us and through us in the world!"

We are accelerating toward a point of no return, becoming ill, permanently harming both present and future generations, the environment and the fabric of society due to a lack of moral beliefs and practices, and by and large we no longer know how to get out of our self-promoted dilemma.

There is hope however, if people are willing to allow *Reason* its honorable position alongside the *ego*, adopting a shared responsibility which would allow for a whole person approach to the development of a viable set of moral considerations and ethical behavior, both in the workplace and in society at large. There is a desperate need for us to return to ensuring there is a balance between pure, rational, conscious, ego minds with decisions based upon the intellect, with Reason, which is more value-based discernment with the greater capacity to lead us toward mindful, reasoned, compassionate, intuitive decisions which arise from our unconscious.

2.18 REASON as an Anchor for Ethics and Morality

The terms mind and reason are often not clearly understood. It is important for this book and the arguments puts forward in it to clearly define how these terms are intended to be understood. Mind relates to thinking, to the intellect and other cognitive functions. The mind arises from the ego and its learning process. REASON, as used in this book, refers to the ability of human reason to *intuitively* recognize universal relationships and establish conclusions and actions based upon them.

> As far as reason relates to principles of recognition in the sciences, one speaks of *theoretical reason*. It is the reason we use to act upon something aligned to our standard of living, it follows the principles of *practical reason*, which can be oriented towards moral questions of values and towards economic principles (Extracted from Wikipedia).

However reason has a double meaning, with two polarities; nature and creation as a primary polarity and human reasoning as a secondary polarity.

> In addition to this human "subjective" (theoretical) reason, some philosophers postulate the existence of an "objective" REASON, this being an ordering principle (in a metaphysical or a cosmological sense, a world reason, a world Spirit, Logos, God). These philosophers include Heraclitus, Plotinus and Hegel. Both colloquially and in the history of philosophy the term "reason" has several overlapping meanings. On the one hand it is considered as the basis for knowledge and insight. It creates the conditions for recognition by promoting and adhering to a systematic approach and a framework for knowledge. Distinguished from reason is usually the mind as cognition or as the interaction of many different cognitive skills. On the other hand reason is used in the sense of acting reasonably. In this sense, REASON establishes a normative, philosophical ethic, which admits no appeal to other instances. It is found, for example in Aristotle as "*the right measure*" or in Immanuel Kant as the "*Categorical Imperative*". In his universal history Voltaire describes a steady development of mankind from primitive barbarism to supremacy of reason.
>
> Finally REASON is used in the meaning of "a higher order". This view usually bears the features of a religious belief, as in the *German Idealism* where reason is the "Mind of God". Mankind, the whole of humanity has in idealism contributed to this REASON, but it takes place more within him rather than he having an influence upon it. Even without accepting traditional religious dogma many people are now convinced of a world of higher REASON of creation, including Intelligent Design. Physicists like Erwin Schrödinger were convinced of the existence of a supernatural, super rational order.
>
> The *European Age of Enlightenment* is based on the idea that REASON is able to bring the truth to light. The religion of REASON shall overcome the dogmatic repression and authoritarianism of the Christian religion and bring freedom and prosperity for all. Rationalism defined REASON as "pure", a recognition independent of the empirical experiences which formed the basis of Descarte's, Spinoza's and Leibniz's philosophical systems. The concept of human reason was often equated with consciousness, self-consciousness or spirit. In Rationalism, reason represents the central element of the cognitive process. Thus deductive insights, which can be achieved even without sensory perceptions are possible. This compares with the empiricism of David Hume, which disputes the possibility of recognition "*a priori*", i.e. without experience (Extracted from Wikipedia).

However, REASON may be an anchor for ethics and morality *if* people are conscious of its double meaning and *if* they have not lost access to *objective* REASON. But that is exactly the problem today. The anchor chain is broken.

For clarity, *objective* REASON, the ordering spiritual principle implying spirit, God, or Logos will be written in this book as REASON.

2.18.1 The Abuse and Decline of REASON

This is the title of the famous book by Friedrich August Hayek, philosopher, psychologist and economist. Few could write so knowledgeably about the severing of the anchor chain. Can we get out of the dilemma in which we are entrapped by our minds so as to be able to find our connection to REASON? Friedrich August Hayek states,

... the common idea that the human mind is, as it were, to pull itself up by its own bootstraps springs from the same general approach: the belief that by studying human REASON from the outside and as a whole, we can grasp the laws of its motion in a more complete and comprehensive manner than by its patient exploration from the inside, by actually following up the processes in which individual minds interact ...

The presumptuous aspiration that REASON should direct its own growth could in practice only have the effect that it would set limits to its own growth, that it would confine itself to the results which the directing individual mind can already foresee. Though this aspiration is a direct outcome of a certain brand of rationalism, it is, of course, the result of a misunderstood or misapplied rationalism which fails to recognize the extent to which individual reason is a product of inter-individual relationships. Indeed, the demand that everything, including the growth of the human mind should be consciously controlled is itself a sign of an inadequate understanding of the general character of the forces which constitute the life of the human mind, and of human society. It is the extreme stage of these self-destructive forces of our modern "scientific" civilization, of that abuse of REASON, the development and consequences of which will be the central theme of the following historical studies.

The individualist approach, in awareness of the constitutional limitations of the individual mind, attempts to show how man in society is able by the use of various resultants of the social process, to increase his powers with the help of the knowledge implicit in them and of which he is never aware; it makes us understand that the only "REASON" which can in any sense be regarded as superior to individual reason does not exist apart from the inter-individual process in which, by means of impersonal media, the knowledge of successive generations and of millions of people living simultaneously is combined and mutually adjusted, and that this process is the only form in which the totality of human knowledge ever exists.

The collectivist method, on the other hand, not satisfied with the partial knowledge of this process from the inside, which is all the individual can gain, bases its demands for conscious control on the assumption that it can comprehend this process as a whole and make use of all knowledge in a systematically integrated form. It leads thus directly to political collectivism; and though logically methodological and political collectivism are distinct, it is not difficult to see how the former leads to the latter and how, indeed, without methodological collectivism, political collectivism would be deprived of its intellectual basis: without the pretension that conscious individual reason can grasp all the aims and all the knowledge of "society" or "humanity", the belief that these aims are best achieved by conscious central direction loses its foundation.

Consistently pursued it must lead to a system in which all members of society become merely instruments of the single directing mind, and in which all the spontaneous social forces to which the growth of the mind is due are destroyed. It may indeed prove to be the far most difficult and not the least important task for human reason to comprehend its own limitations rationally. It is essential for the growth of REASON that as individuals we should bow to forces and obey principles which we cannot hope to fully understand, yet on which the advance and even the preservation of civilization depends. Historically this has been achieved by the influence of the various religious creeds and by tradition and superstitions which made men submit to those forces by an appeal to his emotions rather than to his reason. The most dangerous stage in the growth of civilization may well be that in which man has come to regard all these beliefs as superstitions and refuses to accept or to submit to anything which he does not rationally understand. The rationalist whose reason is not sufficient to teach him those limitations of the powers of conscious reason, and who despises all the institutions and customs which have not been consciously designed, would thus become the destroyer of the civilization built upon them. This may well prove a hurdle which man will repeatedly reach, only to be thrown back into barbarism.

It would lead too far here to refer more than briefly to another field in which this same characteristic tendency of our age shows itself: that of *morality*. Here it is against the observance of any general and formal rules whose rationale is not explicitly demonstrated that the same kind of objections is raised. But the demand that every action should be judged after full consideration of all its consequences and not by any general rules is due to a failure to see that the submission to general rules, couched in terms of immediately ascertainable circumstances, is the only way in which for man with his limited knowledge freedom can be combined with the essential minimum degree of order. Common acceptance of formal rules is indeed the only alternative to direction by a single will man has yet discovered. The general acceptance of such a body of rules is no less important simply because they have not been rationally constructed. It is at least doubtful whether it would be possible in this way to construct a new moral code that would have any chance of acceptance. But so long as we have not succeeded in doing so, any general refusal to accept existing moral rules merely because their expediency has not been rationally demonstrated (as distinguished from the case when the critic believes he has discovered a better moral rule in a particular instance and is willing to brave public disapproval in testing it) is to destroy one of the roots of our civilization (Edited for brevity from *The Counter-Revolution of Science, Studies on the Abuse of Reason* (Hayek 1955).

Hayek clearly suggests that all of the actions, all of the efforts made with the best of intentions by people who have not made the ascent from mind and individual reason to the level of objective, superior, overarching REASON are doomed to failure.

2.18.2 The Leap from Mind to an Ethic of REASON

In his book *Der Gegenlauf: Das grausame Gesetz der Geschichte* (Counter-course: the cruel law of history) my friend Friedrich Gaede (Gaede 2012) deals with the need for a transitional leap from the conscious, rational *ego mind* to compassionate, mindful REASON arising from the unconscious. In so far as people are *essentially* moral, ethical and compassionate creations in nature, surely decisions which affect their well-being and ability to be productive members of a larger society must be based upon reasoned, mindful processes *and* REASON in order to resonate in any meaningful way with them.

Gaede begins his reflections:

The conception of the world as a cosmic *mechanism* is a titanic concept, one which is substantiated by scientific or physical Cartesian minds which try to measure the world with *quantitative* scales and determination. In his study, *Die Titanen* (Jünger 1944), Friedrich Georg Jünger describes the resulting paradox: "This striving for autonomy ego mind is ... titanic intelligence ... It is caught in its own mill, i.e. leading to the counter-course of self-destruction ... For both the present and for the future world the titanic man remains dangerous because of his inherent, necessarily destructive counter-course power" (Gaede 2012, p. 81)

In this conceptualization of decision-making as a purely intellectual, rational process there is no room for a *qualitative* consideration of the value that the application of ethical and moral behavior plays in the economy, and thereby in society at large. Gaede provides several historical examples which illustrate how a course of action which is established by the ego-dominated mind has built-in self-destructive counter-course tendencies which slowly but ineffably assume control. The only course of action which can negate this tendency is to elevate the control of the action from the level of the ego-dominated mind to the level of REASON. To illustrate the difference he quotes *Hegel* (Gaede 2012, p. 17) "The struggle of reasoned discernment is able to overcome what the mind has initiated and set in place."

Gaede continues,

This outlines a contrast that paradoxically, simultaneously represents a unity; the tensely exciting unity called REASON because it sagely understands it must integrate the ego dominated *mind* as its opposite pole. "The locations of the *ego dominated mind* are the clear, conscious, uppermost layers of our soul", writes G. Simmel, REASON however, is rooted deeply within the soul and spirit. Both the conscious and the unconscious need and complement each other; the conscious mind is devoted to arranging the empirical world, especially the conceptual by quantitatively categorizing, measuring, calculating, distinguishing, enforcing rules and finally judging according to the determinations made, and the applicable laws applied, to decide how to act. ... The ego dominated mind and its object are therefore two entirely different entities.

Gaede cites W. Welsch (Gaede 2012, p. 17–19): "Since the *epoch of enlightenment* has assumed the form of intellectualism, the split between subjectivity and objectivity has become the new present reality."

He continues,

The split creates on the one hand the need *to establish*, to increase the dogmatic approach, and on the other hand to ensure that the approach is non-binding. Since the ego dominated mind is seen as the most adaptable of our inner powers, it is also therefore the most irresponsible. Dogmatism and arrogance are fueled by the ego mind ...

The psychophysical dualism of perceiving both subject on the one hand and perceived object on the other hand causes E. Husserl, in his essay *Die Krise der Europäischen Wissenschaften* (The Crisis of European Sciences) (Husserl 1935), to emphatically point out that ... a rational comprehension of the world which is the result of a method should not be considered as "true being". It is therefore imperative to critically question the role and function of the mind and to limit its importance in accordance to its dimension and role. This unavoidable limitation can only be effectively accomplished through the integration of ego mental activity into REASON. ...

Since the beginning of the modern era, and even more so since the beginning of the epoch of enlightenment, the intellect has dominated by creating on the one hand the financial economy and on the other hand the general foundations of natural science. The economic and financial order, and to a large extent science are necessarily dominant intellectual abilities resulting from quantitative thinking. ... The indifference afforded to individuality which results from the logical mind working in an abstract fashion is based upon the lack of understanding of what constitutes individuality in the literal sense, namely the *indivisible* or whole. Its foundation is found within the meaning of *substare* (lat.) = *existing beneath* the substance. This is the combined ordering principle which contributes individuality to all living beings. Theology and philosophy speak of the *substance* as the *essence* of a person.

Individuality is psychoanalytically defined by C.G. Jung as the SELF, that is, the exciting *unity* of his conscious and the unconscious ...

The inability of the ego mind to grasp the potential of the power of the soul has resulted in catastrophic consequences, as has been reinforced by the philosopher Schelling in his following cautionary note:

"If the connection between the mind and the soul is interrupted the result is the most terrible thing, namely madness."

Exclusive intellectual systems when they are related to living beings contribute to the germ of destruction and self-destruction ... The tendency towards perversity of the logical mind corresponds with its inability to grasp the creative principle. The nascent principle of growth, the opposite of destruction, is dependent upon and bound to REASON because only REASON comprehends nature and its potentiality, as growing. REASON is about a dynamic understanding of nature.

The overwhelming ongoing crisis due to the formation of the eurozone which has placed European unity at risk is an excellent example of how the well-intentioned ego-dominated minds which gave birth to the eurozone must now recognize the chaos resulting from the counter-course of unreasonableness of their decisions. The members of the eurozone states along with individuals fueled by egocentric behavior and greed egotistically strive to achieve the best for their country and themselves, forgetting that the unification of Europe is the main focus. So far it seems to be that the eurozone, because of conflicting, competing interests, is unlikely to result in a lasting united Europe. Evidence the recent decisions made by the citizens of the UK to vote for Brexit; the message expounded in Gaede's book (Gaede 2012) *Der Gegenlauf* (The counter-course) can be seen to have lasting relevance!

The American Nobel laureate economist Milton Friedman in a short essay on the introduction of the new currency wrote that the new euro will not unite the continent as hoped, but rather divide it because economic adjustment by way of changing the exchange rate of the now-common currency will lead to controversial political issues ... The euro has proven to be a wealth destruction machine in more than one half of the member countries, not a wealth-creating one as was hoped. If we would have to make a decision on the euro again today, we would not decide to adopt it. However, the eurozone countries are now so intertwined that the structure cannot be disentangled without enormous political damage (*FAZ* 2015).

Following is a quote from the constitutional lawyer Udo Di Fabio (Gaede 2012, p. 31): "If we separate the state and law, and REASON from each other, then any compass for humans and for a wise conception of the 21st century is lacking." Of course we can also relate this conclusion to the economy. If in spite of all laws we are not able to realize the leap from the level of the ego-dominated mind to the level of REASON, then managers even in spite of their responsible intentions will continue to damage society, which is dependent upon the economy. It is worthy of note that while we are able to read daily of managers' detrimental behavior that there are few if any publications touting the many managers and entrepreneurs who have solved the counter-course paradox so as to benefit *both* the economy and society. Learning to trust in our ability to REASON intuitively ensures that the activities initiated by our minds follow an ethical framework which precludes unethical practices."

2.18.3 Friedrich Schiller's Freedom of REASON

Inge Brose-Müller (Lecture *Humboldt Society Meeting* Mannheim/Germany October 3, 2015) enlightened us with Friedrich Schiller's thoughts on freedom by REASON in his *Aesthetic Education of Man* in a series of letters.

> Schiller is not naive in his plea for beauty and art; again and again he starts from the physical state of a nation, he has our basic needs in mind. Man is still very primitive, he must stay warm and have enough to eat, but when these needs are met, then his better nature can be realized ... Only when the mind can be detached from the yoke of necessity can he be led to the freedom of REASON (Schiller 1793).

Today, even though we are well fed, the recognition of and desire to REASON is lacking in humanity, continuing to shackle us from the freedom of the realizations necessary to embrace a New Ethic.

2.18.4 Promoting the Faculty of REASON within Individuals

Gaede (Gaede 2012, p. 87f.) recognizes an opportunity in what he calls *monadic chance*. He promises a discussion of the *monadology* of *Leibniz*, but asks our indulgence as he first gives us an illustration from the present day, citing Christa Wolf, in the story *Cassandra*. She had her Trojan heroine berate Western thinkers, saying that for them there is only "Either truth or falsehood, right or wrong, win or lose, friend or enemy, life or death ... it is the *other* that they crush between their sharp distinctions. The *third* option, which does not exist in Western opinion, is the smiling living substance that is capable of producing again and again, by itself, the *Undivided Spirit* in life, life in the *Spirit*." As does Gaede, Christa Wolf recognizes that the development of the living force that grows between the opposite poles has a unifying, connecting power. That which then arises from the opposites is a single harmonious unity.

Gaede comments (Gaede 2012, p. 88):

This *Third*, which Pascal refers to as *sense*, originates in the unconscious – or according to Christa Wolf from the *undivided* influx of creative energy. Jung speaks of it also in connection with Schiller's insight, and calls it the *third* or the *middle way* which is most fruitful when the two opposites, the quantitative thinking of the ego mind and the qualitative intuiting of the essence, the Self, are in balance. Then, according to Jung, the *creative imagination* can act as a *symbol forming power* and can begin the process designated by Christa Wolf, *bringing forth from itself*.

For Hans-Peter Dürr sustainability is only achieved when we can truly say that we have made *living livelier*. This revelation was of crucial importance to him, to the extent that at the end of our five years of friendship he requested that his interpretation be spread around my world of influence. How can we bring about the individuation of the person described by Jung so that new ethical practices can result from experiencing the *Self*? To paraphrase Christa Wolf, how do we go about *bringing forth from the Self*? Gaede (Gaede 2012) provides us with a philosophical answer culled from the turn of the seventeenth and eighteenth centuries:

> In 1695 Leibniz decides, in the revival of his sharp criticism of Cartesian thinking, to implement the *substantial forms*. What this means is found in the *Aristotle Substance Doctrine*, which applies to all living things. The result evolves into the later *monadology* in 1714, considered to be Leibniz's major contribution.

The terms *monas* which is Greek for unity or simplicity, and *monad* which occurs throughout the history of philosophy have slightly different meanings, but their basic intents remain remarkably consistent. Usage begins with the Pythagoreans and unfolds especially in Neoplatonism, in Christian mysticism, Jewish Kabbalah and the Hermetic tradition. Later they all almost unite in meaning in Leibni's *monadology,* before they begin once again to adopt individual interpretations in the nineteenth century (Wikipedia).

Regardless of the diversity of specific mystical pathways chosen by various religions, and sects within religions, ultimately there lies within each of us the recognition that it is all about personally experiencing unity, and projecting this unity upon the external world. This constitutes a widespread agreement that *ethics begin within* and are understood and accepted individually.

Concerning the basic maxim of the *monadology* Gaede states,

> "The monad perceives itself", a statement consistent with Christa Wolf's, "Bringing forth from itself". The meaning of the word *perceives* is of importance here. It means more than simply *bringing forth*. It is self-imagined, internally organized and includes the entire underlying reasoning process which precedes, initiates and supports the *bringing forth*. The *monadology* is an alternative system of REASON to the ever present danger of the counter course of the world of the ego dominated mind.

Gaede (Gaede 2013, p. 5) extends his thoughts in a *Lecture for the Museum Society* in Freiburg, Germany, where he further refers to the biblical story of Adam and Eve in Paradise, and the Tree of Knowledge.

> If, therefore, man who has been seduced to believe that with his knowledge gained through the snake he is already *God like*, then he is addicted to arrogance ... arrogance which is manifested

as ruthless self-will which is later referred to as *will to power*, called by Nietzsche the "Urfactum of History", the basic engine of history. This arrogance-based will carries within it the core of failure ...

This is consistent with Jürgen Manemann's *position* in his *Critique of the Anthropocene* in which he argues the need for a new human ecology (Manemann 2014).

Gaede also referred to Sebastian Franck, who in 1534 raised serious concerns resulting from the serpent-seduced human judgment because it was misused so as to specifically serve in taking advantage of people.

> The "seduced" judgment leads to *acts of will* which primarily serve self-interest. These voluntary actions follow a specific pattern in which the alternative poles of good and evil are expressed in the manner of *either/or* ... Less harmless are either/or statements which express the alternative as a negative or undesirable state, phrases such as either profit or loss.

This *either/or* thinking too often leads modern managers to utilize immoral actions such as false accounting and price fixing, aiming for greater profits and the good of the company as justification for unethical practices. For Gaede the either/or argument is a *Luciferian* curse. He cites Hegel who notes, "either/or ... is expressing a principle of ego mind that renounces REASON."

Because of its importance in understanding the consequences, I have deliberately and extensively illustrated how a course of action which is established by the ego mind has built in self-destructive counter-course tendencies which slowly but ineffably assume control when the flow of actions are not elevated to the level of REASON.

> *When you have initiated decisions and actions with your ego mind they must be transferred to the level of REASON or you will destroy what you have begun!*

Will managers act with REASON when and if exposed to the foregoing historical, soundly reasoned and intuitively rational philosophical positions? Probably not, or at best, only a very few will. Some may be attracted to the idea of REASON being able to liberate them from the limitations of their mind's limited intelligence, but without truly understanding and accepting the reality of the power of the ego-dominated mind they will allow their mind to *limit its own limitations*, thwarting the effort of the unconscious to incorporate *individuation* into the decision-making process. This is a serious problem of paramount importance. The findings of philosophers and spiritual intellectuals who preceded us are a cultural asset of tremendous value. They are available to assist us in finding our way through difficult situations which are perhaps new *to us*, but not novel. Unfortunately most of us today have no conscious awareness of historical philosophies. The treasure is thus stored in the collective unconscious where it cannot be accessed by the mind, but solely through the soul which is our guide to the unconscious. Once the leap to spiritual consciousness is undertaken and a body–soul–spirit unity is established, we are guaranteed the emergence of viable, defensible ethical behavior in all of our activities, both professional and personal.

If performance-based managers have difficulty raising their ethical actions to the level of REASON from that of the mind, then at the very least they must understand that their potential for success is compromised. That would be a beginning, and perhaps ultimately also a motivation for change. How can we facilitate this leap to spiritual consciousness so as to benefit from managers of the economy who access their individuation? There is also access to REASON through the heart, for example in Sufism and in the mysticism of Islam. Pope Francis refers in his recent Encyclical Letter *LAUDATO SI'* REASON to a source for ethical principles. "The ethical principles capable of being apprehended by REASON can always reappear in different guise and find expression in a variety of languages, including religious language."

Blaise Pascal: "There is a REASON of the heart unknown to the mind."

"Moral reasoning" was also very often connected with Business Ethics by numerous other authors during the last few decades. For example, Linda Klebe Trevino (Klebe Trevino 1992, pp. 445–459) writes:

Beginning in 1958, Kohlberg revived interest in moral psychology. His theory of cognitive moral development (Kohlberg, 1969) emphasized the cognitive basis of moral judgement and its relationship to moral action. A number of ethics researchers have been guided by Kohlberg's cognitive moral development (CMD) theory. Although not without critics, Kohlberg's CMD theory has become the most popular and tested theory of moral reasoning, and it remains among the most cited work in contemporary behavioral science. CMD theory focuses primarily on the cognitive process involved. ... judging what is morally right.

It is important to be clear that "moral reason" is not REASON. It may be a smaller part of it, or even a consequence of REASON. As this theory relegates the cognitive process to the ego mind it must be considered out of date and out of touch with recent revelations.

How about the possibility of change as a result of education, or through suffering? Many of us have directly experienced that suffering often leads us to make changes, at least in our actions if not in our intentions; often a *sine qua non*. Through a comprehensive education which focuses not only upon expanding the ego-dominated mind, but pays equal attention to morality, ethics and the higher education of the spirit, future generations would be better prepared for life, including being able to transfer their learning into marketable, *reasonably* ethically sound business practices. Hans-Peter Dürr summed up the limitations of our knowledge and the vastness of our experience in the statement: "We experience much more than we know!"

What about the education of our children and young adults? Is there hope that we will move toward an education which includes instruction in spiritual philosophy, or at least some exposure to it? Can we hope for a future that includes a population which is once again literate in the fullness and richness of ideas which have been espoused by philosophers and educators for countless centuries? Unfortunately, for the past half century our formal educational institutions have moved *away* from *educating* the whole person, and *toward training* the ego-dominated mind. Historical, well-reasoned and fully functional educational ideas are discarded in the race for new ideas. *Modern* educators wish to be published with their new *fashionable* ideas. These ideas far too often cannot stand the light of historical scrutiny, and are thus destined to be replaced within a decade or two by *newer* irresponsibly unsound practices; this all at the expense of generation after generation of young fertile minds which are devoid of the ability to REASON, to see the *big picture*, or to develop a functional social or economic consciousness. Witness the OECD which advocates for PISA (Program for International Student Assessment), which tests educational concepts that are based upon economic fiction.

2.19 OECD Guidelines Are Seriously Misguided

Silja Graupe and Jochen Krautz take the following critical position in the FAZ on December 6, 2013.

> PISA and its results determine how future generations are formed. It is a comparative measure and evaluation of the skills and abilities of students in over 30 countries. PISA directors openly confessed that this measure does not take into consideration the educational traditions, constitutions and regulations of the countries surveyed ... By its own account, since the 1960's the OECD has played a central role in the provision of indicators on educational services and wants not only to evaluate educational policies, but also to contribute to their design ... The plan for this was formulated in 1961 at a conference entitled, *Economic Growth and Education Expenses*, convened in Washington, D.C. The plan was then recommended, as noted by the Cultural Commission of Europe, without taking into account any criticism from national ministries or parliaments. The positions outlined as a result of the conference were major determinants for the public discussion of pedagogical and educational programs which ensued. It is rare that a single conference has so visibly changed the policy of so many countries. It was not an expressed intent of the conference to consider the varying and diverse standards which had historically evolved to meet the educational traditions of each country's needs and cultural diversity. Rather, the proceedings were designed such as to *disregard* individual traditional norms. The result was that in developing countries tens of millions of people were to be denied traditional knowledge and wisdom that reached back many millennia. The educational focus of the schools and the communities in these countries had previously been consistent with social and religious goals, some of which promoted resignation and spiritual consolation, things that are contrary to economic progressivism.

Entire societies were deliberately cut off from their spiritual roots in order to be placed at the service of economic growth. Jung's statement "Throughout my practice, I have never found a patient where, at the end of a detailed medical history, the separation from the numinous (spirit) was not the cause of the disease," is pertinent here. It follows that educational policies and practices which focus entirely upon the mind and actively avoid the education of the spirit will lead to mental and physical distress. It is evidenced by burnout, a lack of purpose, immoral and unethical attitudes and practices, and depression and suicide among students and young adults.

Graupe and Krautz continue,

The OECD Program condemned the growing pluralism of educational goals and the practices resulting from those goals and renewed the fight to replace them with a single new idea: *At school only those attitudes, wishes and expectations which help a country to strive for progress, to think and to act economically, will be fostered. People should not learn to set their own standards of responsibility for their community.*

With the stroke of a pen the possibility for making responsible decisions regarding the economy, as demanded by John Maurice Clark, was abolished with the blessing of the OECD!

To ensure compliance, the OECD enacted a *Code of Ethics* and *Codes of Conduct*:

Citizens expect public servants to serve the public interest with impartiality, legality, integrity and transparency on a daily basis. Core values guide the judgment of public servants about how to perform their tasks in daily operations. To ensure that the standards are enacted a vast majority of OECD countries have established written, formal codes of behavioral standards. They can set out in broad terms those values and principles that define the professional role of the civil service, for example integrity and transparency, or they can focus on the application of such principles in practice, for instance in conflict of interest situations such as the use of official information and public resources, receiving gifts or benefits, or working outside the public service and post public employment. Ideally, these codes combine aspirational values and more detailed standards on how to put them into practice.

The forgoing are guidelines for the public sector. What about the OECD guidelines for the economy? Angel Gurria, OECD Secretary General delivered a paper at the *European Business Ethics Forum* (EBEF), titled *Business Ethics and the OECD Principles*, on January 22, 2009, addressing *What can be done to avoid another crisis?*:

The current global economic crisis is costing the world trillions of dollars, a protracted recession, millions of lost jobs, a huge loss of confidence in financial markets and a reversal in our efforts to curb global poverty. It is the result of the combination of several failures. A failure of business ethics is one of them, one that lies at the epicenter of this financial and economic earthquake. In the coming months the rules of the global financial and economic system will be rewritten. The incentives for proper behavior have to be included in those new rules. A new balance between governments and markets will also be established. The crisis will give us the opportunity to build the foundations of a new business culture, one which is more ethical and responsible. The OECD is already working to develop a framework to ensure that these events will not happen again. We are working for a fairer, cleaner and stronger economy.

That paper was delivered in 2009. Is there any evidence of change in the economy? Do we increasingly find more responsibility and ethical behavior in the economy? I don't think so. We simply have another set of guidelines on our bookshelf.

Graupe and Krautz continue,

In 1961 the OECD stated in unequivocal openness that the goal of education is dynamic adaptation, adaptation to the abstract needs of the economy. Today, it goes without saying that within the context of the influence of the economy on the educational system, it is just as necessary for the economy to prepare *people* as material assets and equipment. But our educational systems are little more than reflections of highways, steel plants and fertilizer factories.

This is reminiscent of the phrase *human capital*. From what dark corner of what misguided minds could that phrase have been coined and accepted? How can *human capital* learn to behave ethically when they have been *trained* rather than *educated*, so as to be of use in increasing profits without scruples; to increase productivity as would be expected of a machine? The OECD appears to be of the opinion that the accumulation of *intellectual capital* benefits us as much as the accumulation of *financial capital*, and in fact in the long run it is likely even of greater benefit. The OECD endorses the *human capital* theory.

Graupe and Krautz continue,

> In an OECD release in 2007 we are told, *individual abilities* would be considered as *a form of capital*, as *a factor of production, like a spinning wheel or a flour mill, which generate cash returns.* Willingness to adapt and ability to apply oneself is a core key competence for the OECD. What once constituted a *literacy* competence was the ability to read with comprehension and to formulate ideas and form opinions as a result. The *literacy* competence has now become the ability to *use information to function in society so as to benefit the economy* ... But that's not all. The environment to which the students are asked to adapt is not the real and experienced economy but rather a mere ideal, created by the economists of the *Chicago School of Economics*, one which is now being applied to education: the idea of the market as a purely abstract, super-conscious price and coordination mechanism towards which all human action is to align. Conversely, this unrealistic designation prevents any criticism or individual willingness to change, because it is not just perceived in the public as a theoretical construct, but *viewed by most people as an immediately obvious truth*, as the neoliberal August Hayek writes ...

Graupe and Krautz are of the opinion that

> teachers and students are being encouraged to believe that pedagogy is no longer a role of education, having given way to diagnosing and evaluating ... The legacy of measuring is ultimately much more far reaching than the mere results of the measurements undertaken. Regardless of what PISA measures, of how accurately, or of the good or poor results which emerge, the *power* is in the measuring *process* itself. The processes accustom people to impart value to *quantitative* distinctions of *more* or *less*, without consideration of the *quality* of the education being delivered. Students are taught to prepare for a world in which success is measured in economic growth, rather than being presented with philosophical positions which encourage them to *qualitatively reason* analytically and abstractly, suspending belief in only the *quantitative status quo*. It is time to end this planned cultural uprooting of education which undermines democracy and the *real* economy.

2.20 Educating the Whole Person

What the people have lost, that which is degraded by the will of the OECD to mere train human capital focusing only upon economic success, was clearly elucidated by Inge Brose-Müller when she spoke at The Semi-Annual Meeting of the *Humboldt* Society in October 2015 about "The City-The Art-The Human," referring to Friedrich Schiller. In her opinion, Schiller wishes to guide us in the investigation of the instinctual structure of the individual to the totality of man, something which had been lost by the theoretical culture of the Enlightenment. She goes on to say that he wants to overcome the opposite aberration, an era of "crudeness" on the one hand and "slackness" on the other hand, which are encouraged by our "beautiful culture," but he wonders what the remedy against such antipodes could be.

I think we can agree that the "crudeness" and "slackness" continue to be a dilemma. People are suffering without the knowledge that their own self-centered "crudeness" affects the entire collective, and then proceed to blame, in a classic projection, that the collective is "crude." Too often they lack an inner orientation toward wholeness in the outside world. They are "slacked" by all their aimless wandering in their affluent society but are unable to break free from it due to a lack of a holistic education which otherwise could offer them a meaningful personal orientation (lat.: *oriri* =rise).

The remedy to the dilemma proclaimed by Schiller is to be found throughout this book. It is designed to guide us to the New Ethic through a personal commitment to inner growth.

According to Inge Brose-Müller, Schiller sees the task of man to be in his approach to the idea of his humanity. Idealistically, this is an infinite process, one which can at best achieve only partial success in an individual's lifetime. However, achieving the consciousness of wholeness and humanity *is* possible in our life time, and can be achieved through the methodologies of individuation, meditation and Christian contemplation. We will expand upon this shortly.

Brose-Müller refers us to Wilhelm von Humboldt:

> As an idealist Wilhelm von Humboldt formulated a similar idea, albeit without the dualism of the instincts. In his letters to Charlotte Diede he writes: "… every human being carries, independently of how good he is, an even better Being in himself, which accounts for his actual 'SELF.' But he is probably even unfaithful to the SELF. One must rely on this inner and unfluctuating Being and not on the fluctuating and everyday being, which must be repatriated to this inner and not so changeable Being. Only then can one forgive the many things of which the deeper Being is innocent (Leitzmann 1910).

Humboldt also targets "internal improvement and refinement", but he does not appear to inform us of how man experiences his inner core as far as I know.

How current is this message! Humboldt's "actual Self" and "the core" can be recognized as the SELF as defined by C.G. Jung, our Divine Core, unlike our worldly Ego. He also advises us, as do proponents of all spiritual approaches, how we can advance ourselves to experience this core through the process of individuation and inner growth which may lead to the achievement of a unique experience of enlightenment.

2.21 Our Society Is Unhealthy for Children's Souls

There continue to be efforts to overcome the current negative attributes which *schooling* has adopted. Private schools such as the anthroposophical *Waldorf* schools are one example.

Another counter movement is the *Class 2000* being undertaken in German primary schools. With *Class 2000* and its symbolic figure *KLARO*, children experience what they can do for themselves, and what it takes for them to feel satisfied and fulfilled. From early childhood through grade 4 children are exposed to healthy, active, vivid and vitally enjoyable experiences. Teachers and specially trained health promoters and facilitators devote about fifteen *Class 2000* hours per school year entirely to health and life skills, helping to develop in children knowledge, attitudes and skills that will enable them to cope with everyday life in a manner in which they may remain comfortable and healthy.

Goals of *Class 2000*

- Children learn to be healthy, and equally importantly that they must participate in promoting their own health.
- Children learn to know their body, and to know what they can do to keep it healthy in a manner which makes them feel comfortable.
- Children learn important life skills such as dealing with emotions and stress, collaborating with others, solving conflicts and thinking critically.

Themes incorporated in *Class 2000*

- Healthy diets
- Movement and relaxation
- Loving yourself and forming friendships
- Solving problems and conflicts
- Critical thinking and learning to say no

Currently one out of every eight students in elementary school is participating, with more than one million children having participated since the program began in 1991. In the school year 2012–13 over 420 000 children in 18 376 primary school classes took part, which corresponds to 13.6% of all primary classes.

At the high school level there are also some very positive approaches such as that on which Juliane Cernohorsky-Lücke (Cernohorsky-Lücke 2015, p. 77–79) reports in the Journal *Bewusstseinswissenschaften* (Consciousness Studies). Her approach is that students consider themselves as a project under the motto: "Everyone is a good idea that wants to become a reality." According to Juliane, an individual's talents and their individual fate are starting points from which to create and direct their lives, which is to be seen in the context of a larger *Whole*. This is the approach to the teaching of ethics. Students learn mindfulness exercises which assist in affirming themselves and others. They also study art which deepens and enriches their dialogue. In addition opportunities for empathetic experiences and personal expression are facilitated.

These schools also promote:

- Balance of personality: Using games, group and individual tasks, self-knowledge is promoted in terms of strengths and weaknesses in a protected environment.

- From thinking about to thinking ahead: How to philosophize? Thinking from the future! My life. Who lives it? If not me, then who?
- Autogenesis, yoga practice, time management and vitality: "No one is an island unto himself."
- Being alone in nature: What is the farewell to childhood? What do I really want from my life?

The focus is upon holistic personality development with the thesis: "One who is grounded in himself as a human being will ultimately have the most to give to society." Here we can recognize the emphasis upon ethics. Horst Eberhard Richter wrote, "Only he who is reconciled with himself can work with others in a caring way!"

How unfortunate that these positive approaches are the exception!

The *WAZ* (*Westdeutsche Allgemeine Zeitung,* a Daily German Newspaper) wrote on 2nd March 15 under the heading *Our Society Is Unhealthy for Children's Souls*:

> The number of children, adolescents and young adults who have been diagnosed and hospitalized with depression has increased significantly. In 2004 there were 4176 young people between the ages of ten and twenty treated with depression according to figures from the Federal Office of Statistics, by 2012 that figure had increased to 12 567 …

"Environmental factors play a decisive role," says Prof. Johannes Hebebrand, chief physician at the LVR Clinic of Child and Adolescent Psychiatry in Essen. Death, divorce, a move, a change of school, work pressure and stress are risk factors. For Hebebrand it is equally clear that the changed structure of the workplace is also responsible for ensuring that increasingly more and more young people with depression are seeking help. In his clinic children and young adults from all backgrounds are advised and treated. But, he writes, "Depression is more common in lower social classes. Perhaps this is a consequence of the stress caused by increased economic pressure …"

It is always possible to speculate upon *external* causes for this ever-increasing depression in our young people, but we must also examine personal lifestyle choices. What sort of model do we, as parents present? Do we have a *purpose*, other than getting through the daily grind? Do we spend our leisure time in fruitful, healthy, vitalizing activities, or is it filled with mindless television, digital toys and shallow entertainment to try to fill the spiritual void of which we are intuitively aware? The lack of a meaningful, *purposeful* balance in life inevitably leads to physical, mental and spiritual disorders.

Are the Universities Slaves to the Economy? This is the title of an article in *Die ZEIT* (The Time – German Weekly Newspaper and Magazine) published in March 2015. "The close relationship of the economy to the universities is too powerful," says sociologist Michael Hartmann. As university financing by the economy increases so does the influence of the economy upon the universities.

> Those who wish to solicit money from the economy must deliver goods or services which are in the interest of the economy. Rarely does this happen as spectacularly as when oil corporations

solicited reports from the American scientist Wei-Hock Soon, of the Harvard Smithsonian Center for Astrophysics. For a secret payment in excess of one million dollars he published a report in which he denied the link between global warming and carbon dioxide emissions.

Even without any financial support from the industrial sector the focus of many universities is increasingly becoming one of *training* students for the *business* world, at the expense of *educating* them for *life*. Young people are not receiving an education appropriate to facilitating their personal growth and intuitive development prior to entering the world of business. If we have predominantly experienced rewards only for quantitative gains we cannot be expected to be adequately prepared to successfully carry forward qualitative goals into our career. If we have never been encouraged to develop a sound moral, ethical base, how can we be expected to be able to apply these principles to reasoned decision-making, or to be able to show personal resolve and leadership in crisis situations, in either our personal or professional life? Experience in REASON prior to entering the workforce is essential for making ethical decisions once professionally employed.

Gerald Hüther describes the dilemma from his point of his view as a brain researcher.

> I am convinced that for all of us the lone-fighter phase is over and we are at a point where we need to develop a new culture of living together and working together based on trust and cooperation. In this form of cooperation it is no longer a matter of using his knowledge for his own career plans, but to provide it to the community and society. This form of cooperation has rarely succeeded, because the school system and the corporate incentive system that we have created do not support the desire, experience and knowledge to share with others in confidence. (Hüther 2015)

Hüther also explains how new experiences and thus new interconnections in the brain are possible through strengthening community experiences, which in turn are powerfully enabling.

We are **disempowered** as a result of our educational system abrogating its responsibility to educate, replacing it with business skills training. Since access to the soul is missing disempowerment is inevitable, because we need our soul as a guide to our unconscious. In the words of J.G. Herder, man is "disabled of his higher powers." He has lost access to his unconscious where his higher powers reside. Spiritually disabled people are not able to access sound intuitive guidance in order to make reasoned decisions concerning ethical or moral practices. Yet, society has an expectation of ethical practices from the spiritually disabled. If we were to pass judgment upon them it must be, *not criminally responsible*, as we as a culture have failed to ensure that they have the necessary preparation to *enable* and *empower* them to act ethically.

People who have received traditional performance-based training begin a new management career with clear and enthusiastic expectations of succeeding. They have every belief that they have received all the *tools* that they need to do so during their training. But before long they realize that something is missing, that while they apply all the principles that they learned during their training there seem to be aspects of *interpersonal* relationships for which they are not prepared. They too often do not have a spiritual center, a place of depth upon which they can rely when crisis situations call for resilience. The ethics surrounding appropriate, productive practices have not been developed and internalized. Quickly the easier, attractive path of immoral decisions and unethical behavioral practices reveals itself appealingly, entrapping the unsuspecting victim. While society has complicity in the resulting *disabled* ethical behavior, each of us must assume responsibility for our personal awareness and the expansion of our consciousness toward a higher life, allowing us to energetically access and sustain high ethical and moral standards. Each of us has a clear mission for our lifetime: uniting and aligning with that higher energy which may be ascribed many different names, including God, Divine Principle, Emptiness, Allah, Yahweh, Brahman, Higher Being and Spiritual Dimension.

2.22 Is It All about Performance

My first teacher, Karlfried Graf Dürckheim (Dürckheim 1988, p. 27f.) told the story of a manager who had *performance* as his life mantra, and puzzled over why he found himself chronically unhappy. He related that once a very successful manager with a great reputation came to him and lamented,

> Professor, please tell me what I am missing. I am very healthy. I have no financial problems. I have nothing to apologize for. I have a so-called clean record and am well respected by my employees and numerous others. Many could envy me. Yet nevertheless, something is wrong in my life. In spite of all my privileges I have an incomprehensible fear, in spite of my own wholesomeness I have feelings of sin and guilt, and in spite of all my wealth I have the feeling of darkness and emptiness.

> Dürckheim: "May I ask you, what is your life's guiding principle?"

> "It's all about performance," said the top manager.

> Dürckheim: "You are a poor man. I am not surprised that you are unhappy. Do you really believe that performance is the most important thing in life; that life has to be focused only on performance?"

> "What else is important?" asked the manager.

> Dürckheim: "Have you ever heard about the inner path which the human being has to fulfill in addition to the outer path, the work in the world ... Have you considered that inner growth may be a condition for your inner peace?"
>
> With a disrespectful gesture the manager said: "Do you mean something like religion or such? My dear professor, we as top managers do not have any time for that kind of stuff. We cannot use it to manufacture our products or to achieve leading positions in the business world!"

> Dürkheim concludes. "These people, very often busy, well educated, conscientious and orderly, well-meaning people are so greatly limited by their mania to be successful that they believe it can replace all need for their inner growth. The result is a high performance animal which because of his one sidedness is a mere caricature of what a human being is meant to be; a unity of body, mind, soul and spirit ... If you would paint such a human being he would have a giant head, a blown up breast and mechanical limbs of steel which are directed by a tenacious will. But in the middle,

where the guiding center of soul and spirit resides, would be a vacuum which is sheltered by an anxious and easily vulnerable ego. The human being who corresponds to this picture remains, inside, a child in spite of all that he knows, all he can do and all he has achieved, because the soul remains small and is blocked from being able to develop in the person and in his attitude ... The result is emptiness, guilt and fear. These symptoms frequently occur in people who seem to be at the top of their career. Others, who aren't aware of this internal dilemma may admire their visible façade, but behind the façade is an unhappy human being whose suffering soul and lack of inner peace is the result of having remained an immature individual.

Very often these individuals don't see any other possibility for maintaining a modicum of inner peace than to practice an ironclad self-discipline in order to keep their inner tensions under control. But the suppression of the tensions will not lead to any improvement. It will result in frustration, anxiety, nervousness and mood swings, which will be followed by a lack of zest for life. These inner problems may be kept under control in business, but at home family members will suffer the consequences. When the pressure cannot be contained any longer explosions of impulsiveness will follow. In many cases it ends up as Burn Out, depression or some other form of psychological or psychosomatic illness."

Burnout may be considered the implosion of the self-centered ego when outside pressure is increasing. If at that point nothing has been developed inside that can keep you strong you undergo a breakdown, a *Burnout*, from which *healing can only be achieved by inner growth, not through any wellness programs or a simple reduction of work load.*

2.23 Decoding Leadership: What Really Matters

Under the headline *Decoding Leadership: What really matters*, McKinsey writes in *McKinsey Quarterly* 2014 No 4, that new research suggests that the secret to developing effective leaders is to encourage four types of behavior.
1) Solving problems effectively
2) Operating with a strong results orientation
3) Seeking different perspectives
4) Supporting others

These four kinds of behavior account for 89% of leadership effectiveness. This is based on a survey of 81 organizations that are diverse in geography, industry and size (Source: McKinsey's Organizational Health Index). Unfortunately too many managers still have no idea of how best to manage for optimum results.

2.24 The Broken Elite

Benedict Herles, elite student and former management consultant, refers in his book to these one-sided, fixated upon performance managers as "The Broken Elite" in an interview with *Der Spiegel* (A weekly German Magazine) in 2013. An edited version of which follows.

Spiegel: Your descriptions read as if consultants are engaged in a meaningless profession.

Herles: It is not a profession valuing reflection and the search for meaning. It's about being able to juggle one-time events. As a beginner you are little more than a human calculator ... You do not have to be Chairman of the Board to recognize that what is being taught in business schools is nonsense! Must your business card read Managing Director in order to notice that many companies are being analyzed to death? On the contrary, "Those who have been too accepting of the *system* for too long are unaware of what is self-evident to others."

Spiegel: You studied economics at the private WHU – *Otto Beisheim School of Management* in Vallendar, a German Business School. Did you enjoy a regular, traditional student life?

Herles: No, of course not. At WHU there is no student life. During the breaks, *Wall Street Journal Europe* is read, or the next student private equity club is organized. In Vallendar students run with their laptops between lectures and the study hall, back and forth, back and forth, so as not to lose time. We collectively studied all night before exams. The examination room smelled like *Red Bull*. There is no time, encouragement or consideration of free thought because the entire focus is upon training for business. The curriculum is fully packed with facts and strategies. There is no room for reflection. In the little spare time everyone drinks a lot. Work hard, play hard ...

Spiegel: Would you describe graduates of WHU as academics?

Herles: The curriculum there is simply to be learned, memorized and then regurgitated on an exam. Any intellectuals in attendance are only there *despite* the institutional philosophy, not because of it. Intellectual, creative and divergent thinking necessitating qualitative investigation is neither promoted nor facilitated at WHU. Business universities are about qualitative, repetitive training. Humanities components are completely absent.

Herles has the following to say concerning the skills and experiences of the consultants:

Loads of schematic business knowledge is produced but it is all carefully designed and controlled. They promote themselves as having the perspective of an outsider, but at the same time the knowledge of an industry expert! That they can accomplish both is difficult to believe given that most consultants in this industry are under the age of thirty five. When, and from where have they achieved their industrial experience? But the students are happy to go along with the deception. It allows them the easy route of simply following directions and thus not assuming personal responsibility for any future difficult decisions which may necessitate tough actions ...

Spiegel: Which students rise to the top?

Herles: Performance is the only mantra in this system. Anyone who fears risk and welcomes conformity survives best. The students are anxious and brutally ambitious, status symbols are important to them. Final assessment is of a technocratic nature, there is no credit given to rational analysis or forecasting.

Spiegel: Very linear thinkers, then?

Herles: Definitely not the people I would wish to assume leadership responsibilities in our economy. The result would be a society in which I would not wish to live.

Spiegel: A young consultant recently died in London. Are you aware of the circumstances?

Herles: Yes, he was at WHU. I do not know the exact nature of the circumstances, but it adds credence to the fact that something is seriously wrong with the system.

It is sad that some of Herles statements sound radical. They could only be perceived as radical in a society which has become numbed by the incessant downward spiral of rational thinking and qualitative education. Would it not be wonderful if more leaders of our business communities had learned the benefits of developing inner growth, allowing them to perform their duties with serenity, joy, humor, empathy, congruence and compassion for others? If we wish to break out of this *race toward the bottom*, future generations must be educated, not just trained.

There is good news concerning WHU. Beginning in 2015 a new course entitled Business Ethics was introduced by WHU's Chair of Organizational Behaviour. Equally encouraging is that the course will take into consideration the individual experiences of WHU graduates. The more educators recognize and control for the incessant demands of the ego-dominated intellect by encouraging the individuation which follows from inner growth and moral development, the more we will be able to look forward to leaders in society who demonstrate the principles of ethical behavior.

2.25 Business Ethics: The Lost Generation

This title was coined by the well-known professor of economics from St. Gallen, Switzerland, Fredmund Malik (Malik 2005), who said that since managers now only think in terms of numbers and only about money, a lost generation must re-learn morality. He believes that with a few exceptions, there is no shortage of managers with intrinsic morality. The issue is with their training. Students who have completed a typical American-embossed program for a Master of Business Administration (MBA), no matter at which university, graduate without the essential ability to assume leadership positions. Business education is enamored with case studies, with the result that critical reflection is no longer encouraged or valued. The question of what is right for a company, for managers and for their management style has become simply *that it be modern*. A whole generation of managers will have to be "educated" if they wish to manage effectively. The two greatest misconceptions of economics, beliefs which will surely lead to failure, are that shareholder value and the increase in the value of stocks are the ultimate purpose and objectives of a company. These dreadful misconceptions have become entrenched in the minds of many, especially younger executives, worldwide. These dysfunctional beliefs continue to be the only management theories that are taught in the English-speaking world. The very best efforts at morality, in the absence of relevant knowledge concerning corporate management, will not compensate for this deficiency. Conversely, when enlightened management training occurs it is not necessary to indoctrinate students with moral codes of conduct, because it will intrinsically arise within them.

While Malik has the best of intentions his position that our economic issues can be resolved through better education is inaccurate. We have a serious ethical and moral problem in the economy and a change in educational practices alone will not solve it. Imparting management knowledge does not automatically lead to a sense of morality or ethical behavior.

Malik is not convinced that Anglo-Saxon management is the best model. It has led to undesirable developments, which though seen as distinctly moral shortcomings are actually something else. This management style has elevated people *who previously had no chance of advancing*, to the leadership of large companies. But, tragically *not* to leading positions in companies which are sustainably managed. Those who are being advanced are driven by greed, operating in a winner/loser style. Their economic understanding of the world is limited by the quantification of business plans in monetary terms. These managers believe that only that which is quantified can be effectively managed, whereas in reality effective management necessitates taking effective actions in situations which *cannot* be quantified.

There is a widespread perception that materialistic greed has become the new norm. While it is true that there are those driven by human greed, they are rare. Moral arguments are lost on these few, those that do eventually recognize the error of their ways generally do so in accordance with *Hofmannsthal*'s observation that it occurs only in the final days of their life. Anxiety concerning money including a focus upon earning money is not the same as greed. Money anxiety results from the apparently best, internationally recognized education offered by certified universities during which one learns that only what can be expressed in economic terms matters, namely money. This is then legitimized by those receiving MBA degrees which are inculcated with the belief that there are no other values except monetary ones. Because of the exaggerated importance of MBAs in our society, which holds them in reverence, this belief becomes expanded beyond money simply being of primary importance in the economy, to all other sectors of society as well.

Life is measured by such people in monetary terms not because they are unskilled or innately immoral, but because they have been taught and have internalized the belief that this is the ultimate truth. They do have quite a strong sense of morality – the morality of economic reductionism, which was, however, never represented by any one of the true liberal thinkers; not by Friedrich von Hayek, Ludwig von Mises or Wilhelm Röpke. The Scottish moral philosophers of the eighteenth century who were the founders of true liberalism were opposed to such economic thought. It is due to neoliberal superficial knowledge that the basic components of the economy are now at risk.

What liberalism requires is that all of us, including managers must assume responsibility for our own actions. True liberalism does not mean that all of its objectives must be assumed by the economy. Numerous positions of liberalism have undergone scrutiny recently with the result that they have been rescinded. It is harmful to preach to people that the market economy is a wonderful system. The market economy is dysfunctional at a societal level. It is unsustainable. We experience the truth of this daily. It is experienced as brutal, pitiless, inhumane and unjust. Leaders continue to defend the market economy as they know that all other systems commonly taught are much worse, and even more inefficient. But this is shallow praise for a failing system that operates immorally and inefficiently.

2.26 Expanding the *Status quo* is Insufficient for Ethical Development

In the *Harvard Business Review*, May 2015, in an article entitled *How to Outsmart Your Bias and Broaden Your Thinking* John Beshears and Francesca Gino write:

> All employees, from CEO's to frontline workers commit preventable mistakes: We underestimate how long it will take to finish a task, overlook or ignore information that reveals a flaw in our planning, or fail to take advantage of company benefits that are in our best interests. It's extraordinarily difficult to rewire the human brain to undo the patterns that lead to such mistakes. But there is another approach: alter the environment in which decisions are made so that people are more likely to make choices that lead to good outcomes.
>
> Leaders can do this by acting as architects. Drawing on our extensive research in the consulting, software, entertainment, health care, pharmaceutical, banking, manufacturing, retail and food industries, and on the basic principles of behavioral economics, we have developed an approach for structuring work to encourage good decision making.
>
> Our approach consists of five basic steps:
> (1) Understand the systematic errors in decision making that can occur.
> (2) Determine whether behavioral issues are at the heart of the poor decisions in question.
> (3) Pinpoint the specific underlying causes.
> (4) Redesign the decision making context to mitigate the negative impacts of biases and inadequate motivation.
> (5) Rigorously test the solution.
>
> This process can be applied to a wide range of problems, from high employee turnover to missed deadlines to poor strategic decisions.

2.27 The Business School Approach to Ethics

Business schools promote too little, if any personal development. Young professionals must confront questions such as who am I, why am I here and what is my life's task? *Learning to Live* would be an excellent course! One must be encouraged to come to the realization that life is best understood as a process of reflection and learning. Perception and mindfulness are key attributes leading to an understanding that all of mankind is connected, each one of us with every other. The best teachers will join forces with their students and together work upon the development of inner growth and maturity.

Our greatest hope for the economic sector as well as for society in general is that more business leaders will undertake personal reflection leading to an increased awareness so that they may begin to carry out their duties with serenity, joy, humor, empathy, congruence and compassion for others. We need to bring our young generation to this awareness. There are business schools which do focus not only upon the external presentation of business and management knowledge, but also encourage their students to develop their own inner, personal ethical morality. One example is ESADE in Barcelona, Spain. Eugenia Bieto, Director General of ESADE welcomed participants to the World Congress on *Spirituality and Creativity in Management* between April 22nd and 25th, 2015 in Barcelona, with the following wisdom:

> Spirituality is synonymous with freedom. Does it make sense to study the importance of spirituality from a management perspective? Is it worthwhile for business schools to highlight the importance of cultivating executives' inner selves? At ESADE, we are convinced that it is. Our institution is dedicated to guiding the development and growth of committed people in the leadership of organizations. I am therefore delighted at the organization of this international conference, and I invite you to participate in as many sessions as possible.
>
> Through business schools the management field must make a two-fold contribution. We mustn't concentrate exclusively on helping executives grow as professionals. It is a mistake to overlook a second essential component: the personal growth of leaders. Here at ESADE, we are committed to building a more just world. Our aim is not to train professionals concerned solely with their own success. Instead, we instill in our students the importance of cultivating their *inner selves* and staying connected to their basic values. By focusing on spirituality we are providing organizations with *free* individuals and helping executives understand that their purpose is greater than themselves. In short, spirituality makes people free. Free to accept criticism, free to avoid idleness, free to innovate, free to find new opportunities, and – as the name of the conference suggests – free to be more creative. I invite you to highlight your commitment to training leaders capable of integrating their professional careers with their inner lives. A growing number of organizations, companies and business schools have realized that this is the way to avoid repeating the mistakes of the past, to improve the society, and to build a more principled economy.

I attended this conference at which I also facilitated a Professional Development Workshop on the topic of *The Golden Path to Creativity*, and I can attest to the widespread, international desire for business schools to begin down a similar pathway as has ESADE, developing awareness and facilitating the development of greater personal inner growth amongst business school graduates.

The *European SPES Institute* is another good example of an organization where the inner growth of business managers is an important focus. The President of the Institute is Professor Laszlo Zsolnai, author of the book *The Spiritual Dimension of Business Ethics and Sustainability* (Zsolnai 2014). This book embraces the spiritual dimension implicit in business ethics and sustainability management. Spirituality is understood as a multiform search for meaning which connects people with all living beings, as well as with God or one's own personal Ultimate Reality. In this sense spirituality is a vital resource in our social and economic life. The book examines the spiritual orientations toward nature and business in different cultural traditions, including Christianity, Judaism, Islam, Sufism, Hinduism, Buddhism and Taoism. It explores how spirituality and ecology can contribute to the transformation of contemporary management theory and practice. It also discusses new leadership roles and business models that have emerged for sustainability in business, and demonstrates how entrepreneurship can be inspired by nature and spirituality in meaningful ways. The mission of the institute is a spiritually based humanism.

The *European SPES Institute* (formerly the *European SPES Forum*) was founded in 2004 in Leuven, Belgium. It is part of the SPES Forum, a formal nonprofit organization under Belgian law. The origin of SPES goes back to the year 2000 where it was started as a "personalist study group" in the Center for Economics and Ethics at the *Catholic University of Leuven*, Belgium in cooperation with the *Center for Ethics at the University of Antwerp*, Belgium. In 2004, as SPES Forum it became an autonomous nonprofit organization under Belgian law. The initiative was successful and resulted in setting up the Belgian *SPES Academy* (2004) and the *European SPES Forum* (2004).

The *European SPES Institute* is an international network of individuals and organizations promoting spirituality in economic and social life. It is the belief at the *European SPES Institute* that spiritually motivated individuals who define success in multidimensional and holistic terms may serve the common good of nature, future generations and society. The mission of the *European SPES Institute* is expressed in the key word of SPES, being on the one hand an acronym for *Spirituality in Economics and Society* and on the other hand the Latin word for *'Hope'*, the virtue that sustains our belief in a better future. Spirituality is defined in broad and pluralistic terms so that the *European SPES Institute* may bring together people from different spiritual backgrounds and traditions. As SPES understands spirituality to be our multiform search for meaning interconnecting us with all living beings and to God or Ultimate Reality, within this definition there is room for differing views, for spirituality with or without a God and for an ethics of dialogue. The spiritually based humanism for which the *European SPES Institute* stands has been defended on philosophical grounds by European "personalist" philosophers, along with their colleagues worldwide.

The *European SPES Institute* organized its annual conference for 2015 in Amsterdam, The Netherlands on July 3rd and 4th. The title of the conference was: *Management in the VUCA World*. The conference aimed to discuss how spiritual values help managers to navigate the VUCA World of Volatility, Uncertainty, Complexity and Ambiguity. As a participant in the conference, presenting a lecture on *How to Survive the VUCA-World with Your Mind, Soul and Spirit Inspired by Depth Psychology Based Spirituality*, I can once again attest to the overwhelming support of participants from around the world for a greater emphasis by educational institutions upon facilitating moral and ethical growth in their students.

Another good example of ethical-based business training was the *Business Ethics Center of the Budapest University of Economic Sciences* under the leadership of Laszlo

Zsolnai. Unfortunately, in a retrogressive step, Business Ethics has recently been removed from the curriculum.

Several Business Schools in the USA take ethics education seriously. The following is a course description at MIT.

> This will be a seminar on classic and contemporary work on central topics in ethics. The first third of the course will focus on *Meta Ethics*: we will examine the meaning of moral claims and ask whether there is any sense in which moral principles are objectively valid. The second third of the course will focus on *Normative Ethics*: what makes our lives worth living, what makes our actions right or wrong, and what do we owe to others? The final third of the course will focus on *Moral Character*: what is virtue, and how important is it? Can we be held responsible for what we do? When and why?

All of these institutional undertakings are excellent first moves, but the development of ethics does not come from teaching. It evolves within us as a result of reflective spiritual exercises, our interactive experiences with others and a daily routine of vigilant, disciplined effort.

2.28 The Power of Ethical Management

There are numerous books which promote ethics in the economy. An excellent example is *The Power of Ethical Management* by Norman Vincent Peale, author of *The Power of Positive Thinking*, and Kenneth Blanchard, co-author of *The One Minute Manager* (Peale and Blanchard 1988). Peale and Blanchard prove that you don't have to cheat to win. They explain how to bring integrity back into business while at the same time offering hard-hitting, practical and ethical strategies that result in increased profits, productivity and long-term success. Their useful tools are a three-step *Ethics Check* and the so called *"Five P's"* of ethical behavior. These well-known authors show how integrity pays dividends. They are convinced that ethical behavior is related to self-esteem. People who feel good about themselves have what it takes to withstand outside pressure and to do what is *right* rather than doing what is merely expedient, proper or lucrative. They believe that a strong code of morality in any business is the first step toward success. Ethical managers are the winning managers.

To avoid unethical behavior Peale and Blanchard suggest completing a so-called *Ethics Check* prior to taking any significant action.

1) "Is it *legal*? Will I be violating either civil law or company policy?
2) Is it *balanced*? Is it fair to all concerned in the short term as well as the long term? Does it promote win-win relationships?
3) How will it make me *feel* about myself? Will it make me proud? Would I feel good if my decision was published in the newspaper? Would I feel good if my family knew about it?"

The following five core principles of ethical behavior are their five P's:

1) "*Purpose*: I see myself as being an ethically sound person. I let my conscience be my guide. No matter what happens I am always able to face the mirror, look myself straight in the eye, and feel good about myself.
2) *Pride*: I feel good about myself. I don't need the acceptance of other people to feel important. A balanced self-esteem keeps my ego and my desire to be accepted from influencing my decisions.
3) *Patience*: I believe that things will eventually work out well. I don't need everything to happen right now. I am in peace with what comes my way!
4) *Persistence*: I stick to my purpose, especially when it seems inconvenient to do so! My behavior is consistent with my intentions. As Churchill said, 'Never! Never! Never! Never give up!'
5) *Perspective*: I take time to enter each day quietly in a mood of reflection. This helps me to get myself focused and allows me to listen to my inner self and to see things more clearly."

"These five principles are also the ingredients for genuine, lasting fulfilment in life. Highly successful satisfied individuals practice these five principles with great consistency." The authors have developed an additional 5 P's for organizations.

"The Five Principles of Ethical Power for Organizations:
1) *Purpose*: The mission of our organization is communicated from the top. Our organization is guided by the values, hope, and a vision that helps us to determine what is acceptable and unacceptable behavior.
2) *Pride*: We feel proud of ourselves and of our organization. We know that when we feel this way we can resist temptations to behave unethically.
3) *Patience*: We believe that holding to our ethical values will lead us to success in the long term. This involves maintaining a balance between obtaining results and caring how we achieve these results.
4) *Persistence*: We have a commitment to live by ethical principles. We are committed to our commitment. We make sure our actions are consistent with our purpose.
5) *Perspective*: Our managers and employees take time to pause and reflect, take stock of where we are, evaluate where we are going and determine how we are going to get there."

In their explanation of what they mean by patience the authors say,

> Once we have a clear purpose and our ego is under control, the third principle for sound ethical behavior is patience. One reason why people sometimes get off course is because they lack faith; and with a lack of faith they become impatient.

This sounds great but it is not easy. It is the dilemma! Most people *cannot* get their ego under control, and therefore they are not only impatient but they are also destabilized and ready to act unethically when they are under pressure. The authors do not address the reality that our dark side is the main influence of our ego. There is a slight indication that spirituality may solve the dilemma. The authors obviously mean a lack of spiritual faith as opposed to faith in a more general sense. For them *Positive Thinking* is another aspect of faith. They assume that spirituality is related to God or a higher power. But positive thinking is a *creation* of our ego mind. The ego mind will never create a tool for its own control! Only our spirit can do this.

Peale and Blanchard are asking for balance because with balance we may have the self-confidence to hang tough when confronted with difficult ethical situations. True enough, but balance is complex. We cannot *decide* to be in balance. It is the result of the development of our personality. Balance is an equilibrium between ego, soul and spirit, male and female, and our bright and dark sides.

Peale and Blanchard state, "If you are committed, you find ways to suppress your rationalizations. Even when it's inconvenient you keep to your moral commitment. Persistence in life is characterized by this ethical toughness."

In accordance with Depth Psychology, this suppression of our rationalizations is precisely what leads directly to catastrophic results. We can *only* be patient when we have recognized, accepted and *integrated* our shadow, but the authors recommend *suppression* of the dark side. By so doing we will extend our shadow, empowering it. The results are tragic if we don't recognize the forces that are actively acting behind the impatience, indeed actually promoting it! This is the weakness of "Positive Thinking," which is an auto-suggestion of our ego mind. It works to a degree, but it will not last when individuals or organizations come under pressure.

It is of some encouragement for the lost generation that more and more companies in the *New Economy* have realized that the indoctrination of the young generation with a one-sided, intellect only concentration of facts is a dead-end approach, and have adopted approaches which incorporate practices which facilitate educating the whole person.

In *Easy zum Ziel* (Easy to Target), Andreas Ackermann states

> We live in a time in which the megatrend is self-realization. I submit that in the future those com-
> panies that make self-realization the goal of their employees while providing optimal conditions
> for their customers and suppliers will take off like rockets (Ackermann 2004).

2.29 Wisdom 2.0: Hope for the Younger Generation

Soren Gordhamer, the initiator of the *Wisdom 2.0 Conference*, wrote the highly recommended *Wisdom 2.0* book (Gordhamer 2013). It focuses not on ethics but on improving our work/life balance and creativity through mindfulness and compassion. He
calls the fourth chapter *Go for Truth* and explains:

> In this fourth section of Wisdom 2.0 life, we explore the importance of becoming aware of the
> frame from which we view the world, of our ideas we hold, and of seeing and aligning ourselves
> with the truth in any situation.

We may assume that he is of the opinion that a focus on mindfulness and compassion
will lead to a code of morality from which acceptable ethical behavior will result. He
considers wisdom and technology, seeing the use of modern technology as the source
of many human distractions. But there are also many other reasons why humans
severed the connection to their inner world centuries prior to the implementation of
the new technologies. It is certainly true however, that the new technologies do tend
to further destabilize those who are already isolated from their inner world, accelerating this isolation.

The following is a quote from his book:

Now that we have access to unparalleled amounts of information, certainly getting the right information matters, but it is the inner dimension that is the most vital element for any creative person or company. In fact, this will likely be the primary factor in the great companies of the future.

He also reports about a discussion with the Asana and Facebook co-founder Dustin Moskovitz and his Asana co-founder Justin Rosenstein, who believe that

Companies who are not mindful (have stopped paying attention to what's going on) lose their way: they lose their best people, become complacent, and stop innovating ... In the same way that mindfulness and reflection help individuals with personal growth, they help organizations evolve and find their full potential.

The highly successful first *WISDOM 2.0* conference was held in Mountain View, California. It was supported by numerous corporations, including Zynga, PayPal, Google, Microsoft, LinkedIn and Cisco. Other conferences followed, each with increased participation. I was fortunate to be able to participate in the *WISDOM 2.0* conference in Dublin at the Google Headquarters in September of 2015. The topic under consideration was *Mindfulness and Compassion in the Digital Age*. Mindfulness is considered to be the beginning of inner, spiritual growth. More and more companies are supporting this progressive movement, realizing that both employer and employee mindsets can be permanently changed for the better by an adoption of a *mindfulness* approach. There is a growing awareness of an intense desire on the part of the younger generation to work in companies which take employee's values seriously. Those companies which are adopting this awareness are the winners. They attract the best, most creative and motivated employees. Companies which respect their employees by treating them responsibly generate greater earnings. Clark's equation *does* work.

These companies are on the way to become *Caring Companies*. Their employees like their work environment and the resulting profits illustrate the wisdom! A *New Ethic* is growing inside these companies, but even though this is a cause for celebration we must not forget that companies themselves cannot be the sole basis for our development of a spiritual center. It is a personal quest which must be undertaken holistically, not just in the workplace. When the effort is made to do so, our spiritual path leads us to unprecedented individual liberty and freedom.

Mindfulness and Compassion which are expressions and practices from Buddhism have had considerable influence on Google. It is reported that when Thich Nhat Hanh joined the management team of Google, so-called Mindful Lunches were initiated. The Zen master Thich Nhat Hanh, a global spiritual leader, poet and peace activist urged the staff of Google to meditate in order to expand their creative minds. His intention is to implement Buddhist practices into the economy. Together with the President of the World Bank, Jim Yong Kim, he organized a walking meditation (*Kin Hin*) in Washington which attracted 300 bankers and 20 monks. It caused quite a sensation! He does not deny the reality of the economy but he chooses to affect it with his spirit. At the *World Economic Forum* in January 2015 in Davos, Switzerland, Thich Nhat Hanh led participants through a practice of Mindfulness Based Stress Reduction, which was invented by Jon Kabat-Zin. There was a panel discussion on the topic "Leading Mindfully," during which the Goldman Sachs Board Member William George mentioned that now many hundreds of investment bankers would meditate on Wall Street.

The intention of embarking upon meditative practices in business enterprises is to create inner peace, and to utilize our resulting greater personal awareness and inner balance in business decisions, thwarting the efforts of our dark side to become dominant.

2.30 Inviting Greater Peace into Our Lives

Noah Elkrief, a previous consultant and hedge fund manager is now training business people. The introduction to his video blog reads:

"To help you stop suffering and to bring greater peace into your life." All videos are intended to have an immediate impact. They are all constructed to help you stop suffering now, to stop your anxiety, to stop your stress, to stop your feelings of anger, to experience more love and peace, to have more enjoyable relationships, to have more enjoyable time at work … Like everyone else I was brought up pursuing happiness through success, wealth, travel, girls, getting everybody to love me. That's what I thought would make me happy. I spent a lot of time and energy, nothing wrong with that. Somehow by the time I was 23–24 I thought I had achieved all these goals. I had worked on the trading floor with Goldman Sachs, I was a strategy consultant in London, I was travelling around the world a lot, I got girls, I was smart, everybody loved me, I enjoyed my job, I got everything I ever wanted, but yet I was not in peace, I felt something was missing.

I had anxiety about the future, I worried about what people thought about me, I had to maintain their love, to maintain their positive thoughts about me. I had to do things I did not want to do, I had to maintain my thoughts about myself, I had stress, I had all the stuff everybody else does, even knowing that I had achieved everything I ever wanted, my life was perfect, right?

At the same time as all my pursuit of all the stuff, I was brought up to meditate, every day. From the time I was 6 years old I was meditating on my own, I really gave myself to it, I really cared about this practice. So, seemingly as a result of all of that, when I was 24 in 2009 all at once almost all my thoughts completely vanished from my mind and did not attempt to return. So, as you can imagine, this completely changed my life. From that moment on I was left with the peace, freedom and wholeness I have been searching for my whole life. This was everything I ever wanted and it did not go away regardless of what happened in my life, peace stayed with me. It did not matter whether I was behind in a deadline or if somebody insulted me, or if my father was in the hospital, or whether I hurt myself. It did not bother me. I was at peace in every moment.

And the reason why was simply because I did not have thoughts to make me suffer. And that made it very clear to me that the only thing which created my suffering were my own thoughts.

So, from the moment I lost my thoughts, every once in a while new thoughts would show up and I would begin experiencing a sudden sense of tension, sadness, anger. I would immediate see it was created by a thought in my mind and not by anything happening factually in my life. And once I saw this I could instantly see that this thought was not true, and then ... BANG ... the thought was dissolved and the emotion was dissolved and I came right back to this natural state of peace, the natural experience of the present moment.

Spontaneously my friends opened up with their suffering. I was able to help them to see what thoughts were creating their suffering and to help them to see that these thoughts were not true. Then completely astonishing me; shocking me, to my surprise, each time my friends emotions were just dissolved their suffering was dissolved in a moment. I did not think it was possible, I did not think it was happening, but somehow it did, over and over and over again. It did not matter whether this person was spiritual or not spiritual ... everybody could watch their suffering dissolving in a moment, when they could stop the thoughts creating the suffering. When I saw this it completely changed my life, I quit my job, I wrote a book *A Guide to the Present Moment* that shared 5 steps to identify and stop the thoughts creating the suffering. I created my video blog: https://www.youtube.com/user/NoahElkrief

2.31 Happiness, Bliss and Compassion

In March of 2015, Adrian Lobe reported in the newspaper *Die Welt:* "In the US there is a new Job Title, *Chief Happiness Officer* (CHO), whose mission is to make people happy and so to increase sales." But is it that easy? Tony Hsieh, the founder of the online store Zappos wrote a book in 2010 entitled *Delivering Happiness.* The entrepreneur received great press reports and the book became a best seller. Zappos sells shoes, and with its progressive corporate savvy it has equally been purchasing great good fortune! Today Tony is not only Chief Executive Officer (CEO) of his company, but also Chief Happiness Officer (CHO). More and more managers of start-ups and advanced technology companies in the Silicon Valley bear this name in their title. What actually constitutes a CHO? What explains the rapid movement to adopt this policy?

Alexander Kjerulf is CHO of the Danish start-up company Wohoo. "Companies notice that happy workers have happy customers and earn more money," says Kjerulf. Studies illustrate that happy employees are more productive, innovative and motivated. They remain loyal to their company longer, and take fewer sick days. "Happy customers are loyal and recommend products or services to others." Kjerulf asserts that "The best way to make customers happy is to have happy employees, because they take the best care of their customers." It is becoming recognized that designating a board member specific responsibility for creating *good fortune* is a wise business decision. "He or she need not be called a Chief Happiness Officer, but it must be an individual who recognizes their responsibility for ensuring happiness within the organization ... Sometimes the role is limited, intended to address employee contentment internally, but other times it can equally include customers outside of the organization," explains Kjerulf. "The position is both inspirational and practical. The individual accepting the appointment must be one who exudes happiness, someone who can inspire others by nature of their happiness, someone who recognizes the importance of the feel good factor at work," says Kjerulf. "The task of the CHO is to carry out initiatives which encourage employees to do a good job, to organize celebrations, training, events, and similar activities in the workplace that help to educate and motivate employees."

The position of CHO is not a frivolous passing fad. Chade-Meng Tan has the official title of CHO for Google. The staff members of the Google Internet Group are recognized as being very happy. At their headquarters in Mountain View, California staff on every floor can slip into re-purposed chairs to *de-stress* while discussing their creative ideas with colleagues. Google's many campuses reflect the philosophy of "creating the happiest, most productive workplace in the world," as enunciated by spokesman Jordan Newman. "Google is a *happy making machine*. In secret labs engineers tinker even with the algorithms of happiness. In corporations in the Silicon Valley happiness is not something you merely find, but something which is consciously facilitated and successfully delivered."

"Companies like Google want to codify something that is individual and personal, and spread it within the organization in order to make effective and efficient workers," said the economics professor Martin Ihlig from the Wharton School of the University of Pennsylvania. The CHO is not just there to keep the employees happy, but also to attract new talents. "It is especially in the Silicon Valley that there is a considerable demand for highly skilled workers, so it is understandable that companies like Google are investing in the happiness of their employees." At the same time, companies want to increase customer satisfaction. "Knowing how to satisfy the fundamental needs of the main customer segments is becoming increasingly important," says the management expert Ihlig.

Dan Haybron teaches philosophy at Saint Louis University in the USA and has published several books on the subject of happiness. He says, "I think it's really important for entrepreneurs to take seriously the concepts of happiness and quality of life, because a pleasant or unpleasant workplace can make a big difference in a person's life." In companies with a bad reputation even the most positive person is incapable of spreading optimism. Happiness researcher Haybron has himself worked in the Silicon Valley, and he knows the mood very well. "The people have high expectations of their lives. At the same time there is a lot of stress and job dissatisfaction ... Behind the masquerade of euphoric optimism there is a great deal of displeasure. Good mood and an optimistic attitude cannot be prescribed, and happiness is not necessarily produced through a position or a title ..."

David Steindl-Rast prefers the expression Joy rather than Happiness which has a greater dependency upon external events. Joy, on the other hand, can just manifest within us without request, action or expectations (Wisdom 2.0 Annual Conference 2014).

2.32 Beyond Happiness: Bhutan's Philosophy of Gross National Happiness

If an awareness of the desirability for happy employees is based upon mindfulness, compassion and inner growth, then it can be seen as a serious and potentially beneficial move on the part of management. Moral decisions and ethical behavior will increase. But if the impetus is not based upon the promotion of inner growth, then the program can have at best, limited results. The trite, *don't worry, be happy* approach can be of an egocentric origin, potentially harmful rather than helpful.

Real happiness based on inner values is well described in some essential remarks made concerning Bhutan in *A Short Guide to the GNH Index*, published in 2012:

> In the GNH Index, unlike certain concepts of happiness in current western literature, happiness is itself multidimensional, not measured only by subjective well-being, and not focused narrowly on happiness that begins and ends with oneself; being concerned for and with only oneself. The pursuit of happiness is collective, though it can be experienced deeply personally. ... Gross National Happiness (GNH) measures the quality of a country in a more holistic way than does GNP and believes that the beneficial development of human society takes place when material and spiritual development occurs side by side to complement and reinforce each other.

What is the history behind Bhutan's phenomenal orientation? Tashi Dorji (Dorji 2015) writes with the headline *Father of GNH – The Story of the Birth of the Development Philosophy of Bhutan, Gross National Happiness (GNH)*:

> The message was clear and simple – happiness of the people is more important than economic development of the country ... When His Majesty Jigme Singye Wangchuck formally ascended to the throne in 1974 at 19 years of age, two years after he was deemed too young to do so following the demise of his father, the country was still an agrarian economy ... Literacy level was painstakingly low with a handful of primary school graduates occupying the highest levels of the young civil service. The country had just entered the world map, joining the United Nations in 1971 ...
>
> His Majesty outlined his vision for the country with the same message; that collective happiness of the people was his ultimate goal. No single incident is recorded as the first time when His Majesty asserted this idea, one which gave birth to a new development philosophy centered on the intangible human emotion of happiness. At that time it did not have a name. His Majesty inadvertently christened his philosophy in 1979 at the Bombay International Airport when returning from the sixth Non-Aligned Movement Summit in Havana. Giving a rare interview to a group of Indian journalists, one reporter asked: "We do not know anything about Bhutan. What is your Gross National Product?" "We do not believe in Gross National Product" His Majesty replied, "because Gross National Happiness is more important."
>
> The media reports that resulted from the interview did not really focus on the new development philosophy Bhutan was pursuing. Eight years later on May 2, 1987, John Elliott of the Financial Times of London, published an article "The modern Path to Enlightenment" ... It was the first news article ever to highlight GNH as a development philosophy. His Majesty was quoted in the article, "We are convinced we must aim for contentment and happiness".

No doubt His Majesty added the word "contentment to happiness in order to clarify what he means by happiness. *The Center for Bhutan Studies* considered that ethics would be positively impacted as a result of GNH:

> Most educational systems, all over the world, are implicitly penetrated by the predominant economic ideology. As a consequence, competition is more valued than collaboration; one-sided intellectual knowledge is more rewarded than social, ethical, emotional, relational, artistic and spiritual skills (October 25, 2015).

Johannes Hirata has linked GNH and ethics in several publications:

> The link between happiness and ethics can be thought of as two-fold, making a distinction along the lines of the classical separation between teleological ethics – basically the "private" questions of the good life, of who I want to be and how I want to live – and deontological ethics – the "social" question of legitimacy, of one's rights and duties vis-à-vis other moral subjects. Psychological hedonism, to take up my point of departure, supposes a very mechanical relationship between happiness and ethics. With respect to teleological ethics, it says, first, that happiness is the only thing that counts when it comes to choosing who one wants to be and how one wants to live, and, by implication, that the things from which a particular person derives happiness are predetermined by nature and therefore beyond this person's own will. To use economic terminology, a person is assumed to simply have, rather than choose, a consistent set of preferences which provides the algorithm to calculate, in any given situation, the optimal decision, i.e., the decision that will maximize her happiness. The kind of rationality involved here is purely instrumental rationality, i.e., it is a matter of optimization with respect to a given end.
>
> With respect to deontological ethics, the deterministic nature of psychological hedonism renders the very idea of rights and duties meaningless because one cannot sensibly demand from predetermined beings (which resemble a clockwork more than a person) to behave in another way than that which they are programmed to follow, the reason being that morality as such requires indeterminacy of human behavior. In general, therefore, whether others are affected by one's choices or not, psychological hedonism claims that an individual's decisions are always and exclusively the deterministic manifestation of one's preferences, whatever these happen to be. Thus, psychological hedonism subscribes to a solipsist conception of the person and does not know the concept of morality.
>
> In a self-transcendental perspective, by contrast, voting would be explained – to the extent it is explainable – by an intrinsic motivation to act in accordance with those moral principles which one has found to be irrefutable. Of course, living up to these principles will most often be a reason for a person to feel satisfied, but then only as a symptom of one's successful commitment to one's principles, rather than its cause or motivation (Hirata 2003).

The GNH concept is based on this self-transcendental perspective in accordance with moral principles.

From *Bhutan-2015* with the headline *Father of GNH – The Story of the Birth of the Development Philosophy of Bhutan, Gross National Happiness (GNH)* another quote:

> It was only in 1998 that Bhutan first mentioned GNH as its development philosophy at the Asia Pacific Millennium Summit in Seoul. … In 2004, Bhutan organized the first international conference on GNH in its capital Thimpu. In July 2011, history was made when the UN General Assembly unanimously adopted the Bhutan led resolution on *"Happiness: towards a holistic approach to development"*.

Kinley Dorji, editor in chief of *Kuensel*, Bhutan's national newspaper, summarized what GNH really means in August 2008:

> What is GNH? If it is a national development goal, how can it be measured? How do you translate it from a philosophy into a policy for development programs? ... GNH is not a promise of happiness. In fact, it is not even about happiness. All spiritual practices teach us that happiness lies within the self, after all, we look inside ourselves to seek happiness because there is no external source of happiness. In Bhutan, therefore, GNH is understood as a mandate of the state to create an environment in which citizens can pursue mental equanimity. What is important here is that this becomes a direct responsibility of the government. *The GNH premise is that the right to pursue happiness already lies with the people, government is meant to serve the people, and hence it must deliver, not rob the people of this right.*

In an attempt to translate GNH from an idealistic concept into a realistic guideline for development, one of the early initiatives taken by the Royal Government of Bhutan was to identify four *measurable* pillars of GNH:
1. Socio-economic development
2. Preservation of cultural heritage
3. Protection of the environment
4. Good governance

GNH is not exactly a new concept, but rather is the expression of the values that have sustained Bhutanese society through the ages. As a responsibility of the government these values and priorities must continue to be the basis for national policy and programs. The following expands the four pillars of GNH into nine *domains*:
1. Psychological well-being
2. Health
3. Education
4. Time use and balance
5. Cultural diversity and resilience
6. Good governance
7. Community vitality
8. Ecological diversity and resilience
9. Living standards

Tobias Pfaff writes in *Tashi Delek 2010: The GNH Principles*:

> These thematic areas (the nine pillars) cover the broadest perspective of human life within society and its various environmental factors. This multi-faceted approach toward quantifying the factors that determine the quality and richness and, yes, happiness of a human life reflects the strong Buddhist foundations of GNH. The holistic Buddhist world view is, if nothing else, underpinned by the conviction of the interdependency of everything. Happiness could easily be seen as the main dependent variable of the GNH model, but the survey itself is designed with up to 290 questions that deal with the myriad aspects that influence personal and societal happiness. If it is true that God is in the details, this comprehensive survey seeks to find the

answers to no less significant a question by scrutinizing all the infinite parts, small and great, that make up what we collectively term "happiness". The core of GNH is the equilibrium of economic and non-economic goals of development.

In 2015 the Prime Minister of Bhutan, Tshering Tobgay, explained what GNH means for him:

> We are balancing growth carefully with social development, environmental sustainability and cultural preservation; all within the frame of good governance. We call this a holistic approach to the development of GNH. We will improve the happiness and well-being of our people ... Our King, His Majesty Jigme Singye Wangchuck made it very simple for us to understand GNH when he says: "GNH simply means development with values!"

Yes, we can learn from Bhutan. By following the concept of Buddhism in general, and of Bhutan's GNH in particular, we will progress toward the development of inner growth, moral attitudes and ethical behavior. Even in the economy.

Dan Haybron reminds us that

> It (GNH) includes harmony with nature which is absent from Western notions of happiness, and concern for others. The brilliant nature alluded to consists of the various types of extraordinary sensitive and advanced awareness with which human beings are endowed and can fully manifest.

This happiness may be referred to as *bliss*. And *only* this bliss will influence people to exercise their ethical responsibility. The question remains whether this paradigm shift, which is currently focused within companies, will influence the behavior of these companies in the marketplace. Those still adhering to the old economy *must* follow or they will become uncompetitive. Entrepreneurs in the twenty-first century want to live and work differently. A healthy work/life balance is crucial for them in their decisions about which companies attract them. The average age of the participants at the Wisdom 2.0 Conferences was 35. It is regrettable there were fewer elder managers and representatives of the Old Economy. There was much to be learned at these conferences about what it means to practice mindfulness and compassion, and to implement the resulting inner growth into both our business and our private life balance.

2.33 The CEO of the Future

"CEO of the Future" was a competition, an initiative of Bayer, e-fellows.net, Bertelsmann, Porsche, Thyssen Krupp and Vodafone, the media partners, Manager Magazin, n-tv and Spiegel Online as well as the career network. The competition was aimed primarily at young professionals, generally those with one to four years of professional experience, but also includes select students and doctoral candidates with practical experience. As the first check of their potential as a future top manager they were asked to put their critical thinking skills to work and create a "message from the future." Their instructions are as follows:

> Suppose you had the opportunity to have a look into the year 2030. What would you say to a CEO of today? Use structured, creative and stimulating reasoning and condense your message to today's CEO into a headline for your essay in one poignant sentence. Upload your essay by September 16, 2012 together with your CV onto this website and automatically qualify for final participant selection. For daily updated information about the course, please visit our Facebook fan page. Or become a member of our Xing group. We wish you much fun and good luck.

My son Philipp, participating in the completion, wrote the following essay:

Dear leaders

I write to you, as leaders of the global economy in 2012, from a post-collapse perspective in 2030.

You, in 2012, are currently fighting for the preservation of an exaggerated level of wealth in a global crisis of nations. This crisis is rooted in our desire for more and more growth, more welfare and more consumption. More everything. Even more 'free lunch'. Free lunch? Didn't somebody once say there was no free lunch? Absolutely! There is not! So why do you act as if there was a free lunch and build your prosperity on a glass house of debt? Simply, because you can, and your opposition is not strong enough. You, leaders in power, know that the ultimate payback will likely not happen under your reign, possibly not even in your lifetime.

There are insufficient mature leaders whose power is rooted in their dedication to their own inner growth. As soon as interior growth supersedes exterior growth the game of *more* and even more ends, because those leaders will retreat from inflicting harm on their environment and future generations.

But why should you embrace a harmless approach? Prosperity has never been greater. Elites, as well as middle and working classes have a higher standard of living than ever before. Growth seems to be the universal answer for failing states and companies. So you, the leaders of today, decided to create artificial growth. With trillions of government and central bank fairy-dust money artificial demand is created, currencies are weakened and the financial markets are once again pumped to all-time highs. This time, it's different you say. Everything is under control!

I assure you that the inevitable collapse of financial markets and with it the down-turn of global economies is only delayed. Central banks have entangled themselves in the fraudulent practice of quantitative easing. With every fake dollar invested in the markets you have increased the destructive power of the eventual down-turn. Markets are meanwhile more leveraged than before 2008. But when growth is your mantra, growth it must be, whatever the consequent cost to future generations. The natural business cycles cannot be prevented and are healthy. Trying to prevent them and postpone them will only exacerbate the swings and make the eventual down-turn more painful.

But to where does this artificial growth lead? The idea of exterior growth as the only way forward leads inevitably to collapse. The consequences of unlimited growth in nature materialize as a cancer. The same is true in business. An unconditional focus upon growth drives sickening behaviors, as you have just witnessed in the form of the sub-prime crisis in the United States, which subsequently sent its shockwaves around the world. Now the excessive indebtedness in Europe and the US is staggering, weakening the foundations of the global economy.

What are you doing to prevent this devastation of the future economy, or at least to initiate healing of the fatally ill patient? Next to nothing. In retrospective I have to say, that the pain is not yet large enough. You are still living too well. You have already recognized the danger, but with very few exceptions you – along with most of the political and business elite – don't want to assume the responsibility for change. The changes would have to be too drastic. You do not want to take the risk, because the top management would probably not survive the political fallout. The urge to remain first at the feeding trough is too large. Greed is too strong of a driver, when it is not balanced by other motivations.

What changes lie ahead? Inevitably, the standard of living and wealth will dwindle in the Western industrialized countries if the necessary reduction of over-indebtedness and misma-nagement is not made a priority. The wealth gap between the majority and the 0.1% will widen further.

As CEOs you have to change in order to successfully compete given the reality of reduced growth accompanied by a levelling off or even a contraction of the economy in many countries. You have to rethink added-value, which *does not only* mean growth.

Your wealthy lifestyle at the beginning of the 21st century is founded upon the exploita-tion of natural resources. Companies carry out the task of conversion of natural resources into products, and service providers have established their turf. Such a consumer economy will flou-rish only as long as the resources are still available in sufficient quantities. With depletion of these resources change is inevitable. We are living like junkies, mostly oil junkies. It is desirable, indeed essential that you initiate the necessary changes without delay.

The undeniable imperative is the creation of a sustainable economy. You simply have no another choice. Sustainability means providing a product that creates quantitative and qualita-tive value and consumes only resources that are short to mid-term renewable, thereby causing no harm to humans or the environment. The suffering of the world's population by environmen-tal degradation and exploitation is increasing and unsustainable. Companies which lack sus-tainable management and practices will become less and less accepted in their societies. The demand for products from non-sustainable and unethically operating companies will therefore decrease over time. This has a direct impact on the bottom line and will lead to the extinction of companies that have not recognized the trend and taken on the challenge. In the long term companies that align their business models on a *Sustainable Economy*, will be the winners.

How can companies commit to this change? It begins with the search for the purpose of life, out of which arise sustainable business practices predicated upon moral decisions and ethical practices. This is essentially determined by the management of a company. In companies which are committed solely to growth, leaders at all levels are enticed and trapped by the short term rewards, making it exceptionally difficult to change their purpose or their practices.

A mature person however, with advanced inner growth will recognize the challenges of this time and make decisions based upon a multi-dimensional new structure of values in favor of our society, rather than on monetary performance alone. The company's goals are then increa-singly dedicated to sustainability in the long term, ensuring that the company, humanity and the environment will all benefit. Because this change is slow it will not be immediately apparent to everyone, but it *will* continue to spread and spill over to other companies as soon as the pressure is sufficiently felt.

The finite nature of external growth has become visible. It is ugly and it threatens the world as you know it.

My concluding questions:
–   Why did you promote, in so many cases, the ruthless egoists?

- Why are ethics and morality not central to your business plans?
- Why did you not use your leadership to develop your employees ethically?
- Why are mindfulness and compassion still foreign to you?
- Why did you not realize that this new culture is essential to the ways of working of the New Economy?
- Why did you not create a culture which valued innovation?
- Why did you concentrate on optimizing the *status quo* rather than establishing an *elevated status quo*?
- Why did you let investment bankers and consultants persuade you to execute mergers and acquisitions that were inappropriate?
- Why did it not bother you if your actions resulted in thousands of individuals losing their jobs?
- Why did it not bother you that so many people became ill due to the stress of mismanagement?

I can only assume that you have not yet realized that the target is not only successful external quantitative performance, but equally, at least the initiation of inner development from which then outward qualitative performance grows.

That, and only that, is the "life balance" of the future.

I appeal to all of you who are political and/or business leaders to devote yourself to inner growth so as to realize that only sustainable business practices have a future in top management. I know only a handful of "Wise Leaders" in Germany; individuals who lead from their heart with a dedication to moral decisions and ethical practices, and they are very successful. I sincerely hope that the number will grow in the years to come, to give me confidence in a brighter future for us young professionals.

2.34 The Philosophical and Christian Vision of Ethics

Peter Knauer SJ, Catholic Theologian of Ecumenical Fundamental Theology, admirably established basic principles of ethics which are consistent with his philosophical and Christian vision of reducing the all too evident immoral abuses in the business of the economy. He did so in his book, *Handlungsnetze* (Action Networks) (Knauer 2002). The following are some of his core ideas.

On the fundamental problem of traditional ethics, he writes,

Just as with other knowledge, ethical knowledge is not innate; to know which actions are justifiable and which are not is not innately instilled within us. Ethics have been learned by humanity through tedious experience and through the tedious transfer of the insights gained … One learns from one's mistakes, but paradoxically, at the same time history seems to demonstrate that we always tend to shy away from *actually* learning our lessons … Only through the care of other humans do we achieve consciousness of ourselves. Therefore, we experience ourselves from the outset as ethically obliged, before we even begin upon an ethical reflection. Otherwise we would not even be able to understand what is meant by the question of whether we are responsible for our actions.

2.34.1 The Golden Rule of Ethics

An excellent summary of all ethical reflection is contained within the Golden Rule. Affirmatively it states: "all things whatsoever you expect from others, also do unto them." The inverse version is contained within a proverb. "What you do not want to have done unto yourself, do not do unto others." The Golden Rule remains a commonly accepted criterion for ethical and moral behavior. Knauer believes that the general public can understand and realize the truth and wisdom inherent in this criterion for how to behave. He remarks,

> It is often formulated as an ethical principle: *to do good and to avoid evil.* This formulation is a tautology, as it does not answer the crucial question of how to recognize whether something is good or evil. Further, does one actually have an absolute moral and civic duty to do *good* in everything imaginable? Some would call *good* that which corresponds to REASON. However, it remains open how to recognize reasonableness ... Kant's categorical imperative, *act as if the maxim of your will can always serve as a universal law* begs the question of how to ensure that a maxim is likely to claim universal validity.

On the concept of action Knauer writes:

> In traditional ethics, even the concept of action itself, is in many ways unclear ... It is also striking that the ethics manuals seldom accommodate the reality that our actions are always performed under less than ideal conditions, that there is seldom sufficient time to ponder, in the abstract, various courses of action and to choose the most favorable ... Some ethics manuals include an assessment component, suggesting that actions taken be assessed for their favorable/unfavorable results as pertain to those affected by the actions. However they seldom make allowances for the fact that we do not act as isolated individuals, but rather that our actions, both in their emergence and especially in their results, are influenced by the actions of others and thus are difficult to assess in isolation. Our actions are usually intricately associated with the actions and with the reactions of others, and thus we need to consider the larger reality of a feedback structure of ethics (Knauer 2002, p. 19).

2.34.2 The Principle of Double Effect

Knauer (Knauer 2002, p. 27f.) recognized that our actions most often have more effects than simply the initially desired one.

> Frequently the others may be undesirable. In order to assess when this was occurring, scholastic ethics formulated the *Principle of Double Effect.* The principle of double effect addresses the question of under which conditions one may agree with the undesired effects as well as the desired effects. Traditionally the principle is formulated as follows. The approval or causation of damage is permitted if:
> – the action is not *intrinsically evil.*
> – the damage is not specifically intended as a purpose.
> – the damage is not specifically intended as a means to an end.
> – in the approval of damage to occur there is a corresponding basic REASON.

If any one of these conditions is not met, then authorization for the action is not ethical. It is important to consider that the acceptance of a morally objectionable action is not ethical. We often think only of the intention of our own behavior, but this definition is also critical of *nonintervention*, or looking the other way.

Knauer (Knauer 2002, p. 33) is also concerned that conventional ethics does not adequately address the universality of actions. He believes one needs to consider their effects over time, and in concert with other actions.

The *Principle of Double Effect* in its conventional formulation and in its conventional understanding is confined to marginal cases of ethical considerations. Almost all of its terms remain unclear. This ambiguity can lead to serious mistakes. Perhaps this is the reason why this principle is no longer included in many modern books on ethics. To overcome the inadequacy of the traditional interpretation, the following is a reconstruction of the principle.

Knauer (Knauer 2002, p. 37) continues:

The pertinent question of the principle of double effect is: under what conditions is the authorization or causation of loss or harm ethically permissible? This question pre-supposes that an action can only be characterized as undesirable when it directly *causes* harm, or *allows* for harm to occur to either the recipient or the instigator. However, the following also applies. Not *every* authorization or action resulting in harm necessarily makes the action undesirable. Justification is only required for the approval of damage or for causing damage; on the other hand actions designed to result in a benefit or profit, as long as no harm results from them, need not be specifically justified. Conversely, an action can only be ethically good if it seeks a profit. It is however not the case that every action that seeks a profit is actually ethically good ...

Knauer (Knauer 2002, p. 39) comes to the realization that there is no other ethical principle that could adequately replace the *Principle of Double Effect*.

Further, that it requires no additional corollaries, that it has universal significance and that it tolerates no supplement ...

To the extent that the *Principle of Double Effect* indicates the precise boundary between harmful and non-harmful actions it determines the universe of irresponsible actions and that of responsible actions. The universe of responsible actions includes not *only* the best possible actions, but also those with good intentions, even where possibly better actions are possible. In reality, *there are no actions other than those with a double effect*. Experience shows that for each desired value there is always a cost, even if it is only the time and effort expended, or the resulting fatigue.

Knauer (Knauer 2002, p. 67) comes ultimately to a hermeneutic revision of the principle of double effect:

Only an act that leads to damage, without appropriate cause, can be bad in itself. However, one can allow a damage or can cause a damage when
- the action has an "appropriate reason."
- there is not another "intrinsically bad" action by the same actor enabling the action.
- it is not used to enable another "intrinsically bad" action by the same actor.

When considering ethics in business it is important to distinguish between *ethically correct* and *ethically sound*. Knauer (Knauer 2002, p. 93) points out the distinction in the following.

> He who does not steal from a self-service store because he is afraid of being caught can be considered, in a sense, *ethically correct* in so far as no one can accuse him of a bad action. However, the intent behind his action is far from being *ethically sound*. The latter would only be the case if the person on *principle* would not steal, even if there were absolutely no possible risk of being caught.

This distinction is what Clark was referring to when he demanded that the managers of the economy should behave ethically *even outside the areas regulated by laws*.

Knauer (Knauer 2002, p. 141) also comments on ethics and the Christian faith. He points out that

> the previous considerations were philosophical arguments. But they beg the question of how to address the Christian message that is regarded by many as an ethical authority. In what sense can a church get ethical authority? The Christian message is concerned with the moral obligation of the people. The Christian message is claiming to be able to redeem man from the root of his inhumanity. This root of inhumanity is man's inherent fear which is due to his vulnerability and mortality. It causes him, if necessary, to kill others to save himself. The Christian message claims to be able to liberate man from this inherent fear by exclaiming that subjugating oneself to God results in the certainty of everlasting communion with Him, which is absolute and certain, even beyond mortal death.

Knauer (Knauer 2002, p. 141) argues that one does not need to recognize the existence of God to justify acting with ethical integrity. Since God is not subject to our human conditions one cannot logically deduce something from Him. He also finds it problematic that people *must* turn to God's word for ultimate authority in the matter of morality. Does that mean that those people who have not heard of God are unable to internalize the recognition of morality? Knauer recognizes other ways that lead to sound ethical behavior, ways not necessarily dependent upon knowledge of Christian principles. With the churches emptying and more and more people no longer believing in an almighty God, the Christian ethical orientation for moral action in the economy is suffering. But it need not be the case. One can deny the existence of God but still try to live up to intuitively reasonable and sound moral and ethical principles espoused by the Christian church. In so doing, one may well find to their surprise, that they *experience* God!

2.35 An Appeal from Pope Francis for Ethics and Morality

In his Encyclical Letter of June 2015 entitled LAUDATO Si': ON CARE FOR OUR COMMON HOUSE Pope Francis engages very intensively with the immoral behavior in the economy, especially concerning environmental issues. The words "ethics" or "ethical" are mentioned twenty-eight times. The following is a summary of his statements and appeals:

- He wishes to provide a concrete foundation for the *ethical* and spiritual itinerary.
- He discusses an *ethics* of international relations.
- He considers environmental deterioration and human and *ethical* degradation to be closely linked.
- He considers the principle of the subordination of private property to the universal designation of goods, and thus the right of everyone to their use, to be a golden rule of social conduct and the first principle of the whole *ethical* and social order.
- He states that we cannot claim to have sound *ethics*, culture or spirituality.
- He advocates that science must take into account philosophy and social *ethics*.
- He states that there are no genuine *ethical* perspectives to which one can appeal.
- He believes that the present ecological crisis is one small sign of the *ethical*, cultural and spiritual crisis.
- He advocates that we constantly reevaluate our goals, effects, overall context and *ethical* limits.
- He points out that a technology severed from *ethics* will not easily be able to limit its own power.
- He admonishes that an integral ecology is inseparable from the notion of the common good, a central and unifying principle of social *ethics*.
- He warns that many problems of society are connected with today's self-centered culture of instant gratification and an *ethical* and cultural decline.
- He believes that reduction of environmental damage is primarily an *ethical* decision, rooted in solidarity between all peoples.
- He believes that the financial crisis of 2007–2008 provided an opportunity to develop a new economy; one more attentive to *ethical* principles.
- He points out that the *ethical* principles capable of being comprehended by reason can always re-appear in a different guise, and find expression in a variety of languages, including religious language.
- He admonishes that we have had enough of immorality and the mockery of *ethics*, goodness, faith and honesty. It is time to acknowledge that light-hearted superficiality has done us no good.

He is powerfully demanding that we find our way back to our spiritual treasures and make the leap toward the transcendent! In his Encyclical Letter Pope Francis makes the following statements about spirituality to guide mankind back to the path of spirituality:

> There needs to be a distinctive way of looking at things, a way of thinking, policies, an educational program, a lifestyle and a spirituality which together generate resistance to the assault of the technocratic paradigm ... The rich heritage of Christian spirituality, the fruit of twenty centuries

of personal and communal experience has a precious contribution to make to the renewal of humanity. Here, I would like to offer Christians a few suggestions for an ecological spirituality grounded in the convictions of our faith, since the teachings of the Gospel have direct consequences for our way of thinking, feeling and living. More than in ideas or concepts as such, I am interested in how such a spirituality can motivate us to a more passionate concern for the protection of our world. A commitment this lofty cannot be sustained by doctrine alone without a spirituality capable of inspiring us, without an interior impulse which encourages, motivates, nourishes and gives meaning to our individual and communal activity ...

Christian spirituality proposes an alternative understanding of the quality of life, and encourages a prophetic and contemplative lifestyle, one capable of deep enjoyment free of the obsession with consumption ... An adequate understanding of spirituality consists in finding out what we mean by peace, which is much more than the absence of war. Inner peace is closely related to care for ecology and for the common good because, lived out authentically, it is reflected in a balanced lifestyle together with a capacity for wonder which takes us to a deeper understanding of life ... Everything is interconnected, and this invites us to develop a spirituality of that global solidarity which flows from the mystery of the Trinity ...

The technocratic paradigm also tends to dominate economic and political life. The economy accepts every advance in technology with a view to profit without concern for its potentially negative impact on human beings. Finance overwhelms the real economy. The lessons of the global financial crisis have not been assimilated, and we are learning all too slowly the lessons of environmental deterioration. Some circles maintain that current economics and technology will solve all environmental problems, and argue, in popular and non-technical terms, that the problems of global hunger and poverty will be resolved simply by market growth. They are less concerned with certain economic theories which today scarcely anybody dares defend, than with their actual operation in the functioning of the economy. They may not affirm such theories with words, but nonetheless support them with their deeds by showing no interest in more balanced levels of production, a better distribution of wealth, concern for the environment and the rights of future generations. Their behaviour shows that for them maximizing profits is sufficient. Yet by itself the market cannot guarantee integral human development and social inclusion. Admittedly, Christians have not always appropriated and developed the spiritual treasures bestowed by God upon the Church, where the life of the spirit is not dissociated from the body or from nature or from worldly realities, but lived in and with them, in communion with all that surrounds us ...

This appeal by the Pope is unlikely to be fully understood or adopted by the managers in the economy. If more and more people no longer believe in God and the churches remain empty, then the Christian ethical orientation for moral action in the economy has no apparent base from which to be instilled. But, even a nonbeliever in God can still experience God. Unfortunately even the representatives of the churches are often no longer able to lead men into the experience of God, because they themselves have not experienced the reality which we cannot describe with words, but to which we give the name God. Their preaching has been reduced to doctrines and dogmas with the result that their audience becomes disenfranchised.

In Germany in 2014 a record of 217 000 people renounced their Catholicism. About 200 000 left the Evangelical church. The number of candidates for the priesthood in the world is declining sharply. This is regrettable as the churches are an important social institution for leading mankind toward an awareness and exploration of spirituality. In light of this decline in church affiliation we need to look elsewhere for teachings and practices which promote the internal growth which can lead to the development of a New Ethic.

Fight against Corruption: Francis Rebuilds Vatican Bank. This is the headline of an article in *Spiegel* online on December 4th 2013.

> For decades, the Vatican bank IOR gave us plenty of material for dark mysteries. It was involved in corruption, money laundering, even murder. Initially Pope Francis wanted to close the Institution, now he is determined to make the IOR a small, neat house bank.

Sexual abuse in the Roman Catholic Church is a phenomenon that has received considerable public attention worldwide since the mid-1990s. The awareness of this previously taboo subject has encouraged many victims to make their traumatic experiences public, even 30 or 40 years after the events. Cases of sexual abuse, especially by priests, monks and nuns, but also by educators within the Roman Catholic Church as their wards are reported ... (Wikipedia).

Immoral behavior, unethical practices, fraud and corruption flourish everywhere, not only in the Catholic Church. Fraud and corruption are also reported in Evangelical Church-affiliated organizations. Ironically, in the nonprofit *Organization Augustinum*, one of the leading Elderly Group Homes in Germany that is consciously committed to Christian values, where Christian faith, charity and welfare for these values are predominantly *why* one enters the Augustinum, fraudulent transactions and corruption have been reported. Prosecutors investigated deals involving millions of euros. The Diaconal Group which runs the Augustinum is a leading social services company in Germany, maintaining twenty three residential homes with 7,500 nursing home residents, nationwide.

The *Allensbach Institute* reports that according to surveys, in recent decades the sharp decline in the reputation of Germany's public institutions is not nearly as severe as is the decline in the reputation of the priests and pastors. These undesirable developments illustrate that the suppression and repression of the dark side into the shadow, in accordance with the practices promoted by the Old Ethic, even by the representatives of the Churches, lead to the dark side suddenly gaining control and acting out with a vengeance. Mankind *must* integrate the dark side in order to move forward into an era which embraces the New Ethic. It is time to recognize that spiritual paths alone are often insufficient without the additional insights of Depth Psychology.

2.36 As Individuals We Must Find Our Own Way

When the spiritual teacher J. Krishnamurti was asked in 1974 to define his own teachings he wrote the following:

> The core of Krishnamurti's teaching is contained in the statement he made in 1929 when he said "Truth is a pathless land". Man cannot come to it through any organization, through any creed,

through any dogma, priest or ritual, not through any philosophical knowledge or psychological technique. He has to find it through the mirror of relationship, through the understanding of the contents of his own mind, through observation and not through intellectual analysis or introspective dissection.

In a 2008 interview with David Ian Miller of the San Francisco Chronicle, the Astrologer/Philosopher/Humorist Rob Brezny quite aptly summed up Krishnamurti's statement: "I subscribe to Krishnamurti's principle ... he said that 'we need four billion religions.' Now that number is up to 6.5 billion – a religious tradition for everyone on the planet, 6.5 billion paths to God." Now, in 2017 we are more than 7.2 billion.

2.37 Mysticism and Ethics

If we cannot trust or rely upon any organization to tell us what is right or wrong then we have to rely upon our personal experiences and the resulting wisdom which promotes our inner growth leading us toward a higher level of consciousness. Karl Rahner, concerned with ensuring the preservation of our species and our ecology, developed a transcendental theology on the basis of transcendental experience, one wherein the experience of God is a prerequisite to ethical behavior. His vision may be summarized as, "The man of the future will either be a mystic or will become extinct!"

In a lecture in Cologne/Germany in 1967 entitled, *The Future of Faith and the Church*, Karl Rahner stated:

> We humans can only remain Christians if we are mystics. The Sermon on the Mount can be understood only by someone who has the courage to radically question himself – himself not others – and thus the Church must be experienced and lived in the years to come in a lively spirituality. These people will be mystics who have "experienced" something, or they will cease to exist ...

Perhaps it is then reasonable to conclude that individuals of the future who work in the economic sector must also either become mystics, or they will cease to exist. What is the connection between ethics and mysticism?

My current teacher Willigis Jäger represents a non-denominational spirituality in which in contrast to Catholic doctrine God is understood not as an entity but rather as a pure, *unifying consciousness*. We become aware of this unity in divine experiences. The following comments summarize his thoughts on *Zen and ethics,* and *ethics and mysticism.*

There are critical books on Zen and Buddhism, perhaps you have even read some of them. Buddhism and Zen are very much in the headlines currently. Some books have torn the mask of innocence from traditional beliefs. It has been long believed that Buddhism played no part in wars and conflicts, but unfortunately this is not the case. While the question of ethics in Zen must be reconsidered, ultimately, it's not just about Zen and ethics but about the larger question, *from where do all ethics arise?* The ethics of Christianity and mysticism are not excluded.

All mysticism of the world rests on two pillars, *awareness* and *love* or as they are usually referred to in Eastern mysticism, *wisdom* and *compassion*. Any really deep mystical experience results in a great openness and tolerance of all beings and in an all-encompassing love. Those who experience themselves as one with all others also feel the pain and joy of others as their own pain and their own joy. Compassion and love are the moving forces of the universe. Demarcation, enmity, hatred and war are initiated by a lack of awareness and wisdom. One who experiences who he really is also experiences all of the suffering and joy of others as their own suffering and their own pleasure. Mystical recognition manifests in unconditional love. Enlightenment leads only to actions that are initiated by compassion. Much of humanity already knows this, they feel the pain of the repressed, tortured and oppressed in this world as their own pain. Why is it that the lessons of Zen, and of those arising from other enlightened masters of other faiths are so often ignored by so many? It is because they are conditioned by parents, school, society, politicians and religious leaders to conform, to accept false authority, to look outwards at the expense of inner growth.

This conditioning undermines the deep experience of personal enlightenment which each and every person is capable of achieving. One needs to be constantly vigilant to avoid these traps. Zen has not failed, individuals have failed in not having been sufficiently vigilant. An experience of enlightenment which fails to be relevant in everyday life is not an experience of reality. How do we proceed? What is the way? Achieving enlightenment does not negate the limitations of our personalities. It does not keep us from acting unwisely. We must still be open, receptive and aware of our surroundings, our material world, of what is happening in our environment, and in so doing recognize the *relativity* of our views. Imperialism, nationalism, racism, religious fundamentalism and a rigorous, misguided, self-centered morality are not, unfortunately, eliminated by enlightenment. They have done much harm in the world. They are the source of war and oppression.

It's strange. Much of the suffering that some people cause other people often arises from the desire to defeat and eliminate everything that we believe to be evil. Satan as a symbol of evil is our dark brother. To bear him, to suffer by him is often better than to fight him. We must embrace our dark shadow in order to experience it, and through this experiencing we are able to integrate our dark side rather than projecting it outwards. Once integrated within us we can assume control over it, ultimately disenfranchising it of authority over us. We need a healthy skepticism toward ourselves. The experiences which result from Zen meditation allow the motives of our ego to become clearly recognized for what they are: image building, personal gain and self-aggrandizement. Once realized we are guided toward a greater tolerance of both others and ourselves. We become aware that we should not blindly follow any guru, spiritual guide or coach on our journey toward spiritual awareness. We must be *critically self-responsible.*

Each of us is unique. We are all confused, deceived or entrapped by different people, events and ideologies. In particular, reflect upon the 55th anniversary of the uprising against Adolf Hitler. Some were sufficiently self-aware to be able to see through the madness of Nazism. But even among these not all rejected his policies entirely out of a sense of philanthropy. Selfish interests are seldom very far beneath the surface of our proclaimed beliefs and actions. Following healthy reflection this can lead to the recognition of the error of one's ways. This is an opportunity for apologizing, making restitution and moving forward, for allowing oneself to shed the burden of past transgressions. Self-forgiveness is an essential, wholesome quality; it cleanses the mind so that it is free to examine each new idea within the context of past lessons learned. This assists us in freeing ourselves from the dogma of rigorous, restrictive religious authority with its threat of damnation to those who do not conform, which in turn opens the door to our ascension through an honest, uncluttered study of trans-denominational spirituality which is *liberating and expansive, not limiting and confining.*

The following text, the author of which may be Lao Tse, the first *Taoist* philosopher, is a clear appeal to the reader to consider that knowledge can never replace wisdom, and that wisdom without love can never represent enlightenment.

Duty without love makes us morose
Responsibility without love makes us inconsiderate
Justice without love is difficult and
Truth without love makes criticism addictive.
Education without love makes us contradictory and
Wisdom without love is incomplete.
Friendliness without love makes us hypocritical and
Order without love makes us merely petty.
Expertise without love makes us opinionated and
Power without love is violence.
Honor without love makes us arrogant and
Possession without love makes us stingy.
Faith without love is fanaticism.

Nelly Sachs, a German Jewish poet also highlighted the importance of love when she wrote: "Love is the only thing that increases as we spend it."

In his book *Jenseits von Gott* (Beyond God), Willigis Jäger writes about overcoming self-centeredness, that debilitating character trait which hinders ethical behavior.

A real mystical experience leads us away from egocentric thinking. Every thought, every action has an effect on the whole. Only when we are able to understand that this comprehensive reality constitutes our real life will we finally stop killing each other and have the possibility to survive as a species. The mystery of life is immediate and ever present. It takes place in every instant of our lifetime. We experience the REASON for being here, this *Ground State of Being* while sipping tea, while working, while driving ... It is the very basis of everyday life.

2.38 What Constitutes a Whole Person

Ultimately, for each one of us it comes down to whether and how we undertake the journey toward maturing into a whole person; one unified, balanced and harmonized in body, soul and spirit. Buddhism, Christian Mysticism, individuation and an understanding of the spiritual ramifications of knowledge gained through quantum physics provide an excellent foundation from which we may gain a strong ethical sense. There are numerous pathways *up the mountain, but they all lead to the summit.* The route is a personal decision, as is if, when and how we decide to embark upon it. But let there be no doubt that without making this inward journey our consciousness will never be expanded in its awareness and our inner growth will be stymied. We will remain a moral *child*, with the ego-dominated mind influenced by the controlling dark side, resulting in immoral, unethical thoughts, words and actions. People stuck in this mode are characterized by the following:
- feeling immediately offended
- needing constant recognition and praise
- always blaming others

Our dark brother or sister is evidenced by greed, envy, embezzlement, extortion, deception, resentment, ruthlessness, injustice, anger, oppression, aggression, abuse, hate, injury, destruction, arrogance, deceit, jealousy, delusions of grandeur, impatience, malice, slander, impudence, intrigues, lies, denial, falsehood, humiliation, betrayal and intolerance. We exhibit these characteristics in order to gain advantage over others. As we continue to express our *dark side* we have no control over it. This sort of projection has become rampant; our behavior is ego centered, devoid of meaningful ethical guidelines. Those who are currently employed in the business sector relate that during the past 20 years they have noticed a significant increase in ruthlessness in the commercial world. Compassion, empathy for others and working together toward common goals and rewards are far too seldom encountered.

But our network of concerned and increasingly self-aware and compassionate individuals is growing!

> Compassion can be taught. It must be taught, it should be taught. It needs to be taught with the same sense of urgency and gravity as math skills or verbal skills. If you think about it, what could be a more important legacy to leave this generation of children than the ability to be compassionate? (Jeff Weiner, CEO, LinkedIn).

Karlfried Graf Dürckheim stated that when we embark upon and embrace a spiritual pathway, in order for it to be completely liberating it must be accompanied by a deeply personal, intuitive exploration of our inner Self, our spiritual center, in order that the pathway followed *originates* from our spirituality, rather than attempting to *formulate* that spirituality. While spiritual pathways such as Zazen (Zen-meditation), meditation, yoga and prayer may also lead to liberation from the ego-dominated mind, without a clearly established, personal spiritual center which integrates our dark shadow that shadow we will continue to act to block our progress as we follow *any* pathway. After having practiced Zen-meditation for more than 40 years I sensed that additional knowledge and experience in the sense of Dürckheim's process of maturation and Jung's individuation into a whole person were still necessary. I spoke with Walter Schwery about my search in this direction. He chuckled and said, "Yes, that's very familiar to me. Recently a Tibetan monk came to me and said, Mister Schwery, I have a big problem. I have meditated for 20 years, but I still get angry too easily."

Despite following a very intensive and disciplined spiritual pathway for many years, I nevertheless found I continued to occasionally experience unsettling symptoms which I did not expect after such a prolonged period of meditative practices. The triggers I will describe which many others have also experienced and reported upon are a phenomenon which while apparently common have received very little attention or examination. Meditation literature generally only speaks of the progress one achieves through meditation. "Meditate and you'll be fine." As consoling a thought as this is, it is not always the case. Despite all of our mindfulness and our spiritual practices, when we entertain various opportunities for consciousness expansion we may all of a sudden be triggered to experience our dark side. This frequently occurs when we

- are angry
- argue
- are greedy
- want to be a hero or heroine
- do not want to lose something
- are afraid
- hurt others
- wish to dominate others
- want to be always be right

This all comes out of our shadow in which all of our bad habits and failures are suppressed. We are hiding this dark side of our person behind a mask. The integration of the shadow is a necessary condition for our evolution into a *whole person*. Then and only then can inner growth and creativity develop without encountering blockages.

When we fail to recognize and accept our dark side we remain at the mercy of our shadow. The *Jungian* approach is particularly well suited to guide us toward a new ethical approach for decision-making in the economy. Why Depth Psychology? Can other psychological approaches also help managers in the economy? Of course. Psychologists from a variety of disciplines have attempted again and again to identify ways to assist in providing suggestions which would lead to behavioral evidence of ethical practices in the economy.

2.39 Corporate Leaders and Psychology

The *American Psychological Society* reports about a meeting in 2003 of the Society for Psychologists in Management (American Psychological Society 2003):

> Helping corporate leaders develop guiding ethical principles to avoid the problems of such fallen companies as Enron was a hot topic at the *Society for Psychologists in Management* (*SPIM*) mid-winter meeting held Feb. 28–March 1, 2003 in Tampa, Fla.
>
> *SPIM*, an organization of psychologists who either consult with high level executives or who themselves are in high level management positions, hosts the meeting annually to examine how psychology can be used in business and executive level settings.
>
> In 2003 the meeting featured two events that specifically addressed businesses and ethical decision making ... How do CEOs get into hot water? While some corporate woes are due to deliberate greed ... *unconscious* bias can also play a dominant role. For example executives may discount facts that aren't consistent with their expectations – also known as self-serving bias. As such biased decisions are prone to escalate over time, speaking up and admitting to the string of poor decisions becomes harder, and executives may try to conceal the problems.

What can be done to prevent such dilemmas? The speakers offer these ideas:

- *Pass clear laws with consequences.* While legal regulation is a first step, Profitera says, more preventative measures are also needed because punishing businesses for violating the law only occurs after the fact.

"Also, because something is legal doesn't mean it's ethical, and because something isn't illegal doesn't mean it's ethical," says Crosby.

- *Help companies develop an ethical business culture.* An environment in which employees can discuss ethically ambiguous situations puts the focus on supporting responsible behavior as opposed to preventing wrong doing. For example, psychologists can recommend that companies assign a person to play the devil's advocate when discussing important decisions.
- *Avoid ambiguous situations when possible.* Setting regular checkpoints and agreeing on the course of action before a project begins minimizes the chances that ambiguity – and the need to decipher what is ethical – will arise.
- *Address ethics at the executive level.* As business consultants and coaches psychologists can help CEOs understand what general values and aspirations they hold, and then help them translate those values into their leadership styles, says Fogelman.

"We might all be better off if we could talk about business purpose and personal meaning more explicitly." Parchem explains: "People seek meaning in their lives and, if encouraged, many will seek it in their work."

- *Implement training on self-serving biases and judgment errors.* Just as many organizations offer sexual harassment or diversity training, businesses can train employees to identify and discuss disconfirming evidence.

Greenberg reminds us that many business ethics courses fail to include applicable psychological research, such as work on decision-making by the Nobel Memorial Prize winning psychologist

Daniel Kahneman, and the late Amos Tversky. Psychologists, he says, could be designing courses that include such research.

- *Develop more measures and methods for businesses to select people with good character.* It's difficult to train an unethical person to make ethical decisions, Fogelman says.

"You may not steal from the company, but you certainly may make decisions that will violate accounting principles and may better you and the organization at the expense of somebody else," Greenberg explains. "The tests out there right now aren't getting at what businesses are trying to establish as more ethical decision making."

The conclusion today, 15 years later, is that all of these serious suggestions will not create more appropriate moral decisions or ethical actions in the economy. They assumed in the summary above that the *unconscious* has a major influence. Exactly! That is precisely why Depth Psychology, which guides us toward a working relationship with our unconscious, is the appropriate tool for instigating the necessary changes.

2.40 Depth Psychology and Integrity

Robert C. Solomon has pointed out (Solomon 1992) that cooperation and integrity have to work together to achieve an excellence based on ethics. The abstract of his book reads as follows:

The Greek philosopher Aristotle ... called people who engaged in activities which did not contribute to society "parasites". ... Solomon asserts that while capitalism may require capital, it does not require, much less should be defined by, the parasites it inevitably attracts. Capitalism has succeeded not with brute strength or because it has made people rich, but because it has produced responsible citizens and – however unevenly – prosperous communities. It cannot tolerate a conception of business that focuses solely upon income and selfishness while ignoring traditional values of responsibility, community, and integrity. Many feel that there is too much lip service and an insufficient understanding of the importance of cooperation and integrity in corporate life. Solomon stresses the virtues of honesty, trust, fairness, and compassion in the competitive business world, and confronts the problem of "moral mazes" and what he posits as its solution – moral courage.

For many of us it is not so easy to follow these well-meaning appeals. Most of us do not understand why, in spite of predominantly behaving with integrity, we sometimes all of a sudden act immorally. A powerful understanding is evidenced once we link the request for integrity with the experience of Depth Psychology.

Christopher Reynolds and Jane Piirto (Reynolds and Piirto 2009) write about *Depth Psychology and Integrity*:

Investigators of depth psychology turn studies of the psyche toward the unconscious, believing that the ego consciousness typically receives excessive emphasis. When depth psychology is applied to high ability and creativity, often hidden aspects of human ability come to the fore.

These include notions of the collective unconscious, the transcendence of the psyche, the presence of the archetypes, unbidden, positive inspiration, and the darker side of human nature. Consequently, the gifts of bright, creative people can be both blessing and poison, and can have strong influence on moral/ethical issues ... It follows that if the depths are the unconscious, any penetrating discussion of ethics will require us to always see through our ego consciousness into what lies hidden, forgotten, unacknowledged, just below the surface in even our best intended judgements and actions.

The *Jungian* approach of Depth Psychology recognizes the *wholeness* of the individual both as an individual entity *and* as an individual who is part of a collective. In his *Collected Works 6*, Jung tells us that there is a new understanding of psychological types, a classification which includes the influence of *shared egos*. These result from the influences to which an individual is exposed through education, parents and mentors, indeed all of the influences which help to shape an individual. These *ego parts* are expressed as one goes about their daily affairs in the world. Jung made the revolutionary discovery that a portion of the four consciousness functions, thinking, feeling, sensing and intuition, remains relatively *unconscious* and forms the *inferior* personality, what Jung later refers to as the shadow. But out of the inferior personality spring the impulses that enable diversity within the individual, impulses which when accepted and intuitively adopted can lead one away from the dangers associated with unilateral development. Applying these insights into the processes in which we engage in our business life we can see very quickly that different types of people work together differently, and that the make-up of teams working toward a common goal can have a decisive influence upon the quality of their performance. A skillful manager who wishes to maximize performance must carefully consider the compilation of teams assigned to specific tasks in order to maximize performance.

The insights of Jung concerning the development opportunities of the individual aspect of the depth of the person are far reaching. The aforementioned inferior aspect of the personality supports other functions of consciousness by questioning the existing *status quo* and opens the potential for conflicts. Only in this way can a re-orientation be enabled, because the too rational, ego-dominated mind leads to constriction. This too rational, egocentric dominance has the potential to cripple the individual, and through the individual also to cripple the creative innovative corporate decisions necessary in the business world.

In contrast to the numerous psychological and behavioral therapeutic approaches, the Depth Psychology approach probes deeply into those areas of the individual which are suppressed, repressed, embarrassing, undesirable and rejected. But they are not viewed, as Freud did, as merely unconsciously repressed emotions which need to be discarded. Rather, they are a *rich source of unused energy and ideas*. This creative potential would never have been discovered only by the ego mind and its rationalizations. This approach to examining our unconscious and liberating us from the limitations it imposes upon us results in the freeing up of a great reservoir of creative energy! When an individual has access to this reservoir of rich resources and boundless energy, business decisions which result from this previously untapped depth have the potential to be considerably wiser and more profitable.

A company can also be considered to have an unconscious. It is formed as a result of permanent suppression and repression of everything which doesn't fit with corporate philosophy, including what is inconvenient, what doesn't meet its own corporate targets and what seems to be completely insane.

C. G. Jung, in *Collected Works, Volume 5*, emphasizes that every psychological extreme contains its secret opposite, or has in some other way a most essential relationship with its opposite. It is from this dichotomy that beliefs derive their peculiar dynamics. A superabundance of anything inevitably produces its opposite. There are no sacred beliefs which are exempt from this tendency. Ironically, the most firmly held platitudes are the most threatened by this devilish twist, because they result from the greatest suppression of their opposites. Recall the earlier remarks of Friedrich Gaede who argued that this destructive "counter-current" can only be avoided if the actions are guided up to the level of REASON.

The futility of management alienating their labor force, expediently ignoring important issues such as environmental impact, working conditions and recovery and regeneration of human resources are a few examples of undesirable business practices and of undesirable corporate developments. Paying attention to these aspects is a crucial beginning along the road of appreciating the business case for ethical behavior as a corporate strategy. In addition companies must master the dynamics of the internal impact of implementing changes upon the staff, the Board of Directors, the workers council and the union, as well as the external impact upon customers, suppliers, public relations personnel and the media. It is well worth the effort. An appreciation of the power that humanistic changes within a company can manifest when put into action holds the potential for an exponential increase in the value of the company for *all* stakeholders. Increasingly, companies are using the techniques of the *Myers Briggs Type Indicator* (*MBTI*), which is based upon Jung's psychological profiling of individual personality types, to improve the constellation of work teams established for specific tasks.

It is clear that Jung's individuation approach is already being utilized and is benefitting the economy. The next step is greater consideration of Jung's work and its application in the business world to prevent immoral decisions and encourage the implementation of ethical policies for the benefit of *all* of the various players in the corporate world.

2.40.1 The *Red Book* of C.G. Jung

In 1913 Jung began writing down his dreams and inner experiences in a book which was covered in red leather, subsequently known as the *Red Book*. His journey of self-analysis had begun. One of the important motivations for this book was the intellectual schism which had been developing between Jung and Freud, a fundamental difference of opinion as astounding as if Jung had committed patricide, considering that Freud had become his mentor, almost as a father would be.

How can lessons from the *Red Book* help us?

Jung's great *"patricide* predicament" resulted in his *Red Book* in which he documented the tremendously important *experiences of the unconscious in his own body*, as Jung described his "difficult experiment." When, fifty years after Jung's death, an English historian of science published the book, it was an immediate and tremendous success. Investigations of unfathomable breadth and depth continue, investigations which promise to open the door a little wider upon the workings of the unconscious mind. It is a treasure trove not only for those who want to further explore the process of individuation; the process of individual personal development, but also for those who wish to *directly experience* their *Inner Self*, to open receptively, giving this process a practical form. Even companies, at least successful ones, go through a process of individuation. Companies are living forms of organization that require, like individuals, self-control processes and feedback systems in order to maintain the highest possible energy efficiency while ecologically managing their natural resources, and ethically managing their human resources. The vitality of a company can be *improved* significantly, and this improvement can be *sustained* by the application of the information available through Depth Psychology.

Here is an example to illustrate the difference between approaching a corporate employee issue conventionally, and using the psychoanalytic approach. Assume a company has evident problems with employee satisfaction. A department manager, taking notice, discusses the situation with his superiors. Conventional psychology would dictate that one proceed as follows. The supervisor asks specifically who is dissatisfied. If a scapegoat can be identified and removed, then the problem is solved!

In the psychoanalytic approach, the department manager would ideally already have at least some psychological and spiritual training, and have demonstrated openness and receptivity to other points of view. The manager would gather information, focusing upon the alleged dissatisfaction, not upon the individuals who have drawn attention to it. The manager's superiors would be notified, emphasizing the importance of ensuring a flexible approach, and then, in an ethical fashion, ask the employees for their suggestions for remediating the problem as they perceive it. This approach has a high likelihood of success, as it ensures authenticity at all levels, and as such will be respected by all parties concerned. Success is due to the ability to create a win/win situation. This is the sign of an "individuated" manager who will be able to resolve the dichotomous situation on a higher level than otherwise would have been possible. What is to be gathered from this example is the personal responsibility of the department manager who has to decide how the employee dissatisfaction can be resolved in a fashion which results in a change for the better, to be well prepared as a result of intensive personal inner work leading to consciousness expansion. That's *authenticity*. And in just such a manner is respect garnered.

2.40.2 The Contemporary Meaning of the *Red Book*

My friend the Jungian Walter Schwery (Schwery 2014) gave a speech on Jung's *Red Book* in Rütte / Todtmoos, Germany, in September 2014. Some key, relevant highlights are as follows.

Jung states that one of our greatest current challenges is in dealing with our shadow. The future will be about the *unity of the Holy Spirit*, as the ultimate act of salvation which God, in an act of grace disseminated to mankind through the example of Jesus Christ. The matter of this salvation act which contains the divine secret can be discovered everywhere. According to the alchemists it can even be found in a dung heap. This *opus* is hence no longer a ritual *officium*, but an individual *opus* which can be identified by the philosopher through the *donum spiritus sancti* (the divine art). This *energie vital* which can be found everywhere is the energy that fascinated Freud in the form of sexuality and Reich as *Organ energy*. In modern times this energy can be seen as the trigger for youth revolts, beginning with the hippies, continuing with student riots, the 68-movement all the way to Russia's Pussy Riot and the youth revolution in the Middle East. This matter is also represented by the penetrating libido, the essence of which Jung identified as pure energy which is given the name of *Kundalini* in Eastern spiritual traditions. The alchemists have stressed that experiencing the effect of this energy is a completely individual and transformative event.

From a psychological perspective this means that the dependence resulting from a master-student relationship prevents change. If we are both wise and adept we will face this matter of spirit alone, at least until we realize that we and universal spiritual energy are one and the same.

In accordance with the dogmatic requirements of Christianity, God is "complete" in any of the three persons. Thus he is also complete in every part of the Holy Spirit, as well as in the "matter" of the alchemists. Jung says that in this way every human being can experience the complete God as well as *filatio*, the divine childhood. Thus, the *complexio oppositorum* of the divine image penetrates the individual not as a unit but as a conflict in which the dark side of the image is confronted by the concept that God is *only* "light." Jung then states,

> It is the process which takes place in our present time that is not recognized by the corresponding teachers of mankind even though it would be their task to do so. Everyone is convinced that we are in a place of dramatic change. But we are mistaken by thinking that this process was induced by fission and fusion of atoms or space shuttles. As usual, one ignores that which takes place inside the human soul at the same time.

2.40.3 Depth Psychology and the New Ethic

This chapter heading is the title of Erich Neumann's book (Neumann 1990) which he wrote during the Second World War. He rejects the misguided practices arising from the old ethical concept of only being able to win at the expense of someone else losing, and accepts the enriching content of a new ethical approach which results from the deep, personal psychological development of the individual. This understanding is crucial to the understanding of the behavior of managers, employees, suppliers, customers and indeed all stakeholders in today's business economy. This personal individuation is a *golden pathway* to more fruitful cooperation in the development of a new ethical framework.

For this reason, Neumann's book (Neumann 1990) is the backbone of this book. I will borrow liberally from the content of his book in an effort to introduce his concept of a new set of practical ethical considerations into the consciousness of the representatives of the economy.

According to Lance Owens it is of great importance that we, in the forefront of a New Consciousness, bring up the issues of past wisdom, experiences and recognitions, supporting people in their own current transformation.

Two eminent psychologists, Gerhard Adler and C.G. Jung expressed their admiration for Neumann's approach in the foreword to his book. Adler writes,

> Among all of his books the *NEW ETHIC* has a special place. It is a passionate appeal to the conscience and consciousness of our time, a deeply personal statement of faith in the future of modern man, a future based on an ever growing awareness of his psychological problems and their solutions. To Neumann the basic problem is the presence of evil which conventional ethics have proven incapable of either containing or transforming its destructive forces. The *dark* side has invaded modern man's world image with a vengeance, to the extent that he is no longer certain of his position regarding good and evil. Thus what modern man needs most is an awareness of evil, and first and foremost of the evil within himself ... Awareness of evil challenges the individual. He has to learn to realize, to acknowledge and to live with his own dark side. Instead of suppressing, or repressing the shadow and consequently projecting it outward, it has to be *integrated* ... But this can lead to a conflict with collective societal values ... It is a radical ethic based upon the stringent demand for individual choice and courage. It involves man's continuous confrontation with the problem of good and evil, from the honest acceptance of human totality ... (Neumann 1990, pp. 7–8).

Adler quotes Neumann. "The individual must work through his own basic moral problem before he is in a position to play a responsible part in the collective ..." (Neumann 1990, p. 9). He further quotes a letter which C.G. Jung wrote to Neumann.

> I have read your book once more. Again it made a very strong impression on me, an impression that gave me the certainty that its effect would be like a bomb. Your formulations are brilliant and of piercing precision, they are challenging and aggressive, an *avant-garde* in open country where, alas, nothing was visible before ... Already your title New Ethic is a fanfare: "*aux armes citoyens!*" ... Your book will be a *petra scandali*, but also the most powerful impulse for future developments. ... (Neumann 1990)

C.G. Jung welcomes Neumann's book as the first notable attempt to formulate the ethical problems which are raised by the discovery of the unconscious. He writes in his foreword to the book:

> I am happy to comply with this request (to write a foreword), although it is only as an empiricist and never as a philosopher that I have been concerned with depth psychology, and cannot boast of ever having tried my hand at formulating ethical principles. My professional work has certainly given me plenty of opportunity to do this, since the chief causes of a neurosis are conflicts of conscience and difficult moral problems that require an answer ... I do not mean that such a task does not exist, or that its solution is absolutely impossible. I fully recognize that there is an urgent need today to formulate the ethical problem anew, for as the author aptly points out, an entirely new situation has arisen since modern psychology broadened its scope by the study of the unconscious process ... Moral principles that seem clear and unequivocal from the standpoint of ego-consciousness lose their power of conviction, and hence their applicability, when we consider *the compensatory significance of the shadow* in the light of ethical responsibility. No man endowed with any ethical sense can avoid doing this. Only a man who is repressed or morally stupid will be able to neglect this task, though he will not be able to get rid of the evil consequences of such behavior ... The psychological foundation of all philosophical assertions, for example, is still assiduously overlooked or deliberately obscured, so much so that certain modern philosophies unconsciously lay themselves open to psychological attack. The same is true of ethics ... Although every act of conscious realization is at least a step forward on the road to individuation, to the *making whole* of the individual, the integration of the personality is unthinkable without the responsible, and that means moral, relation of the parts to one another, just as the constitution of a state is impossible without mutual relations between its members ... The analyst learns that ethical problems are always intensely individual, and can convince himself again and again that the collective rules of conduct offer at most provisional solutions, but never lead to those crucial decisions which are the turning points in a man's life ... The formulation of ethical rules is not only difficult but actually impossible, because one can hardly think of a single rule that would not have to be reversed under certain conditions ... I do not, myself, think that any of these rules are *absolutely* valid, for on occasion the opposite may be equally true. That is what makes the integration of the unconscious so difficult: we have to learn to think in antinomies (contradictions), constantly bearing in mind that every truth turns into an antinomy if it is thought out to the end. (Neumann 1990 p. 11–14)

Jung continues:

> The ethical problems that cannot be solved in the light of *collective morality* or the *old ethic* are conflicts of duty, otherwise they would not be ethical ... I am nevertheless of the opinion that in working out a difficult problem the moral aspect of it has to be considered if one is to avoid a repression or a deception. He who deceives others deceives himself, and vice versa. Nothing is gained by that, least of all the integration of the shadow. Indeed, its integration makes the highest demands on an individual's morality, for the *acceptance of evil* means nothing less than that his whole moral existence is put into question. (Neumann 1990, p. 14)

Jung points out that the condition for an ethical attitude is the involvement of the *whole person,* and therefore involvement of the *whole psyche.* He continues:

> This is not possible unless the conscious mind takes account of the unconscious, unless desire is confronted with its possible consequences, and unless action is subject to moral criticism ... We might therefore define the *New Ethic* as a development and differentiation within the old ethic,

confined at present to those uncommon individuals who, driven by unavoidable conflicts of duty, endeavor to bring the conscious and the unconscious into responsible relationship. (Neumann 1990, p. 15)

Jung is referring to the principle of double impact, which was earlier explained by Peter Knauer, namely, that one may do both evil and good simultaneously (Knauer 2002). For Jung it is an example of how life is always a process of balancing opposites.

In the introduction to his book (Neumann 1990) Neumann states,

The modern age is an epoch in human history in which science and technology are demonstrating beyond doubt the *capacity* of the conscious mind to deal with *physical* nature ... But it is also an epoch in which man's *incapacity* to deal with *psychic* nature, with the human soul, has become more appallingly obvious than ever before. (Neumann 1990, p. 25)

2.40.4 The Old Ethic

Neumann (Neumann 1990, p. 33) continues:

The old ethic of the West has many sources, the Judaea Christian and the Greek being the most influential among them. ... The ideal prototype at the center of the old ethic may be the figure of the Saint or the Wise Man, the Noble or the Good, the Devout or the Orthodox Fulfiller of the Law, the Hero or the Man of Self-control ... It is always held that the ideal of perfection can and ought to be realized by the elimination of those qualities which are incompatible with this perfection. The *denial of the negative*, its forcible and systematic exclusion, is a basic feature of this ethic. ... It will then become clear that there are two basic principles – two basic methods in fact – which have made possible the implementation of the old ethic.

2.40.5 Suppression and Repression of the Dark Side

Neumann continues:

The basic methods of the Old Ethic are suppression and repression. It is in *suppression*, that is to say, in the deliberate elimination by ego consciousness of all those characteristics and tendencies in the personality which are out of harmony with the ethical value, that the denial of the negative is most clearly exemplified as a leading principle of the old ethic. Discipline and asceticism are the best known forms ... (Neumann 1990, p. 34)

In a modern economy our inheritance through antiquity of discipline and asceticism are only one side of the coin. "If man does not have reverence for and submit to the unconscious, which created his consciousness, he loses his soul, or rather he loses his connection with his soul and his unconscious" (Jung 1933–1941, p. 214).

Neumann states:

It is important to notice that in suppression a sacrifice is made which leads to suffering. This suffering is accepted, and for that reason the rejected contents and components of the personality still retain the connection with the ego ... In contrast to suppression, *repression* may be regarded as the instrument most frequently used by the old ethic to secure the imposition of its values. In repression, the excluded contents and components of the personality which run counter to the dominant and ethical value lose their connection with the conscious system and become unconscious or forgotten, that is to say, the ego is entirely unaware of their existence. Repressed contents, unlike those suppressed, are withdrawn from the control of consciousness and function independently of it; in fact, as depth psychology has shown, they lead an active underground life of their own with disastrous results for both the individual and the collective ... The complexes of unconsciousness which have been shut away from daylight by repression undermine and destroy the world of consciousness ...

We have seen that suppression and repression are the two main techniques employed by the individual in his attempt to achieve adaption to the ethical ideal. The natural result of this attempt is the formation of two psychic systems in the personality, one of which usually remains completely unconscious, while the other develops into an essential organ of the psyche with the active support of ego and the conscious mind. The system which generally remains unconscious is the shadow, the other system is the *façade personality* or the *persona* ... The formation of the persona is, in fact, as necessary as it is universal. The persona, the mask, what one passes for and what one appears to be, in contrast to one's real individual nature, corresponds to one's adaption to the requirement of the age, of one's personal environment, and of that of the community. The persona is the cloak and the shell, the armor and the uniform, behind which and within which the individual conceals himself *from* himself, often enough, as well as from the world. It is the self-control which hides what is uncontrolled and uncontrollable, the acceptable façade behind which the dark and strange, eccentric, secret and uncanny side of our nature remains invisible.

A large part of education will always be devoted to the formation of the persona ... Originally, the old ethic was the ethic of an elite. It was the solution adopted by strong personalities who desired to solve the ethical problem by means of suppression – that is to say, by the conscious denial of the negative ... The aim of the old ethic is expressed in the injunction, "Man should be noble, helpful and good" ... This implies that the old ethic is, basically, dualistic ... The dualism of the old ethic, which is especially marked in its Iranian, Judaea Christian and Gnostic forms, divides man, the world, and the Godhead into two tiers, an upper and a lower man, an upper and a lower world, a God and a Devil. This dichotomy is effective on the practical level in spite of all philosophical, religious or metaphysical declarations of ultimate monism. The actual situation of Western man has been essentially conditioned by this dichotomy right up to the present day ... The fight between good and evil, light and darkness is its basic problem. ... (Neumann 1990, pp. 34–38)

This is the essence of the existential problems of *where does man come from, what is there at the end of life* and *how can we overcome our fear* of death? These questions have been asked throughout antiquity and still need to be addressed in the spiritual realm in order to ensure that an exploration of the totality of the psyche, rather than supernatural, is the essential task of every individual. The collective psyche is as dark as the collective human. Throughout history it has often been demonstrated, all too vividly, how quickly individual psyches can be destroyed by collective furors, and collective shadows initiated by collective forces!

Neumann writes:

By contrast with repression, in which all contact with the dark contents which cause suffering is destroyed by the splitting off of the unconscious components, suffering permits the suppressor to live a comparatively normal life. He is not, like the repressor, attacked and overwhelmed by the dark forces of the unconscious. Voluntary self-limitation by sacrifice and suppression is a way of life which does not make the individual a sick person. For the collective, however, the consequences of this suppression are disastrous, even where the individual escapes injury. There is in fact this much common ground between the two methods of suppression and repression: *in both cases the collective has to pay for the false virtue of the individual.* Suppression, and still more repression, results in an accumulation of suppressed and repressed contents in the unconscious ... The content which has been split off from consciousness becomes regressive and contaminated with other primitive, negative contents of the unconscious with the result that, in an unstable personality, a minor irritation denied access to consciousness is not infrequently blown up into an access of fury or serious depression ...

The more dogmatically the old ethic is imposed on individuals and societies – that is, the stronger the influence of conscience – the more radical will be this exclusion and the greater the split between consciousness with its value identification, and the unconscious, which by way of compensation will take up the opposite attitude. Where there is suppression, conscience shows its strength in the shape of a conscious feeling of guilt ... This guilt feeling based on the existence of the shadow is discharged from the system in the same way by both the individual and the collective – that is to say by the phenomenon of *the projection of the shadow*. The shadow, which is in conflict with the acknowledged values cannot be accepted as a negative part of one's own psyche and is therefore projected, that is, it is transferred to the outside world and experienced as an outside object. It is combated, punished, and exterminated as *the alien out there* instead of being dealt with as *one's own inner problem*. The way in which the old ethic provides for the elimination of these feelings of guilt and the discharge of the excluded negative forces is in fact one of the gravest perils confronting mankind. (Neumann 1990, p. 47–50)

Before turning to a consideration of Erich Neumann's *New Ethic* in his own words, we have to understand that there is a *relationship* between the *stages of the development of our consciousness and the stages of development of our ethical sense*. The following is from this chapter in his book.

2.40.6 Stages of Ethical Development

The evolution of ethics and the evolution of consciousness are closely interrelated, and it is not possible to understand one without the other. ... The starting point of the whole development is the stage of *primal unity*. In this stage, the embryonic ego, an ego which is still largely helpless and dominated by the unconscious, lives in a condition of almost complete dependence on the tribe, the world and the collective unconscious. *Participation mystique* and the dominance of the collective psyche over the still undifferentiated individual psyche are the most striking characteristics of this primal human situation. As is only to be expected, there is no individual or conscious ethical responsibility in this primary stage of ethical development ...

In the primal stage ... the *Great Individual* will represent the *man* personality, he will be, in a sense, the Self of the group, its creative center and it will be from him in his capacity as leader and creator that the collective will receive its values ... Subjection to the collective law does, however, represent an important advance in consciousness. It implies that the evolution of consciousness has reached a stage when the primal unity and with it the tyranny of the unconscious, is broken up, and the differentiation and strengthening of the ego and the conscious mind lead to a separation between the two systems of consciousness and unconsciousness ... The old ethic liberated man from his primary condition of unconsciousness and made the individual the bearer of the drive towards consciousness; so long as it did this, it remained constructive ... This explains why it was that the old ethic played an important and ancillary role in the evolution of human consciousness ... Actually, it is true to say that a certain devaluation and deflation of the unconscious are urgently needed in the initial stages of the development process; the conscious mind is still very weak, and without this tendency to devalue the unconscious it could never have established and consolidated its position, or proved its value as a formative agency in the creation of culture ...

As the individual and his ego consciousness are progressively differentiated and separated out from their matrix in the primitive collective, human development proceeds to a second ethical stage, the stage of individual moral responsibility. To begin with, this individual responsibility expresses itself within the framework of the collective ethic ... Before the appearance of the old ethic the ego had remained to a large extent a victim of the unconscious forces which had now become forbidden. It was subject to and dominated by these forces and instincts, which took possession of it in the form of sexuality, lust of power, cruelty, hunger, fear and superstition. The ego was their instrument and was totally unaware that it was in fact possessed ... But for an ego which is required to accept responsibility, this stage of unconsciousness and possession amounts to a sin ... The collective ethic which, with its doctrine of individual responsibility to conscience represents the classical form of the old ethic, then continues to evolve in two directions. Both these directions correspond to analogous processes in the development of the ego and the consciousness of the individual. The first leads, with the progress of individualization, to the *ethic of individuation, the new ethic;* the second, to the collapse of the old ethic ... (Neumann 1990, p. 59–75)

In 1948 Neumann explained that the old ethic had reached a point of no return. This is still the case today in 2018. There is, in fact, an even more urgent need for a new ethic now: an ethic which builds bridges to our soul and to the souls of others, and connects us with our unconscious and the collective unconscious. As the conclusion to this chapter in his book Neumann describes in detail why it is essential that we relinquish the old ethic and move ahead with the new:

> The old ethic demands suppression and sacrifice, and in principle, also admits of repression, that is to say, it does not consider the condition of the psyche or total personality but contents itself with the ethical attitude of the conscious mind, a partial system within the personality. In terms of the collective this encourages an illusionary form of ethics, oriented solely towards the action of the ego and the conscious mind. This is in fact a dangerous illusion: in the social life of the group and the collective it leads to negative compensatory phenomena in which the repressed and suppressed shadow side breaks through ... The old ethic has not only proved inadequate as a solution to modern man's most pressing moral problem, it also confronts him with an additional hazard due to the splitting tendency brought about by its dualistic conception of the world and of values. The partial ethic is an individualistic ethic since it accepts no responsibility for the unconscious reactions of the group or the collective. That is why the old ethic is inadequate; *the compensatory relationship between consciousness and the unconscious which it fails to take into account, turns out to be a major cause of the contemporary crisis in human affairs, and actually the crucial ethical problem of our time.* (Neumann 1990, p. 74–75)

2.40.7 The New Ethic

The conflict or disease which compels a modern man to embark upon a course of depth psychology is very seldom of such a kind that a simple correction of the conscious attitude, a mere rearrangement of the given material along the lines of a new structural pattern is sufficient to bring about a solution. In most cases it proves necessary to open up and make available to consciousness, levels of the personality which had previously been beyond the range and span of its experience, and were for that very reason termed *unconscious*. In former times a crisis of this nature was experienced as a threat to the soul's salvation ... *Modern man ... experiences his situation in the first place as nothing more than a crisis affecting his conscious mind and his ego.* The conflict is interpreted as a breakdown, a defeat, a failure to deal with a specific situation or vital problem ... Almost without exception the psychic development of modern man begins with the moral problem and with his own reorientation, which is brought about by means of the assimilation of the shadow and the transformation of the persona ... The disillusioning effect of the encounter with one's own shadow, *the unconscious negative part of the personality*, is always to be found in cases where the ego has lived in identification with the persona and the collective values of the period. That is why this encounter is, as a rule, particularly severe and difficult for the extravert, since by nature he has less insight into his subjectivity than the introvert. The naïve self-illusion of the ego, which has more or less identified itself with everything good and fine, receives a shock ... The absence of a *sense of sin* appears to be a characteristic of our own time ...

Now-a-days the situation is thought of largely in terms of exposure to outside influences, such as other people, circumstances, the environment or heredity – in relation to which the personality is a *victim* ... The result is that in a crisis the ego feels itself innocent since it cannot identify itself in a really responsible way with the ego of early childhood. In the encounter with the shadow, however, the ego falls out of its persona identification with the value of the collective. ... But what shakes the individual to his foundations is the inescapable necessity of recognizing that the other side, in spite of its undoubted character of hostility and alieness to the ego, is part of his own personality ... The individual is driven by his personal crisis into deep waters which he would usually never have entered if left to his own free will ...

A process in which the ego is compelled to recognize that it is evil and sick in mind, antisocial, prey to neurotic suffering, ugly and narrow minded ... all this represents such a bitter form of self-encounter that one can readily understand the resistance that it arouses ... In the end, the individual is brought face to face with the necessity of *accepting* his own evil ... The acceptance of one's own imperfection is an exceedingly difficult task. Each one of us, irrespective of his psychological type and sex, has an inferior function and a shadow; that is why we all find the assimilation of this side of the personality equally difficult. By the *breakthrough of the dark side* into Western consciousness we understand that whole complex of parallel developments which has led, in the course of the last hundred and fifty years, to the phenomenon of *darkness* becoming visible and problematic in widely different areas at the same time ... In no previous epoch of human history has the dark side occupied the foreground of attention to such an extent as it does today ...

The collective disorientation of modern man, especially when it remains unconscious and unassimilated ... gives rise to a series of dangerous reactions which have decisively molded the general ethos of our age ... Two main types of reaction can be distinguished, and by a typical quirk of the psyche, both may occur jointly in the same individual. The first reaction is deflationary and collectivist, and devalues both the individual and the ego. The second is inflationary and individualistic. Unlike the first, the second reaction over estimates and over values the individual and the ego. Both represent unconscious attempts to escape from the real problem. Common to both is the desire to conceal the fact that a new ethical attitude is called for to deal with the conflicts by which modern man is oppressed ... *The only person who is morally acceptable in the eyes of the new ethic is the person who has accepted his shadow problem ...*

The new ethic is *total* in the sense that it is oriented towards wholeness, towards two aspects of wholeness in particular. In the first place it is no longer individualistic; it does not merely take into account the ethical situation of the individual, but also considers the effect which the individual's attitude will have upon the collective. In the second place it is no longer a partial ethic of consciousness, but also includes within its reckoning the effect of the conscious attitude upon the unconscious. In fact, responsibility has to be carried by the totality of the personality, not simply by the ego as the center of consciousness. These two expansions of our ethical horizon are intimately connected ... The new ethic was born under the ruling star of fuller insight, deeper truth and clear-sighted awareness of human nature as a whole, which is the real achievement of depth psychology. ... We have in fact first to assimilate the primitive side of our own nature before we can arrive at a stable feeling of human solidarity and co-responsibility with the collective. Since the total ethic includes the shadow within the sphere of moral responsibility, it follows that the projection of this component will cease ... (Neumann 1990, p. 76–92)

The new ethics incorporates the intent, supported by personal internal stability, of never harming others and thus it also has permanence.

2.40.8 Aims and Values of the New Ethic

Neumann concludes,

The aim of the new ethic is the achievement of wholeness, of the totality of the personality. In this wholeness the inherent contrast between the two systems of the conscious mind and the unconscious does not fall apart ... The principal requirement of the new ethic is not that the individual should be *good*, but that he should be *psychologically autonomous* – that is to say, healthy and productive, and at the same time not psychologically infectious. And the autonomy of the ethical personality means essentially that the assimilation and use of the negative forces to be found in every psychic system takes place as far as possible *consciously*, within the process of *self-realization*. (Neumann 1990, p. 102)

Within the individuation of a person it is therefore the *task of life* to become whole. There is no way back to the wholeness of the early childhood. To progress is to become whole as an adult and to act from this inner strength.

Schwery had the following to say on the New Ethic.

The new ethic therefore is no longer based on the ideal of perfection, but on that of wholeness. This new orientation is rooted in the understanding and appreciation of a fundamental duality of human nature. Since the result of this duality is suffering, the solution or redemption from the suffering must lie outside of the duality in a 'Third'. Jung calls this Third the Self, an archetype of wholeness in which duality is removed ... This way is not based upon existing values. It is rather a process of careful observation and recognition of the reality of the soul, of its light and dark side. It is a '*middle way*' on which the development of the personality which is free from dogmatic identifications with 'good' and/or the rejection of 'evil' can occur. (Schwery 2008, p. 37)

2.40.9 Depth Psychology in Leadership

The awareness of the shadow and the integration of it are becoming more and more importance in the economy. The following comments are from a 2013 discussion on

Seeing the Shadow, in which David A. Laveman, who brings depth psychology insights into the business world to help executives and organizations "raise the bar" on performance and deliver breakthrough business results, is speaking to Bonnie Bright, the host of Depth Insights.

Depth Psychology is concerned about leadership because we are part of a global economy in which ecological considerations, interconnectivity, accelerated change and rapid availability of information are realities. Psychotherapy leading to personal growth is not necessarily sufficient to cause one to become engaged with important world issues. It tends to internalize emotions. Psychologist James Hillman, in a 1992 dialogue with Michael Ventura entitled, *We've Had 100 Years of Therapy and The World Has Gotten Worse,* notes that

> psychotherapy may lead us to a deeper understanding of how our psyche works ... it does not ensure that we have a better understanding of how the world works. Our emotions must connect to the world ... converting insight into engagement ...
>
> Those who have spent decades investigating the nature of the psyche must become more engaged with society's leaders, especially those of business and government. This responsibility is currently being filled by a thriving leadership development and coaching industry, one which knows little about the dynamics of the unconscious, how to work with shadow projections on an individual and organizational level or how to recognize archetypal patterns ...
>
> Depth Psychology can inform the corporate world by generating a broad and deep awareness among its leaders of the true nature of the shadow. The "shadow's" fundamental nature that has direct relevance to corporate leaders is that it does not reveal itself as such, but rather is often externalized on to a troubling aspect of the environment "out there", creating an "us vs. them" situation ...

Laveman believes the shadow expresses itself in three ways in many business enterprises; in greed, where no amount of wealth is ever enough; in hubris, where success causes a leader to overestimate their powers to predict the future, and in denial, where the necessary distinction between an understanding of the workings of the economy at large and the knowledge needed to run a company during difficult and complicated market fluctuations is lacking.

He is furthermore convinced that today's business leaders elevate circumstance over psyche, rationality over imagination and externalization over introspection. The reality of the tangible, empirically observable *outer* world takes clear precedence over the cloud like realities of the psyche. As this has been unsuccessful, organizations are constantly interested in "change management."

As the pace of external change has accelerated, the need to *transform* rather than merely "change" has given rise to a large network of "transformation" consultants and Human Resources specialists who do not understand archetypal realities. Thus transformation programs often devolve into a non-productive, energy depleting exercise.

Laveman follows up:

> Archetypal realities in a business context are background patterns of perception and images on the level of the psyche, and cultural values and reflexive behaviors on the level of the organization. They are often unconscious, and operate independent of the ego. Without an archetypal perspective leaders resort to making decisions through an over emphasis on rational analysis,

data gathering and trend analysis. The missing realization that archetypal powers are at work as a company struggles to bring into being a new order of reality leave those who are advocates of the transformation at a severe disadvantage. Without an archetypal perspective they are left with only their own efforts and superficially literal interpretations of challenges they face ...

It is easy to point a finger at business leadership for being too wedded to their collective views of change based on standard organizational psychology, change management and overarching pressures to produce financial results ... However I think it more productive to challenge those who are committed to the perspectives of Depth Psychology to take it out of the highly ritualized and controlled academic and psychotherapeutic environments and test its merits to create meaningful change with the business institutions that for better or worse dictate the pace and direction of today's world. This engagement will force Depth Psychology to endure tensions previously avoided and engage businesses to re-evaluate the role of the soul and psyche in the renewal of our world. (Laveman and Bright 2013)

2.41 The Milgram Experiment on Obedience to Authority

Everything which is suppressed or repressed often and easily rises to the surface when we are following orders, or when we wish to have an advantage over others. The more that we suppress and repress the easier is the seduction for release, and the more destructive the result. The conclusions from the classic Milgram experiment, a description of which follows, are that 62% of us are willing to inflict harm upon others if instructed to do so by an authority figure!

The following description of the Milgram experiment has been extracted from Wikipedia:

The *Milgram experiment on obedience to authority figures* was a series of social psychology experiments, conducted by Yale University psychologist Milgram. They measured the willingness of study participants to obey an authority figure, who instructed them to perform acts conflicting with their personal conscience. Milgram first described his research in 1963 in an article published in the *Journal of Abnormal and Social Psychology* and later discussed his findings in greater depth in his book. (Milgram 1974)

The experiments began in July 1961. They have been repeated many times since with consistent results within differing societies, although not with the same percentages around the globe. Three individuals were involved: the one running the experiment, the subject of the experiment (a volunteer) and a confederate pretending to be a volunteer. These three people fill three distinct roles: the Experimenter (an authoritative role), the Teacher (a role intended to obey the orders of the Experimenter), and the Learner (the recipient of stimulus from the Teacher). Both the subject and the actor drew slips of paper to determine their roles, but unknown to the subject, both slips said "teacher." The actor would always claim to have drawn the slip that read "learner," thus guaranteeing that the subject would always be the "teacher." At this point, the "teacher" and "learner" were separated into different rooms where they could communicate but not see each other. In one version of the experiment, the confederate was sure to mention to the participant that he had a heart condition.

At some point prior to the actual test, the "teacher" was given a sample electric shock from the electroshock generator in order to experience first-hand what the shock that the "learner" would supposedly receive during the experiment would feel like. The "teacher" was then given a list of word pairs that he was to teach the learner. The teacher began by reading the list of word pairs to the learner. The teacher would then read the first word of each pair and read four possible answers. The learner would press a button to indicate his response. If the answer was incorrect, the teacher would administer a shock to the learner, with the voltage increasing in 15-volt increments for each wrong answer. If correct, the teacher would read the next word pair.

The subjects believed that for each wrong answer, the learner was receiving actual shocks. In reality, there were no shocks. After the confederate was separated from the subject, the confederate set up a tape recorder integrated with the electroshock generator, which played pre-recorded sounds for each shock level. After a number of voltage level increases, the actor started to bang on the wall that separated him from the subject. After several times banging on the wall and complaining about his heart condition, all responses by the learner would cease. At this point, many people indicated their desire to stop the experiment and check on the learner. Some test subjects paused at 135 volts and began to question the purpose of the experiment. Most continued after being assured that they would not be held responsible. A few subjects began to laugh nervously or exhibit other signs of extreme stress once they heard the screams of pain coming from the learner. If at any time the subject indicated his desire to halt the experiment, he was given a succession of verbal prods by the experimenter, in this order:

Please *continue*!

1. The experiment requires that you *continue*.
2. It is absolutely essential that you *continue*.
3. You have no other choice, you *must* go on.

If the subject still wished to stop after all four successive verbal prods, the experiment was halted. Otherwise, it was halted after the subject had given the maximum 450-volt shock three times in succession. The experimenter also gave special prods if the teacher made specific comments. If the teacher asked whether the learner might suffer permanent physical harm, the experimenter replied, "Although the shocks may be painful, there is no permanent tissue damage, so please go on." If the teacher said that the learner clearly wants to stop, the experimenter replied, "whether the learner likes it or not, you must go on until he has learned all the word pairs correctly, so please go on."

Results: Ordinary people, simply doing their jobs, and without any particular hostility on their part, can become agents in a terribly destructive process.

Moreover, even when the destructive effects of their work become patently clear and they are asked to carry out actions incompatible with fundamental standards of morality, relatively few people have the resources needed to resist authority.

The *FAZ* reported on August 8, 2005:

> The social psychologist Susan Fiske investigated the incidents (war events) and pulled parallels to the Milgram experiment. 'People can act incredibly destructively when it is commanded by legitimate authorities' says the Princeton professor. This applies not only to war and terror, but also to the economy. The behavior of leaders is decisive in determining the atmosphere which prevails in a company. Those who exploit authority to foment distrust and hatred create a breeding ground for the suspension of moral and ethical actions in their subordinates. The human obviously does not need a strong motive to "strip humanity", as Milgram called it.

Wolfgang Berger, a German philosopher and economist, calls a company's employees "Resonanzkörper" (a body with resonance). If the actions emanating from superiors are ethically and morally sound there is a good possibility that the employees will follow their lead. However, this is not always assured as it may well depend upon the maturity of the employees. When immoral behavior is demanded the majority will comply with only those whose inner maturity is sufficiently advanced, refusing others even at the risk of losing their job. *Bernd Leibig (Leibig 2015, p. 19) writes about the archetype (C.G. Jung) of the resonance:*

> The underlying central principle (in nature) seems to me that all things are connected, so that they are in resonance with each other. The principle of resonance affects the entire animate and inanimate nature, so I would like to speak of an archetype of resonance.

Once we realize that everything is inter-connected with everything else and is in resonance with everything else, one cannot help but behave ethically and morally flawlessly, unless the dark side is allowed to destroy our good intentions.

2.42 Moral Licensing for Immorality

Even *without* being instructed to do so, people collectively are willing to harm others if their superiors and colleagues are engaged in a similar activity. Professor Dr. Bernd Irlenbusch was cited on November 24, 2014 in *FAZ*:

> We know from our empirical studies that our environment and specific situations have a major impact on whether we act morally or immorally ... Our moral judgments and decisions often arise intuitively. We are morally not as consolidated as we ourselves think that we are. Therefore more humility is required.

People with good, positive social connections may use this fact as justification, a type of moral license, thinking, "If I'm a good person, then it is alright if I also occasionally allow some things which are immoral." Often it starts with small violations which then increase. *"Do Banks Encourage Their Staff to Lie?"* This was the title of an article in the same newspaper.

> Trickery, lying and manipulating in the banking sector seems to be the norm of conduct. This is the finding by scientists from the University of Zurich, who have put the honesty of bank employees to the test in an experiment. The results of their tests, which seem to confirm prejudices against the financial industry, are published in the renowned scientific Journal *Nature* ... *If their identity as a bank clerk is revealed, then a significant proportion is dishonest.*

According to Peter Knauer, evil is only bad when it harms others. He postulates that it is only those acts that inflict damage that can ever be immoral. This is at odds with conventional orthodoxy which holds that everything which does not comply with a set of social norms is immoral. It's easier to say of something, "this is bad" if your criterion is simply that "I do not like it, it's unusual." However, this traditional morality leads us nowhere. It simply legitimizes personal likes and dislikes, creating scapegoats while trying to cope with the shadow. It is not an approach which is suited to the furthering of our understanding of ethics. On the other hand, Graf Dürckheim is very clear:

> Wherever you work in our society and wherever you take over responsibility, the blessing of your work depends on the deepness and the maturation of your inner person. It is so important to witness the other world in this world we are currently in. Only the individual can witness the other world, not a group, not an institution, not a society.

This is true not only for our individual contributions to the society in which we live, but equally for our responsible contribution to the economy. The consciousness of humans to accept and honor the individual nature of all sentient and non-sentient beings, and indeed all of the natural world, arises from the deep psychological individuation which can be established through meditation or through rituals established by the mystical branches of religions. This of course includes prayer if it leads to communion with a living, personally experienced, God.

When Meister Eckhart states, *"Nim din selbes wahr!"* (Perceive your own Self), he is referring to the inward retreat which allows for the experience of the divine. But it does not necessarily have to arise from depth psychology or religion.

2.43 Ethics from the Perspective of Quantum Physics

The knowledge and experience of quantum physics can equally lead to collective responsibility and a new ethic, as Hans-Peter Dürr has postulated again and again. While he describes himself as one who does not believe in a personal God, he does recognize a universal principle which can also be called a divine principle. Almost one hundred years after Heisenberg's *Quantum Physics* we have a far better understanding of the nature of reality. Particles, waves and fields are interpreted as quantum fields. Hans-Peter Dürr states,

Quantum physics tells us that reality is a great spiritual connection and that our world is full of possibilities. We live in a much larger world than that of which we are generally aware. Life is an amazing phenomenon. With his consciousness and his ability to deliberate action man has climbed to a new stage of life. It enables him to perceive the world in two quite different ways. First, and most directly, from the inside because man likes everything else is a part of this world. But he is then also able to learn about it from another angle, about its meaning in its bright consciousness as something outside, detached from himself.

Dürr's ethical awareness was honored in 1987 with the Alternative Nobel Prize, and in 1995 with the Nobel Peace Prize awarded to *the Pugwash Group* of which he was a member.

According to Dürr there is a *Permanent Acting Process* which *creates reality* in each and every moment. The field is empty, but has the potentiality to manifest permanently as reality. *Everything* is interconnected within the field. When we act as an individual we influence the field and through it all other individuals, and all of creation, including the economy. If we are responsible individuals we must take this into account when making decisions. If not, we may act irresponsibly and ultimately will fail. We must realize that *life* is the essential background for all that we attempt in the business world. Dürr's advice is to play the "Plus-Sum-Game" (Everyone Wins) and not, as is too often observed, the "Zero-Sum-Game," in which one gains only at the expense of others.

Management, New Physics and Spiritualty was the title of Michael Müller-Camen's lecture in Barcelona (Müller-Camen 2015), where I gave a lecture entitled *The Golden Path to Creativity—Meditation-Individuation-Intuition-Intellect-Invention-Innovation—Creativity from a CEO's Perspective*.

The content of Müller-Camen's lecture is summarized in the abstract:

Over recent years a number of authors have suggested that management theory and practice is still very much influenced by the world view inherent in Classical Physics. Consequently reductionism, determinism and positivism became major building blocks of management studies and practices, and left little room for spiritual and religious ideas. The aim of this paper is to examine how the paradigm of Quantum Physics could inspire management. For this purpose, we examine three phenomena in New Physics namely wave-particle dualism, Heisenberg's Uncertainty Principle and field theory, which suggest that management science should pay greater attention to creativity, interconnectedness, non-duality, non-linearity and qualitative research methods. This could open new opportunities for integrating religion and spiritualty in management research and practice.

2.44 Making Living More Lively

For Dürr the essence of sustainability is in making living more lively. This message was very important for him. Toward the end of five years of friendship with him he asked me to spread his interpretation of sustainability around my world of influence. Bouckaert (Bouckaert 2014, p. 24) in his paper *Spirituality: The Missing Link in Business Ethics* uses the term "Elan Vital," which is another way of expressing Dürr's concept.

According to Bergson's theory of leadership the main function of spirituality in business is to open the mind to the *élan vital* of history. This 'élan vital' cannot be seen as a mechanistic or Darwinian program built into the nature of things which may be revealed by positive science. It is instead the infinity of time that creates new meaning in history and in our lives, which we call the Spirit. Spirituality as a faculty of our mind – to be distinguished from rationality – has an intuitive knowledge of this Presence of creativity in life and history.

It is worth pointing out here that it is not universally accepted that spirituality is a faculty of our mind. It is derived from "spirit" which is our divine source, our "essence" and it, along with our body, mind and soul ensures that we are constituted as a whole person.

The theologian, Jesuit and philosopher Rupert Lay SJ expresses in his book *Ethics for Managers* the principle expressed by Dürr : "Act so that you in yourself along with others increase or enhance your personal life (emotional, moral, social, musical, religious) more than you reduce or demean it."

If we do not act with mindfulness and compassion we will find ourselves outside of the wheel of life. Our energy will not be in harmonious balance with that of all of the rest of creation. Those who are entrusted with economic and political decisions need to take this self-evident recognition very seriously! Even competitiveness takes on another meaning for Dürr. He asks that we consider how two waves when flowing against each other will cancel each other out, but will reinforce each other when they flow together synchronously. Our rewards come not from simple cooperation, but rather from our unique contribution toward the creation of a new dimension. Dürr promotes the process of a "Loving Dialogue" with others as the medium for co-creation of a new, and mutually beneficial understanding. I asked him how companies in the economy could survive. He answered, "*Decentralization* is the solution for survival. Nature has taught us that. One should work with what is within one's reach. There is no reason to include the whole world all at once."

2.45 Embracing Uncertainty May Enhance Our Ethical Practices: Lowering Our Entropy

In a book focusing on Integral Ethics it is prudent, in spite of any prevailing skepticism, to elaborate upon new insights in the natural sciences as a result of the exploration of individual consciousness, the effect of consciousness on the inner and outer world and the realization of the existence of a higher or expanded consciousness, since these insights, when they are practiced have a considerable influence on morality and ethics. For many, especially in the younger generation, the desirability of inner growth both as a contribution to the meaning of life and as an ethical guide may be easier to understand through the doorway of the natural sciences than through religion, mysticism, philosophy or psychology.

For about two decades physicists, mathematicians and computer scientists have preferred to research digital physics on the basis of quantum physics, using this methodology to explore the knowledge of religions, philosophy and psychology. This affords us a greater understanding of reality and enables us to overcome the dualism of mind and matter. Natural Science seems to have both a greater immediate and potential capacity than religion for influencing the transformational process. The physician Thomas Campbell describes in his trilogy, *My Big Toe – Awakening-Discovery-Inner Workings* (Campbell 2007), a unification of philosophy, physics and metaphysics, and how mysticism is *demystified* by applying the findings of Natural Science in order to achieve an expanded consciousness.

Michael Thorn, from his German Interpretation of Campbell's knowledge and wisdom states:

> Nonetheless, the acquisition of knowledge (from Campbell) is never primarily about expanding knowledge, but about the process through which the individual has the opportunity to make a substantial difference where it counts the most. When it comes to development, the subject is always the focus. Every person can make a personal contribution to the enhancement of the quality of the overall consciousness through his or her personal existence alone. Hidden therein are not only claims and responsibilities, but also the closest possible proximity of the individual to the absolute.

Campbell's knowledge and experience may be accessed via his website http://www.my-big-toe.com

Not only scientists, but also opinion leaders of the younger generation such as Mark Zuckerberg embrace this zeitgeist. Internet satellites, virtual reality, even real working AI, it all pales in comparison to the future that Facebook chief executive Mark Zuckerberg (Zuckerberg 2015) has in mind. In a question and answer session with site users, the 31-year-old said he envisions a world where people – presumably Facebook users – don't need these types of communication intermediaries. Instead, they'll communicate brain to brain, using telepathy: "One day, I believe we'll be able to send full rich thoughts to each other directly using technology," Zuckerberg wrote in response to a question about what's next for Facebook. "You'll just be able to think of something and your friends will immediately be able to experience it too."

Not only telepathy, but also near-death and out of body experiences (OBE) suggest that there is a consciousness outside the body, a non-material consciousness. Pamela Reynolds' experiences are considered a classic case in this context (Reynolds 1991).

> In 1991, Pamela Reynolds suffered a brain aneurysm. She was cooled down and was clinically dead for several hours during which she was constantly electronically monitored with every second being documented. After waking up, she reported all the details of the operation as well as her experiences outside of the operating room. But during "standstill", Pam's brain was pronounced "dead" by all three clinical tests: her electroencephalogram was silent, her brain stem response was absent, and no blood flowed through her brain. Interestingly, while in this state, she encountered the "deepest" NDE of all Atlanta Study participants.

Eighteen years have passed since this particularly well-documented case, which astonished many skeptics. In the meantime, the threshold between life and death has been extensively examined. Studies on near-death experiences and para phenomena in the case of dying patients in the clinic have now been taken up by universities and specialist publishers. Several universities operate online portals where people can register and describe their experiences.

It is safe to assume that this otherwise unconscious part of us is continuously present, but only on the threshold from life to death is it particularly noticeable.

Since the internet has been used to bypass the censorship possible in the analogue age, the reports of people who are already consciously in contact with their immaterial part during their lifetime have become more evident. The most common contact medium is probably the dream (Strauch 2006), but all other forms of clairvoyance are also well documented. In 2003, for example, in a dissertation on soil sciences at the Department of Environmental Sciences at the Swiss Federal Institute of Technology in Zurich, the dreams of the doctoral candidate were approved as sources of knowledge (Patzel 2003).

This age old certainty was apparently forgotten by the materialistic industrial age and the inter-subjective validity and repeatability of the results, which the natural sciences increasingly demanded. For example, since the sixteenth century, the *Hypnerotomachia Poliphili* – an extremely meticulously illustrated dream protocol of the professional lucid dreamer Francesco *Colonna* – has been a bestseller in scholarly circles, apparently with immense effects on the production of art (Colonna 1499). This book was translated into German in 2014.

Another example that has only recently become accessible to the scientific community is the *Red Book* by Carl Gustav Jung cited and discussed above.

If the certain realization that our consciousness also exists outside of the body is now growing, then we have to ask ourselves where does that part of ourselves which is not confined by our body exist. What is its reality?

There are several Western pioneers for this new mediation task. One of the leaders of the second generation is nuclear physicist Thomas Campbell, who began his studies with transcendental meditation while working for many years for the American military and NASA, and at the same time out of purely personal curiosity investigated out of body experiences together with the electrical engineer and media producer Bob Monroe (1915–1995). Monroe published his book *Journeys out of Body* in 1971 and soon afterwards founded the Monroe Institute in Virginia/USA. At the same time Targ and Puthoff at Stanford Research Institute (SRI) International in Menlo Park, California/ USA, and their successor aeronautical engineer Jack Houck conducted research on the so-called Mental Access Window in connection with Remote Viewing, Psychokinesis and Psychic Healing, which may be accessed at: http://www.jackhouck.com/maw. shtm. This is just a tiny part of the well-documented and scientifically conducted para research that has historically been carried out in both academies and monasteries.

The leading edge of technical and natural sciences has always been characterized by the utmost discipline, with a penchant for metaphysics in the field of astronomy and space travel, always associated with the knowledge that we are not alone in the universe: which transforms the foundations of everything.

It is time for the implications of the findings from the natural sciences to inform the economy.

Campbell's research on consciousness and out of body experiences has been recognized worldwide. He calls the large, immaterial horizon that opens up, the Larger Conscious System (LCS). His experiments confirm that listening different combinations of frequencies can make listeners either weary or wide awake and active, and that the status of an expanded consciousness which allows access to the LCS can be achieved, during which the experimental candidates are able to solve tasks, even those involving content which was previously foreign to the candidates. These methods turn off the neocortex, and thus active thought. This shutdown is a prerequisite for the limbic system and the thalamus to work undisturbed and without any restrictions by the thinking mind. This state can also be achieved through experienced meditation.

Campbell's own experiences lead him to the conclusion that consciousness is a fundamental aspect of reality itself. Based on this single assumption he can explain "inexplicable" phenomena in quantum physics and give answers to a large variety of philosophical questions. Through his lectures he explains different aspects of the nature of reality. By doing so he offers an alternative viewpoint to a strictly materialistic approach, but in contrast to many other alternative models of reality, Campbell's approach while remaining based upon science as we accept it today, goes far beyond it.

Thomas Campbell distinguishes between two realities, PMR (Physical Matter Reality) and NPMR (Non-Physical Matter Reality). The LCS contains all the information that was, is and will be available in the future. This information may flow to us accidentally or as a result of an expressed intention. In mysticism, which is based upon suspending our active intentions, we speak of "grace" when we receive information. Campbell believes that we must first express an intention to get information about a question. It is then necessary to wait in meditation or some other form of internal stillness, silence and mindfulness. These techniques, along with other opportunities for expanding awareness such as walking in nature, music, dance, art or even illness, are effective tools. As discussed later (**3.1.3**), in accordance with C.G. Jung, in Active Imagination images with information can appear after posing a question.

This appears to be a universally valid process, one which has been espoused by science for several decades which everyone can learn as a mental technique. This would indicate that we are essentially immaterial beings, endowed with previously unthinkable abilities and a kind of immortality which also includes the concept of reincarnation. A new framework for describing our essential nature is possible, one which, while available to everyone, is largely neglected. Campbell constantly implores his students to: "Always be skeptical!" Even dream factories in Hollywood like the magical Disney Empire & Co. serve up with their blockbuster movies and series very solid and compelling premonitions, albeit somewhat distorted! Empirical evidence, however, does establish very clearly that an integral part of this extended horizon of *Our Being* ("I am") is recognition of an elevated level of mindfulness, altruism and globally applied ethical practices.

"Gratitude is necessary for the most important present of each and every moment which we receive, even without our active participation or thought. The moments continue, one after the other" David Steindl-Rast (Wisdom 2.0 Annual Conference 2014).

In order to ascend into this expansion of consciousness we must – expressed in the language of modern natural sciences – participate in evolution by reducing entropy, increasing energy and improving the state of order in ourselves, in other living beings and in nature as a whole. Evolution follows the second principle of thermodynamics which states that in closed systems entropy tends to act against orderliness, allowing for an increase in the state of disorder.

As human beings we are open systems. As a baby we have low entropy, at death we have high entropy. We, along with everyone else and along with our entire environment influence the course of entropy. We are able to consciously reduce the entropy in us, in others and in the system around us as a mission in our life, increasing the possibility that everyone can find greater fulfillment both within their environment and their Being. It actively involves us in evolution.

This leads to an ethically and morally impeccable treatment of all beings and the environment. It leads to a life of mindfulness and compassion, which is based on an order and unity of body, mind, soul and spirit.

Dürr expressed the same concept differently, when he stated:

"Let the living become more alive!"

On the path described above we are able to recognize that every being we meet is a special, unique entity, a consciousness, a creator's consciousness, or even an immortal, divine spark that is formed into matter just as much as are we. Everyone strives to recognize themselves and to develop. Hinduism has introduced the concept of LILA, the cosmic play of the immortal gods, in which the material Earthly dual concepts of good and evil, and even life and death, are abolished.

The deliberate entry into the perspective of LILA erases many anxieties around the concept of our transient existence. Almost everyone with a near-death experience confirms this life-changing epiphany. Campbell also sees anxiety as our greatest source of disturbance. How do we get out anxiety? Dürr and Panikkar consider the question of the nature of the driving force behind the cosmos in their book: "Love is the primordial source of the cosmos" (Dürr and Panikkar 2008).

Dürckheim saw the problem of anxiety in much the same way. He relates the three greatest fears that people voice:
- Fear of loneliness
- Fear of death
- Fear of the absurdity of life

These powerful fears generate anxiety. They have a destructive effect upon our ability to make moral decisions and to act in an ethical fashion. Anxiety integration is a crucial task in our life.

Anxiety is the main source of our immoral decisions and our inability to enact ethical approaches.

Growing up is not about Doing, it is about Being. Growth of consciousness evolution must take place at the *being* level rather than on the intellectual level. ... Physics and Metaphysics, ethics and morality, mind and matter, normal and paranormal, ontology and theology all follow the same rules and derive from the same basic understanding. They all derive from first principles. And these first principles are basically what constitute consciousness. How does consciousness work? What is the digital information field of consciousness? Once we understand the fundamentals of consciousness we understand that the same fundamentals guide us in physics and metaphysics, and the same fundamentals lead us towards an understanding of morality and ethics. Decisions and actions are ethical and moral based upon lowering the entropy of our lives ... (Edited from Campbell 2015), (The whole chapter developed in cooperation with Dr. Inge Kader, München/Germany)

2.46 Radius to Ethics Break

How stable are our ethical principles? Individuals and corporations live in their "comfort zone." When life is running smoothly this zone can be considered to be in the middle of their circle of life where grossly unethical behavior is not required or at least is not readily evident. But if an individual or the collective, which is at the center, is urged to take risks at the *perimeter* of their circle of life, ethical behavior is suddenly jettisoned. Ethical beliefs and behavioral principles are quickly thrown overboard. The radius from the comfortable center of one's circle of life to the outer edge of the stability of ethics I call *Radius to Ethics Break* (REB). The resilience of individuals and businesses differs. In my experience the REB is directly proportional to the status of one's inner maturity. The further the development of individuation in the Jungian sense, or the deeper the internalization of the experience of God, the greater the REB. It is resilience and the preservation of ethics which one acquires through individuation, spiritual wholeness and a personal experience of God which determines the REB, not ethical guidelines, ethics seminars or the imposition of laws. Corporate rational decisions concerning ethics are of very limited use. If personal, spiritual development is not undertaken ethical violations will occur, even at a radius of zero, when, for example, greed may shape our decisions. We can witness this in the media every day. We can emerge from this dilemma, operating under the principles of the new ethic only if we, as individuals and as part of a collective, are actively involved in enlarging the radius. One always acts in the outside world in correspondence to one's inner maturity, consciously or unconsciously. The "royal road" is one of "inner growth," every unethical practice is a reflection of a lack of inner maturity.

3 The Solution

3.1 Allowing Our Inner Growth to Develop

In the following chapters possible individual paths facilitating inner growth will be explained in principle and briefly discussed. Further reading of specific subjects of interest may then add detailed descriptions for interested readers. Inner growth is a condition for ethical awareness. We must always take upon ourselves the initiative for change through the increased awareness which results from an expanded consciousness. There is only one way we will survive in the *VUCA* world of lost orientation. It is by permitting our inner growth. We cannot force it to occur, but we may be able to facilitate it, allowing and encouraging it to grow. We must take the word orientation seriously (from lat.: *oriri* ... to stand up, rise), and return to embracing the unity of Body/Mind/Soul/Spirit. This is difficult *Mind*-work, *Soul*-work and *Spirit*-work, but the consequences of avoiding it are disastrous. The personal unity which results from the following seven practices will facilitate building a strong and resilient foundation for ethical behavior:

- Grounding our ego in our *Self*.
- Building bridges to our *Soul*.
- Balancing the *Male* and *Female* within ourselves.
- Welcoming the return of *Sophia*.
- Avoiding the suppression and/or repression of our *Dark* side.
- Embracing and integrating our *Dark* side.
- Meditating and encouraging our inner values to grow.

Pete Geissler and Bill O'Rourke encourage us with the following declaration: "You can be an ethics ambassador; start with yourself, expand to others ... " (Geissler and O'Rourke 2015).

C. G. Jung often said that *inner growth always requires a psychic tension*, otherwise nothing happens. A life crisis always provides great momentum for growth. It takes a crisis in which we do not desire to remain but rather to resolve, in order to move ahead. Inner growth occurs only when the suffering is too much to bear. Then growth begins with longing and desire.

When we, as Herder stated, are "Invalids of a higher Power" then our longing and the way of inner growth will result in our healing. Our otherwise rigid mask will become permeable to our inner essence. Only then do we achieve wholeness. This is the only way to end our separation from the numinous. Our soul is helping us. If we are able to build bridges to our soul, then it becomes a guide to our unconscious; our great source of power and strength which remains closed to our ego mind.

Soren Gordhamer (Gordhamer 2013, p. 37) refers to the inner journey when he writes: "*Search Inside Yourself,* as taught by Chade-Meng Tan, is a course in

https://doi.org/10.1515/9783110572292-003

mindfulness which is often referred to as 'The Zen of Google'. It helps many employees learn to deal with their fast paced work with awareness and calm rather than stressful reactivity."

Chade-Meng Tan is no doubt aware that in modern times everything spreads around the world quickly, which is good for both individuals and business. The media entrepreneur Ariana Huffington, one of the leading figures of the Wisdom 2.0 movement, said "that everything which is good for both the individual and American companies is of value. Personal happiness is linked to success in business. Meditation relieves the tension between personal and business goals and prevents or relieves symptoms such as burn out, depression, anxiety and isolation."

Soren Gordhamer quotes Tony Hsieh, CEO of Zappos (Gordhamer 2013, p. 37): "The biggest (and hardest) lesson I've learned in my life is that the external world is just a reflection of the world within." That means if we grow inside we will grow outside. We will feel it slowly. It develops in small steps. Our environment will feel it as well. Inner growth is the result of Depth-Psychological individuation and/or a spiritual quest. Dürckheim often emphasized the importance of both ways. Both can heal that which we have lost since our early childhood, and as adults we must now recover: our wholeness.

3.1.1 Growth through Individuation

Recently, after attending a lecture that Brigitte Dorst, Professor of Depth Psychology and Sufism delivered in Essen/Germany, I asked her why she is committed to both Depth Psychology and Sufism. She answered: "Depth Psychology can guide you to the door of God!"

It's always about connecting ourselves with the numinous and thus healing the wounds which resulted from our separation from it. There are many ways for this healing to begin and many pathways for its continued progression. In the following my focus will be upon *Individuation* and *Spiritual Practices.* You may wish to follow other paths, but it is essential to embark upon *some* path of healing, as it is a prerequisite for all of us in order that we may be led toward sustainable moral decisions and ethical practices.

It is essential that we achieve reconciliation with our dark side as previously presented by Schwery (Schwery 2008). We must become complete individuals, a dynamic, balanced integration of our body, mind, soul and spirit. Inner growth cannot be achieved by our rational mind or by our emotions, it takes place in the trans-psycho mental aspect of our Being. Overcoming our ego-centeredness is an essential first step which can be achieved through exercises which are based mainly upon the transcendence which is initiated by our *letting go* of thoughts and feelings. This is consistent with C. G. Jung's observation that separation from the numinous was the cause of all disease.

Wolfgang Berger followed up on Jung's observation in his book *Business Reframing* (Berger 2013). He considers that this separation is not only the reason for psychological illness, but that the lack of the awareness of our unity with all of humanity has also resulted in the loss of our moral center and ethical actions.

3.1.1.1 What Is Individuation

The following is extracted from a publication of *The Jungian Center for Spiritual Sciences*:

> "Individuation" is a term often associated with Jung and his psychology. Our English word comes from the Latin individuus, meaning "undivided" or "individual". The dictionary defines "individuation" as "the process leading to individual existence, as distinct from that of the species". This definition applies the term to both animals and humans. Jung's usage focused on humans and the concept became central to his approach to psychology. Jung recognized the importance he placed on individuation in his 1921 definition of the term:
>
> > The concept of individuation plays a large role in our psychology. In general, it is the process by which individual beings are formed and differentiated, in particular, it is the development of the psychological individual ... as a being distinct from the general, collective psychology. Individuation, therefore, is a process of differentiation ... having for its goal the development of the individual personality.
>
> In later years, Jung amplified his definition in a series of essays, describing "individuation" as
> > ... the process by which a person becomes a psychological "in-dividual". that is a separate, indivisible unity or "whole".
> > ... the better and more complete fulfillment of the collective qualities of the human being, ...
> > ... practically the same as the development of consciousness out of the original state of *identity* ... It is thus an extension of the sphere of consciousness, an enriching of conscious psychological life.
> > ... becoming an "in-dividual", and, in so far as "individuality" embraces our innermost, last and incomparable uniqueness, it also implies becoming one's own self. We could therefore translate individuation as "coming to selfhood", or "self-realization".
>
> Jung felt this process of "self-realization" was a "natural transformation", something that "the unconscious had in mind", something meant to develop our individual personality.
>
> Jung also regarded "individuation" as a solution to what he considered one of the major problems facing modern people: how to link up consciousness to the unconscious; how to bring our ego mind (consciousness) into a working relationship with our inner *terra incognita*, our unknown inner terrain. Consideration of this problem was not unique to Jung: thousands of years ago Taoist and Buddhist practitioners had also seen its significance. Jung recognized this when he noted that "the individuation process ... forms one of the main interests of Taoism and of Zen Buddhism." Coming from a Christian... background, and as the son of a Protestant minister, Jung also recognized a Christian relevance to the concept when he described individuation as "the primitive Christian idea of the Kingdom of Heaven which 'is within you'."
>
> Aware of Western culture's vaunting of individualism, Jung took pains to stress the difference between "individualism" and "individuation". The former concept is ego driven and fosters selfishness and lack of concern for others (Think of the bumper sticker that celebrates "Looking out for #1!"). Individuation is very much the opposite: during the years of inner work the process requires, we experience repeated crucifixions of our ego as it confronts and assimilates contents of our unconscious. This long-term process brings to birth a consciousness of human community

precisely because it makes us aware of the unconscious, which unites and is common to all mankind. Individuation is an at-one-ment with oneself and at the same time with humanity, since ones-self is a part of humanity. Far from being selfish, an individuated person feels deeper responsibility to support and serve others and to foster peace, wholeness and "integrity in the world."

3.1.1.2 Requirements for the Process of Individuation

The following is also from the website of *The Jungian Center for Spiritual Sciences:*

Mention of crucifying the ego brings up the subject of what individuation entails. It's challenging, a task for heroes, not for the faint of heart or for those who can't stand against the crowd and be different. *Divisio* (being divided not only from others but also within oneself), *separatio* (being separated not only from family, friends and collective society, but also from the person you used to be), *solutio* (watching the structures of your life dissolve), discrimination, self-knowledge, "a positive torture" – these are just a few of the hardships likely to be faced in this work. Jung was being honest about the task when he warned, " ... as always every step forward along the path of individuation is achieved only at the cost of suffering ... ."

Why such difficulty? Jung gives several reasons. First, we grow up under the direction of our parents and our society, striving to become what is expected of us, and the result is what Jung called the development of the "persona," or mask. In many cases, the persona is not our true self. We have had to compromise, adapt, even, in extreme cases, betray our authentic nature. The process of individuation requires getting wise to this mask; that is we have to face the fact that for years (if not decades) we have been living a lie. And then we have to give up this lie, put down the mask and begin to change our life so as to live in greater alignment with our authentic being. Such change almost inevitably elicits remarks (maybe even protests) from those who know us best, those most deeply invested in how we used to be, those likely to be most affected by our shifting the parameters of daily life, including our family and closest friends.

Second, individuation is heroic because it is hard to be different, to step out of the mainstream conventional reality and march to our own drummer. The work is not a herd phenomenon. We are not going to find many people doing it. For this reason extraverts, who tend to resonate with the collective and appreciate group activities find the process harder than do introverts.

A third difficulty comes from the self-knowledge that is part of the process. "Self-knowledge" means becoming conscious of the unconscious: facing our shadow and becoming aware of the reality of our "inner partner," the animus (for women) or the anima (for men). The work of individuation takes us through the "swamplands of the soul". While Jung was clear that the *unconscious takes to us the attitude we take to it,* for most people it takes a while (if it ever happens at all) to develop a cheerful attitude toward the unconscious.

By this point you might well be wondering, why bother? Yes, Jung put great emphasis on achieving individuation, but if it's so difficult why make the effort? Because it will make your life immeasurably richer, and through you, the entire world will benefit.

3.1.1.3 The Benefits of Achieving Individuation

The Jungian Center for Spiritual Sciences:

Jung was explicit that the work of individuation was ... absolutely indispensable because through contamination with others, we fall into situations and commit actions which bring us into disharmony with ourselves .... there is begotten a compulsion to be and to act in a way contrary to our own nature. Accordingly we ... feel ourselves to be in a degrading, unfree, unethical condition ... deliverance from this condition will come only when we can be and act as we feel is conformable with our true self.

To be and to consistently and almost effortlessly act in conformity with our true self is both liberating and tremendously empowering. This alone makes the personal undertaking of achieving individuation overwhelmingly beneficial. There are other personal benefits. If we stay on the path and persevere with the work we come to enjoy an expanded circle of consciousness. Our sense of separateness ends and we gain broader, more intense relationships with others.

We also experience the "restoration" or reconstitution of our being that makes our difficult efforts seem well worth the suffering. Life works better. We feel deep in our bones that what we are doing, how we are living, with whom we are living (our new circle of friends) is what our soul intends for us. The quality of the people we draw into our life is better ("like finds like"). We know that the employment we undertake has purchase on our soul. Our values mesh with our lifestyle and our actions speak our soul's purpose. We feel liberated from the unconsciousness of our parents, which permits us to feel " ... a genuine sense of ... true individuality." At the same time as we experience a greater feeling of freedom from our past, we also experience a ... absolute, binding and indissoluble communion with the world at large ...

Time and again Jung stressed in his work that individuals matter. Anyone of us could be "the difference that tips the scales," and so, in our taking up the task of individuating each of us is undertaking ... a healing with universal impact and ... laying up an infinitesimal gram in the scales of humanity's soul. Given the critical nature of our time Jung would regard no other individual activity to be more meaningful and useful than becoming individuated.

3.1.2 Listening to Our Dreams

Methods of modern Depth Psychology include working with myths, fables, pictures, dreams and imaginations. Jung, in accordance with his experience, recommended that we listen to our dreams. We all have dreams. What have you dreamed of recently? You may not remember, but your "dream director" wants to tell you something! It is something important for your life. I encourage you to pay attention to your dreams. The dream director may be able to help you much better than your medical doctor. Everyone dreams. But unfortunately, not everyone can remember their dreams in the morning. Dreams contain important messages for us while we are on our pathway to inner growth. Their study is very important for the individuation process.

Jung's dream theory is the most important dream theory in modern Depth Psychology. For him dreams are the *direct expression of the current situation* of the individual. Jung said that the nature of our dreams is a "spontaneous self-portrayal, in symbolic forms, of the actual situation in the unconscious" (Jung 1967a, p. 505).

Dreams are full of symbols, images and metaphors. They speak to us in the language of the unconscious, in uninhibited symbols and expressions. Because we speak differently in our waking consciousness the "language" of our dreams is very difficult to understand. We may need the help of a *Jungian* expert. Dreams portray the outer and inner world. Thoughts and feelings of the psyche arise.

According to Jung, dreams have two functions. First, they compensate for imbalances in the dreamers psyche. Unconscious contents come up which we have ignored, repressed, suppressed or denigrated. When we learn to accept and recognize these contents we achieve a greater psychological balance. Secondly, they provide prospective images for the future. While dreams are not predictors of the future, they may present us with the suggestion of possible eventualities.

Jung was very much convinced that dreams promote the most important development process in our life, the individuation, the uniting of our consciousness and our unconscious into a healthy and harmonious state of wholeness. Individuation is for Jung the "complete actualization of the whole human being" (Jung 1967b, p. 352). Dreams contain not only personal issues but also those of the collective unconscious. Dreams contain so-called archetypes, universal psychic images like the *Wise Man*, *The Great Mother*, the *Divine Child*, *The Shadow* and numerous others. The archetypical images afford us insights and guidance because they contain wisdom which resides deep within our unconscious. Jung's considerations concerning dreams are based upon an astounding experience of 80,000 dreams during sixty years!

If we take the time to create poetry, paintings or sculptures based upon our dreams it will deepen our insights into ourselves. If we keep these art products with us during the ongoing development of our soul work, we will continue to receive more and more input for our unending growth.

3.1.3 Activating Our Imagination

For Walter Schwery, "Active Imagination" is Jung's method of integration of the shadow. It is a path of practice which enables us to raise, animate and preserve the images of the collective and personal unconscious. Active Imagination offers us the opportunity to open negotiations with these forces and figures of the unconscious so as to gradually begin to accept them. In this respect it differs from dreams, in which we have no control over our actions.

The following explanation comes in part from the book *Active Imagination* by Dorst and Vogel (Dorst and Vogel 2014, p. 9). The authors explain that imaginations are internal ideas:

> They have been and continue to be used by shaman as well as by those leading religious rituals, to change the awareness and extension of our consciousness. The Active Imagination espoused by Jung ... is an intense engagement with inner images ... a free imagination form without guidelines of a therapist as opposed to guided imagination ... The impulses from the Self take over the leadership ...

Dorst and Vogel (2014, p. 3) remind us of Jung's following comment (Wilhelm and Jung 1986, p. 22):

> The let it happen, the doing in the non-doing, the let it be of Meister Eckhart became my key with which it is possible to open the door to the path: you have to let it happen psychologically. This is a true art, of which countless people understand nothing because their consciousness constantly wants to help; correcting and negating it jumps in between, unable to accept the simple being and growing of the psychic process.

Dorst and Vogel (2017, p. 10):

> Active Imagination is a psychotherapeutic method and a spiritual procedure of self-exploration. ... It is a tool to explore the path towards the inside, to orientate in the interior of the soul and to make it possible to move in that space of the soul. ... After some preliminary relaxing exercises consciousness and the unconscious enter into a dialogue which would never have otherwise occurred. ... Picture messages from the unconscious appear only if and when the supremacy of consciousness is overcome. ... The dialogue produces a healing Self recognition which gives us access to creativity and the healing of our soul.

This is progress along the pathway toward Individuation.

How does Active Imagination proceed? Dorst and Vogel (2014, p. 31):

> The procedure is always gradual, step by step. The Jungian Marie Louise von Franz advises us in an unpublished lecture in Los Angeles in 1979 (cited in Johnson 1986, p. 160) to:
> – Empty our mind.
> – Let the unconscious flow into the vacuum.
> – Add the ethical element.
> – Integrate the imagination back into daily life

Dorst and Vogel (2014, pp. 31–32):

> Jung himself recommended in a letter in 1932: "Think, for example, a fantasy and make it available to all your forces. Create and frame it, as if you were the imagination or belonged to her, as you would render an inescapable life situation. All the difficulties you encounter in such an imagination are symbolic of your psychological difficulties and to the extent as you master them in the imagination, you overcome them in your psyche." (Jung and Adler 1973)

In another letter in 1947 he goes into more detail:

> In Active Imagination it comes down to that you start with any image ... Look at the picture and watch carefully as it begins to unfold or change. Avoid any attempt to bring it into a certain shape, just do nothing more than observe what changes occur spontaneously. Each image from your soul that you observe in this way will, sooner or later transform, namely due to a spontaneous association that leads to a slight change of image. Impatient jumping from one topic to another should be avoided carefully. Keep on the picture you have chosen firmly and wait until it transforms itself. All these changes you need to watch carefully and you must eventually even enter into the picture. Is there a figure coming up who speaks, then say what you have to say and listen to what he or she has (on answering) to say. In this way you can analyze not only your unconscious, but you give the unconscious a chance to analyze you. And so you create gradually the unity of consciousness and the unconscious, without which there is no individuation. (Jung and Adler 1976, p. 76)

According to Vogel, developing the Active Imagination does not occur in a passive state of relaxation, but rather through a concentrated, strenuous process of becoming aware of the contents of the unconscious. Active Imagination is also potentially threatening for each trainee due to the possible manifestation of aspects of the dark shadow. He cites the Mexican Octavio Paz (Nobel laureate 1993) (Dorst and Vogel, p. 36):

> The border where the Ego ends and the other, the foreign begins is constantly on the move. A continued erosion: the deeper I intrude into me, the further I move away from me; I myself am my distance, I am in me like in an unknown country. Moreover, it is a country that is produced constantly and goes.

Vogel (Dorst and Vogel 2014, p. 46) continues:

> ... On his inward journey the practitioner of Active Imagination must patiently pass through the personal, conscious layers ... the *Mundus imaginalis* as imaging of the Self and the divine. It is first a therapeutic experience and then a mystical experience. The sequence is pre-determined. Both are realities, but Jung himself, however, tends in its appreciation to the inside (the SELF): According to C.G. Jung "We live only in the world of images". The main criticisms put forward by Martin Buber concerning Gnostic ideas and methods are that the contempt or even the *"de-realization"* of the material world, or the "deification" of the ego do not apply to the Active Imagination in the case where the biographical complexes are being processed and edited and the "Imaginal" is concretized responsibly. Psychotherapy needs in addition the transcendence of Gnosticism by Mysticism, which adds to the *"Via Contemplativa"* the *"Via Activa"* as an indispensable complement.

Vogel clearly is confirming the position previously stated, one which is entirely consistent with my experience, namely, that the contemplative, spiritual pathway must be complemented by individuation as accessed through Depth Psychology in order to ensure that we are able to individually and collectively access our wholeness, ensuring that our shadow side is not blocking our spiritual growth.

3.1.4 Reconciliation with the Dark Brother

In his acclaimed book *Das Böse oder die Versöhnung mit dem Dunklen Bruder* (The Evil or Reconciliation with the Dark Brother), Walter Schwery (Schwery 2008, p. 37–38) discusses the new ethic and offers us a path to reconciliation with our dark side.

> Jung realized that my shadow side is part and exponent of the dark side of humanity in general, and if my shadow is antisocial and greedy, cruel and evil, poor and miserable and when his growing occurs as a beggar or animal in me, then behind my reconciliation with it stands the reconciliation with the Dark brother of mankind in general, and as I am in it and am part of it myself, I accept with him the whole part of humanity, which is as my shadow my associated neighbor. We are to love this shadow, as Jesus said, and to love it as I love myself ... While the idea of the old ethic is focused upon the rejection of evil, of the shadow ... the model for the new ethic is the union of opposites as the goal of a long journey which Jung called the way of individuation. This new ethic does not focus on being *good*, but rather that one accepts both the shadow and the good in his hermetic vessel, which means in his conscious soul, without a need of consent or judgment ... Conversations with Alphonse Goettmann convinced Karlfried Graf Dürckheim (Dürckheim 1986) that at present, when a person is *apparently* at

the summit, blinded by his outer achievements and future expectations, he is actually further away than ever from the truth of life and his personal maturity ... Dürckheim is also convinced that it takes a tremendous amount of personal work, the development of a kind of new ethic, to distinguish the powerful energies of the shadow and to learn how to integrate them.

For Walter Schwery reconciliation begins with the following *distinctive recognition* as taught by Buddhism:

> I *am* not evil, but I *have* evil as an expression of a part of my person. What I have, I can let go of. What I am, I cannot. It is about the recognition of evil, of which I can let go. We can liberate ourselves through awareness, recognition and inner growth and thus escape our self-recognition as culprit. (Schwery 2008, p. 43)

Schwery, who has decades of experience as a therapist, cited Paulus: "So I come up with the law, that evil is present in me, even though I want to do good" (Schwery 2008, p. 44).

Concerning the risk of disorientation Schwery has the following comment:

> In practice we see over and over again how many people, especially the religious, endeavor to be a *better person*. But if we scratch the surface of this facade of religious correctness we soon discover deep uncertainty, a lack of self-esteem and self-acceptance. The quest creates an urgent need for love and acceptance, and at the same time the dangerous desire to cover the narcissistic wound with religious *goodness*, but the root of the problem never heals, to the contrary, it is exacerbated.

As to the temptation of projection, he states:

> But the danger is great that out of this insight temptation arises, first in the world at large, where one preaches this new knowledge in order to mitigate personal responsibility for assuming this difficult and hazardous work, even though it is self-evident that nothing real can be manifested in society without first being integrated by the individual. What is in our reach is our own transformation and our ability to influence similarly minded people within our own immediate, or at least close circle. (Schwery 2008, p. 44)

3.1.5 Designation of the Evil

Schwery continues:

> Following the detection of the dark brother as an autonomous entity, it remains to give this entity a symbolic name. The creation of this symbol affords us the opportunity to take a non-rational entity and give it form ... The designation of the shadow with a symbolic name such as *Dark Brother* prevents us from becoming one with the shadow, so that we can differentiate ourselves from it. Only if this succeeds is it possible to grasp it and deal with it head on. Jung noted that the psyche has a tendency to personalize and dramatize the shadow, resulting in it being experienced as dreams, daydreams, hallucinations and visions. Our *Dark Brother*, our shadow is a vital issue, one which we must face directly. As a next step, we should try to see him not as a moral, but as an energetic problem. The shadow is usually very vital, as such it is hindering live or suppressed energies. But each vital energy which cannot develop naturally is negative and destructive ... (Schwery 2008, p. 48–49)

Rather than always doing, we must learn to just let go, and be.

No longer is the masculine "doing" the answer to the problem of the shadow, but rather the merciful feminine "being". Out of this feminine perspective arises that "Serenity", which finally leads us to awareness and the ultimate redemption of the dark brother. (Schwery 2008, p. 50)

Schwery cited Jung from his commentary on *Das Geheimnis der Goldenen Blüte* (The Secret of the Golden Flower).

The let it happen, the doing in the not doing, the release of oneself of Meister Eckhart became my key with which it became possible to open the door to the way: *you have to allow this to happen psychologically*. This is for us a true art, one which countless people do not understand, rather *directing* their consciousness to leap in to help, to correct and negate, disallowing the simple, natural development of the psychic process. (Schwery 2008, p. 51)

It takes great wisdom, faith and trust in the Spirit, which will always serve us in our own best interests, to step aside, get out of our own way, and allow the transformation to envelope us.

The following comments from the German philosopher Wilhelm Schmidt appeared in *Die Zeit* on May 13th 2015:

Zeit: "What are your sources for your inspiration from the past?"

Schmidt: "For my most recent book about serenity I went back to the ancient philosophy and found it in *Epicurus*: he coined the wonderful phrase 'ataraxia', the 'non restlessness'. This describes exactly what I mean with serenity: not just peace, but less unrest. This is a very lively state, but not hysterical. I recently read in *Seneca* from the *homo occupatus*. Many modern people can find themselves in it: very busy, but no time for the essentials."

3.1.6 Anima and Animus Balance

The terms *anima and animus* were first mentioned by Jung. A condition for the individuation process is the harmony of our masculine and feminine energies. In the Eastern Hemisphere we are speaking about *Yin* and *Yang*. An imbalance has a concrete influence on ethics and morality. A man, who has not yet integrated his anima and therefore is acting in a mainly masculine manner, will easily act in an immoral fashion without any harmony-driven female attitudes. The Anima refers to the unconscious feminine dimension of a male which can often be forgotten or repressed in daily life. However, in order to psychologically progress and reach greater internal balance and harmony, it is necessary for a man to recognize, embrace and connect to this latent element of his character. The man who has connected with his feminine Anima displays "tenderness, patience, consideration and compassion". However, repression of the female element within the man results in a negative Anima that triggers personality traits such as "vanity, moodiness, bitchiness and sensitivity to hurt feelings".

The Animus is the unconscious male dimension in the female psyche. Due to societal, parental and cultural conditioning, the Animus can be often inhibited, restrained and suppressed. On the other hand, some societies and cultures, including much of the Western world, ruthlessly impose masculine ideals as ways for women to excel, succeed and get anywhere in life, contributing toward a negative Animus which reveals itself in a woman's personality through argumentative tendencies, ruthlessness, destructiveness and insensitivity. However, integrating a positive Animus into the female psyche can result in strength, assertiveness, level headedness and rationality.

To achieve wholeness through the process of "Individuation" we must all first encounter, and then work to embrace our internal Anima or Animus.

3.2 Growth through Spiritual Wisdom

It's not about overcoming the ego, or attempting to destroy it as is required by some esoteric practices. In fact in our society many suffer from *too little* ego with disastrous consequences. Our ego plays a very important role in making us individually viable in our society. In the early decades of our life we learn and practice knowledge and skills. "Doing" and "achieving" stabilize the ego. People have greater priority than "being" in the early definition of ourselves. The problem is that we have become one sided. We have left our SELF (Jung), behind, and have given our ego free rein. As Dürckheim clearly argues, man is of double origin. He has a "world based, rational ego mind", as well as an "essence of being". The first is secular in origin and the second of Divine origin. According to Dürckheim (Dürckheim 1986, p. 39): "The essence is the way in which the 'trans-space being' and the 'trans-time being' wants to manifest in us and in the world." Angelus Silesius refers to the development of this essence when he declares: "Oh Man, become essential!" (Silesius 1675).

We may consider a person who has only developed his ego mind, having left behind his inner Divine source, as a "*stretched person*". The wholeness of the person has been lost. The more we develop our mind and leave behind our heart, the more tension we build up. This tension leads to psychological and physical problems, and frequently to disease. Our developmental quest is to become a *whole person*. Person comes from the Latin *personare*, that is, "*to sound through*". In Greek tragedy the message of the gods was delivered by the actors through their masks (persona). This is individuation as presented by Jung. By letting go of the ego, we allow ourselves to become grounded in the SELF.

When P. Hugo Enomiya-Lassalle SJ was asked for the secret of meditation, he replied: "*Ground yourself, rise up and let the mind go!*" (Enomiya-Lasalle 1985). To be a whole person, to extricate ourselves from our childhood's pronounced egocentric and egoistic socialization, we must entertain a daily practice of exercise in which we practice letting go of the ego. Then, as an act of grace the maturation of our essence is allowed to flourish within us. Practices such as meditation, prayer and contemplation, Judo, Kyodo (archery), Aikido, Yoga as well as many other pathways to the experiencing of our essence are available. If we attempt to practice alone we may have limited success; it is preferable to have a teacher. It is also important that our practice is undertaken every day.

Our mind is necessary only for the decision to choose a path and for the determination to stay on it. Then the mind is no longer necessary, as it distracts us with all its attachments. In time, and with dedication we achieve *Transparency for Immanent Transcendence*. This is Dürckheim's definition of the meaning of life (Dürckheim 1976). Once this transcendence is experienced we no longer need a written code of ethics or externally imposed laws. A transcended individual acts out of their given divine experience.

Prominent support for this position was recently voiced by Pope Francis who pointed out the importance of the experience of transcendence in his speech to the members of the European Parliament in Strasbourg, on November 25, 2014 (Francis, Pope 2014). He stated:

> ... It is a message of encouragement to return to the firm conviction of the founders of the European Union who envisioned a future based on the capacity to work together in bridging divisions, and in fostering peace and fellowship between all the peoples of this continent. At the heart of this ambitious political project was confidence in man, not so much as a citizen or an economic agent, but in man, in men and women as persons endowed with *transcendent human dignity*. I feel bound to stress the close bond between the two words *"dignity"* and *"transcendent"* ... To speak of *transcendent human dignity* thus means appealing to human nature, to our innate capacity to distinguish good from evil, to that "moral compass" deep within our hearts, which God has impressed upon all creation. Above all, it means regarding human beings not as absolutes, but as *beings in relation* ... The future of Europe depends on the recovery of the vital connection between these two elements (dignity and transcendence). A Europe which is no longer open to the transcendent dimension of life is a Europe which risks slowly losing its own soul and that "humanistic spirit" which it still loves and defends. Taking as a starting point this opening to the transcendent, I would like to reaffirm the centrality of the human person, which otherwise is at the mercy of the whims and the powers of the moment.

Pope Francis's statement makes it clear that *experiencing transcendence is the gateway to ethical behavior*. This wisdom is essential for the New Ethic in business. It shows us the way to proceed. *All dictates of* "you should, you must, you could" *do not lead to the development of inner growth which is required for high ethical standards*. It may not be easy for us to change our course, but we must.

> *"When you change, the whole world changes!"* (Zen).

Even many very successful senior managers have no idea, in spite of all their external successes, that the development of their inner dimension has been neglected. For them, "performance" is what rules life. In spite of their apparent successes they are often full of fear and discontent. When they come under pressure, as inevitably they will, their apparent code of ethics quickly disappears. They have a low REB.

> *As it is so important for students, teachers and business managers, allow me to cite again how Dürckheim so aptly expresses it, and how he recognizes its importance as a wake-up call for managers.*

Dürckheim (1988, p. 27f.):

> These people, very often busy, well educated, conscientious and orderly well-meaning people are so greatly limited by their mania to be successful that they believe it can replace all need for their inward growth. The result is a high performance animal which because of his one sidedness is a mere caricature of what a human being is meant to be; a unity of body, soul and spirit ... If you would paint such a human being he would have a giant head, a blown up breast and mechanical limbs of steel which are directed by a tenacious will. But in the middle, where the guiding center of soul and spirit resides would be a vacuum, which is sheltered by an anxious and easily vulnerable ego ... The human being who corresponds to this picture remains inside a child in spite of all that he knows, all he can do and all he has achieved, because the soul remains small and the spirit is blocked from being able to develop in the person and in his attitude ... The result is emptiness, guilt and fear. These symptoms frequently occur in people who seem to be at the top of their career. Others, who aren't aware of this internal dilemma, may admire their visible façade, but behind the façade is an unhappy human being whose suffering soul and lack of inner peace is the result of having remained an immature individual. Very often these individuals don't see any other possibility for maintaining a modicum of inner peace than to practice an iron clad self-discipline in order to keep their inner tensions under control. But the suppression of the tensions will not lead to any improvement, rather it will result in frustration, anxiety, nervousness and mood swings which will be followed by a lack of zest for life. These inner problems may be kept under control in business, but at home family members will suffer the consequences. When the pressure cannot be contained any longer explosions of impulsiveness will follow. In many cases it ends up as "Burn Out", depression or some other form of psychological or psychosomatic illness.

3.2.1 Meditation as a Daily Practice

Once we have focused on an object and have observed our thoughts and emotions we know we need to dismiss them, to let them go. In this way we become one with the reality we cannot put in words, only experience. Now, in addition, let the focus go as well! It was only a tool to begin the mindfulness exercise, it is no longer necessary. We were the subject, the focus was the object. When we overcome this duality of subject and object there is no difference between us and the focus. Now we better understand what is meant in Zen Buddhism when it is said that *subject is object and object is subject*. The perceived duality is gone. *As duality is the cause of our suffering the suffering is also gone.* After some time we do not watch our thoughts anymore. They are no longer important to us. We are one with all. We are one with the universe which is boundless and infinite. We are part of it, a wave in the vast ocean connected with all the other waves. It is important to continue our discipline and to maintain the momentum of our practice for as long as is necessary. It may even take years before we eventually experience the totality of oneness, wholeness and complete connectivity with everything.

The following is a summary of the sequences in the practice of meditation:
- longing to feel the end of our suffering.
- self-responsibility.
- selecting a guide; a master for our spiritual path.

- exercising mindfulness – setting our sails!
- selecting a space in which to experience awareness.
- entering that space mindfully.
- selecting our focus.
- calming our restless mind.
- observing our thoughts.
- letting go of our focus.
- having our focus disappear.
- remaining present without thinking, without any emotion.
- becoming *one* with *all*.

Daily meditation should be a daily *Spiritual teeth-brushing,* as my sister, yoga teacher Helga Simon-Wagenbach, recommends to her students.

When we are ready to welcome peace, silence, balance, serenity, kindness, charity, compassion, perseverance, harmony and happiness into our life, mindfulness is the key. Living mindfully in the present, fully embracing the here and now will give our life new meaning. Initial silencing of all the external and internal "noise" around and within us is a prerequisite for meditation.

3.2.2 Meditation on Compassion Manifests in Your Brain

Mindfulness and compassion which result from meditation, both non-focused meditation and the meditation focused upon compassion, lead us into morally defensible decisions and ethical practices.

Neuroscientists have now discovered that meditation on compassion can activate and develop specific regions in the brain. It has always been difficult to explain our meditation experiences to others, but it is a giant step forward for those skeptics of meditation, who have been hesitant to accept anything which does not have scientific validation.

Tanja Singer and Matthieu Ricard, biochemist and Zen master, have presented groundbreaking research in their book *Compassion in the Economy* (Singer and Ricard 2015). Their conclusion is: altruism and the economy are not diametrically opposed. Tanya Singer investigates the developmental, hormonal and neuronal basis of human social behavior and social emotions such as empathy, compassion and fairness. Singer, Germany's leading brain researcher and Director of Social Neuroscience at the Max Planck Institute for Cognitive and Neurosciences in Leipzig/Germany, has published the results of her research trip to the social brain. She wanted to know if we could become healthier through mental training by gaining greater empathy, which is a preliminary prerequisite for the development of compassion. According to Singer, emotions manifest in the brain – just like speaking, thinking or perception. Just as we can train the upper arm muscles, we can also improve the health of the brain through meditation. We can become more mindful; we can open our hearts. To prove this, Singer founded the "ReSource Project" with more than 300 volunteers who meditated regularly with specialized teachers. At various stages Singer's team examined each volunteer's brain, tested their behavior and analyzed their blood.

At first, mindfulness was the goal then followed compassion and gratitude. What can be learned from the data which was gathered? Singer and Co. found that meditating does not only temporarily put people in a peaceful mood or make them more mindful for a brief period of time, rather it measurably and demonstrably strengthens very specific connections within the brain. Follow-up behavioral testing demonstrates that "the training units are working". It is clear that scientifically sound programs can be created with the end of strengthening qualities such as compassion in the world. (Edited from *Die Zeit* No. 44 October 26, 2017)

In addition, Niels Birbaumer, Professor of Medical Psychology and Behavioral Neurobiology, has scientifically proven that we are not only able to influence our breathing and heartbeat with conscious thought, but that we can also direct our brain activity through active concentration (*Die Zeit* No. 47 November 18, 2017).

These findings support long-realized metaphysical knowledge that our thoughts affect our reality. Our concentration upon greed increases the prevalence of selfish behavior in the world, while our concentration upon compassion can alleviate suffering. Through meditation upon moral attitudes and ethical practices we do not simply access these qualities more often, rather those qualities *become* an integral part of who we are!

3.2.3 Opportunities for Increasing Awareness through Mindfulness

Making the opportunity to increase our awareness by practicing mindfulness every day is tremendously beneficial.

If at this time in your life you lack the resolve and discipline to meditate, instead try finding opportunities which interest and fulfill you, ones in which you can practice mindfulness every day. In time you will find that meditation comes calling, asking for a second chance! We encounter these opportunities daily as part of our work, music, art, enjoyment of nature, dance, our experiences of illness, unexpected encounters or a myriad of other possibilities. Our entire daily routine can be used to facilitate our meditative practice, as discussed in *Living in the Golden Wind* (Meyer-Galow 2011, 2014). The result is a life full of equanimity, serenity, humor, compassion, harmony, humanity and a love for others while protecting individual dignity. When we become fully mindful we will never harm others or the environment, and will find inner peace in both our private and business life.

There are many opportunities for mindfulness. A few essential ones are: nature, music, art, dance, religion and love. But our daily work and even illness are very important opportunities for practicing growth. Recognizing these opportunities, according to Graf Dürckheim, greatly increases our likelihood of being able to get in touch with the original ground of our being. If we are not mindful of our experiences during these important opportunities we lack an understanding of our inter-connectedness and may consequently lose a major part of our vitality and our opportunity for growth. We are all able to enter into these realms of experience. When we do so mindfully, we will experience an increased awareness and find that it is the gateway to a better quality of life.

Many of us begin along a spiritual pathway but too often abandon the walk prematurely. It requires a strong discipline to maintain the path of practice and exercise. Often we feel we do not have enough strength and perseverance, especially if living in misery, as when suffering we are focused exclusively upon regaining only the minimally necessary vitality to go on with our lives. But it is exactly at these times that the wonderful human adventure of exploring the wider dimension of being fully present in a situation is offered to us; perhaps one which is but a distant memory from childhood, or maybe even one which we can imagine but have never yet experienced, that we can expand our awareness and deal with our pain. Our pain may linger but we are better able to endure it. It is no longer a heavy burden in our life. Only then, through the meditation of mindfulness, we are prepared to successfully proceed through every phase of life and fulfill our true, natural potential.

3.2.3.1 From Work-Life Balance towards Life-Balance

For all of us employed in the economic sector the opportunity for growth through our "work" is of daily importance. It is currently popular to speak about one's Work-Life-Balance. This is an unfortunate expression, as it creates the impression that work and life are separate dualities; diametric opposites with work being bad and life good. This leads to the desire for less work and more life which many people would interpret as more free time, time for chilling out and wellness. *But everything is life.* Work is life and the time one has off work is also life. Perhaps the phrase Life-Balance is more appropriate. It is desirable to get one's life in balance with the *ever acting process* (Dürr).

When not actively working it is important to make enough time for other important opportunities such as those which may be experienced in nature, music, dance, art, love and religion. Too often we postpone these experiences to the third triad of our lives when we may then be unable to enjoy them due to serious illness or sudden death. My own experience confirms that when our professional work has concluded it is highly beneficial to entertain other opportunities for increasing our awareness through mindfulness, so as to experience our true Being. This important stage in our life can be the climax of our transformation! Experiencing our true self gives meaning to, indeed it is the purpose of our longevity.

We may perform some kind of manual labor (Latin: *labor* = tribulation), or we may spend our days in a profession where we are working toward an *opus*; the mastery of some aspect of society (Latin: *opus*), on behalf of. Either way we often feel that we are just laborers and are burdened by our hours of daily work. Our life is not meant to be like that. It is tempting to work hard in order to gain the prestige of success, a practice adopted by the majority of people in the business world. Because success is a drug we will not question the price exacted from us for it in the beginning. Our ego is both greedy for and addicted to success. Morality and ethics are not of great importance to our ego.

Ego is essentially a feeling or awareness that we live apart from God, separated and distant from our original nature. It motivates us and drives us along our path toward forging a great career for ourselves. Only when we realize the transience of success, and the first signs of suffering are evidenced will dissatisfaction, anxiety and loneliness have the opportunity to pry open the doorway leading to personal change. The experiencing of the moment in awareness, the here and now, is a difficult concept to master. Awareness demands discipline. We need to strive for a constant synchronicity between meaningful work and an attitude of mindfulness, which one may call *contemplation in a world of action*. The founder of the famous Jesuit order St. Ignatius of Loyola spoke of *contemplatio in actionibus*. While our ego is diligent, never resting, this is not necessarily detrimental to our development as long as we remain constantly and directly in contact with our Self, our divine source.

It is the moral responsibility of employers to not simply employ as many people as possible, but rather to create opportunities that allow their employees satisfying, joyful, and peaceful employment so they may ultimately work and "sail" together, motivated. If you ask people what they understand by the phrase *a social market economy* they will often reply that it has to do with ethical behavior in the market place. Many employees who directly contribute to our economy are never encouraged to, or rewarded for taking pride in their work and the pivotal role it plays in the success of a company. A business on the main road to success consists of numerous "feeder" side roads each of which has employees whose service and performance in directing business onto the "main" road determines the overall production or sales volume. For the past 35 years we have had an orientation toward *Sustainable Development* in our economy with individual companies with their unique principles and cultures approaching this sustainable development orientation in diverse ways. Unfortunately, too many have lost their orientation and are in need of a renewed vision; a new compass.

The Loving Dialogue to which Hans-Peter Dürr delights in referring is important in all contact and conversations with others. The quantum physicist Dürr says *"To be connected with everyone and everything is Love"* (Dürr 2011).The Loving Dialogue emerges from a deep compassion for all living beings. This compassion creates serenity, joy and humor as a result of our daily practice. The XIV Dalai Lama refers to our common root of interconnectedness as compassion.

As managers in the economy it is important that we recognize our responsibility to help everyone within our sphere of influence *to relax into trust and compassion*.

Previously, when my responsibilities included assessing managers, I endeavored to ascertain the stage of their wisdom and readiness to assume greater responsibility. I wanted to be able to "feel" the compassion of any manager I intended to employ. Inevitably, our judgment will fail us occasionally, but not as often as if we never even make the effort. Even in the cases where we may find our initial assessment to be wrong, if an open and honest dialogue free from fear or anxiety is maintained then we foster trust and compassion in others. When others recognize that we are engaging people from our heart center it is appreciated both intellectually and emotionally, allowing everyone to move forward productively through both easy *and* difficult times.

In every human encounter the degree of maturity of our wisdom is transparent. Compassion arises out of serenity and certainty, conditions which we cannot either fake or disguise. According to a recent study psychological illnesses are eight times more prevalent in top managers than in the population at large. The one sure-fire way of detecting people with severe psychological issues in business is that they cannot develop empathy for others. Many top managers, in an attempt to inflate their insatiable egos, destroy their employee's creative energies. It is important to be "real" in our life and work, never "veiling" our work persona with ego-based managerial attitudes. Too often when top managers state, "my door is always open for everyone" it is just an empty statement, the transparency of which is evident to all. Our hearts must remain open in order to allow for a mutually joyful attitude in all of our encounters, meetings and discussions with individual employees. Ideally, following every conversation, every compassionate dialogue, all participants will depart with renewed energy, passion and enthusiasm for the common good.

Practicing mindfulness and compassion in our *work* in the economy is an excellent opportunity for increasing our awareness, allowing and encouraging the further development of our inner growth.

3.2.3.1.1 Work-Life Blending

"Forget Work-Life Balance: Aim for Blend Instead" was the headline on October 28, 2015 in *Huff Post*, The Third Metric. The new buzzword is called work-life blending. More and more often free time and leisure activities are blending into our business life, and vice versa. The boundaries between business and leisure are becoming blurred. As with multi-tasking this is not necessarily a positive thing because it does not allow each activity to receive our entire focus. If we look into the offices of investment bankers and management consultants we will observe this new world being experienced. It is fashionably "cool".

New is not necessarily better. The "old fashioned" separation of business and non-business has merit. We cannot fully experience the opportunities for mindful meditation and inner development which facilitate the expansion of our consciousness unless we separate our business and non-business activities. Without this separation we invite destabilizing distractions and diversions which are counterproductive to the development of moral decisions and ethical practices.

3.2.3.2 Nature

For many of us communing with nature provides one of the most fruitful opportunities for experiencing mindful awareness. Far too many children, teenagers and even adults no longer have access to nature in wholesome, fulfilling and satisfying ways. Having grown up with computer games, television, mobile phones and numerous other trappings of a limiting and artificial world, both the desire and ability to interact with nature in a *meaningful* fashion has been lost. It is crucial that we encourage our children and grandchildren to experience the wonder and natural majesty of nature so as to allow its therapeutic effect upon their minds, bodies, souls and spirits. Our ego demands the type of relaxation and re-vitalization which is uniquely experienced in the serenity, beauty and peace of nature. Our original source of being knows that contemplation in nature is an ideal opportunity for experiencing and enhancing our inner growth.

In order to enjoy the beneficial effects of entering into a space of awareness and silence we need to approach it with reverence and respect. Because we are conditioned to being surrounded by noise, loud conversations, electronic media and frantic activity it takes a conscious effort on our part to let go of being the doer and the artificiality of everyday life which accompanies *doing*, and to be receptive to the healing effect which comes from embracing just *being* in the solitude of nature. One way to achieve this letting go is to meditate on the numerous wonders of nature like trees, rivers, lakes, mountains, wildlife or plants. When immersed in nature, hiking in silence or simply observing and reflecting we become the roots, the trunks, the branches and the leaves of the trees. When I stroll through a natural environment I do not attend to the walking, I observe myself as being one with my environment. There is a big difference. It allows for the release of my Self, for it to radiate through my ego. A wonderful enlightenment then carries me through the entire day. If we enter into nature with mindfulness we may leave the forest with an enhanced inner awareness. This precious opportunity awaits all of us.

Willigis Jäger wisely observed: "One who is attentively listening while experiencing nature is transformed into another dimension!" He mentioned this quote very often when he was talking about nature during his sessions.

3.2.3.3 Music and Art

Whether we play a musical instrument or not we all have our own special allowing us to experience the *fullness* of presence.

We hear not only with our ears, but also with our bones and our body fluid. In this way even the deaf can hear. My musical preference is that particular form and variety which may best invoke spiritual mindfulness. Music encourages us to be entirely present in the moment; I experienced this magnificent phenomenon as a participant in the opening ceremonies for a school for hearing impaired children in Bhutan. Full of wonder I watched the children dancing to the music during the celebration. The experience of music clearly transcends simple listening, becoming transformed into a holistic perception. This perception, being much more than simple concentration, is the essence of mindfulness. Bernadette Böll, an expert in music therapy, articulates that "When you play music like a meditation, you don't experience the music, you experience your Self in the music, becoming more and more a whole person." She related that to me when, because of her encouragement, I began to play the piano.

Daniel Barenboim is a proponent of silence. He finds music in restaurants annoying. Buddhists call silence emptiness. The "emptiness of silence" is the actual reality from which everything originates. It is what I refer to in an earlier book as the Golden Wind. Music can lead us toward an understanding of the meaning of life, for which the constant practice of mindfulness is an essential prerequisite. If possible, it is beneficial for us to not only listen to music but also to practice it on our instrument of choice. The possibility of experiencing silence and mindfulness is always there when we listen to, or play music. The intensity of music as a realm of experience results from hearing, being without a doubt, our most important sense. Evolution has given sound the highest priority. Music helps us to find meaning in life. Our inner growth and joy are maximized when we do not just play a piece of music to perfect it, but rather when we let the vibrations of the sound of the music, whether played by ourselves or others, peacefully enter into us. In this way music has magical, psychosomatic healing abilities!

Why do we go to concerts? Because it is a comforting experience. The concerns and problems of daily life melt away, at least briefly. It is important that we do not limit the effect of music to just body and soul. Body, soul *and* spirit are an inextricably interwoven single unit within us. The spiritual dimension is of utmost importance. Our spirit is neither our rational mind nor our intellect, but rather the indestructible essence of our original incarnated being. Yehudi Menuhin speaks of silence being the bridge to God. Silence is infinity. Arising from this infinity is all that is real, including sound, melody and harmony in music. It is infinity expressing itself as music. To experience this reality is the real meaning of music.

Everyone is able to play an instrument. If voice is your instrument, then begin to sing, or if not, learn to play another instrument. It is never too late. There is no age limit! Music is essential for maintaining an energetic, vital life force during the final triad of life. There are noteworthy studies that irrevocably establish the positive influence of music and sports in maintaining optimal brain functioning as we age.

The artist has the opportunity to excel beyond the capacity of his limited ego through his art work. I spoke with Hans Peter Münch, a good friend of mine, about Spirituality and Art on October 28, 2010 in Ettlingen/Germany (Meyer-Galow 2011):

Hans Peter: I once had an initiation experience during my studies in Hamburg. One day my teacher told me to go to the Hamburger Kunsthalle and look at the second apple from the left in a very special painting by Cezanne. When I did so, it was like a flash of lightning shot through my mind. Without intention, without expectation, without forcing it, I *now* experienced the painting. I refrained from any further, deeper examination. I let go of the picture. Then I got it: He meant the modulation, the plastic representation of the color on the surface of the apple.

That was in 1968, but the memory remains with me to this day. This was an experience in an area, and of a quality that had remained closed to me until then. It was not a formal, deliberate technique, but rather of the painter implementing an opening into an initiation. Every painting has the task of being an initiation, of acting as a catalyst between the painter and the viewer. At the time, I was struck by the *knowing* that this is the substantial, intrinsic task of art. Those who do not understand this transcendental potential of art may paint for a lifetime without ever reaching the point where they are able to surpass the formal, the aesthetic and the stylistic.

Erhard: "Only if the mysteriousness can be experienced, it is true art?"

Hans Peter: "That's the truth. It is basically a matter of the inexplicableness, of transcending the capacity that has been present up to then, both sensitively and consciously, in emotion and proportion."

Erhard: "The mystical experience is trans-emotional and trans-rational?"

Hans Peter: "Now, we are, of course, at transcendence, a term that is no longer used at all today. For me, however, this is a very important point. We all live in immanence. It is our daily bread and suffering ... I'm concerned about this transcendence, that is, the crossing over. If I set the color according to certain laws, which there are of course and which I use, then I only get to a certain point. After 40 years of experience, I realize exactly when this point is reached. After a few weeks working on a painting, the moment comes that I have to leave it alone. It paints itself, so to speak. At that point I will just become a tool. At the beginning I apply *active* input. All thoughts, all feelings, techniques and knowledge become images. Then the painting takes on a shape at some point. It begins a dialogue with me. I'll just do what it wants. I am then able to get into this transcendent structure of perception in which one can no longer formulate something with words or clear intentions, but where the painting dictates what more is necessary. This is the realization of the creative.

If I form a desire to recognize some intrinsic aspect of a painting it does not present itself to me. But at the moment when I am completely open and surrender any active request while remaining open to being challenged, then I may receive the gift of experiencing the creative and the transcendence. This may also be called a mystical experience or an experience of God. At this point any words are inadequate attempts at describing the indescribable.

... I became open and receptive to further initiation experiences. My previous revelations awoke in me a desire to move beyond the formal aesthetic towards transcendence."

Erhard: "In painting one can, as you have described wonderfully, not only through one's own work but also through contemplation, experience this inner growth and the healing which is associated with it. It is a gift, a state we can express as grace. It leads us inexorably towards a moral and ethical life."

True art and science is nourished by the experience of mystery. For Albert Einstein art is only authentic when it is initiated by a mystical quality. In the summer of 2007 the theological faculty of the University of Lucerne held a *lecture series on Spirituality & Art* with the theme: *Spiritual traces in the world of art*. A later publication describing the Lucerne lecture states: "If art is considered as a possible experience in the search of the ineffable and invisible towards the ultimate and infinite, then art is in the end a form of spirituality or a means of expressing spirituality."

3.2.3.4 Sports

Sports and music complement one another wonderfully. In the first third of life most of us strive for performance and perfection in all that we do. In the second third of our life relaxation and joy will generally be predominant. In our third triad we have the option of participating in sports as an exercise for inner maturation. Any activity, including all types of recreation can be practiced as a meditation. Through recreational sports we have the opportunity to *re-create* ourselves. Eugen Herrigel in his book *Zen in the Art of Archery* masterfully describes the mindful attentiveness necessary for this sport (Herrigel 1953, p. 14).

> I gradually came to realize that only the truly detached can understand what is meant by detachment and that only one who is contemplative, who is completely empty and detached from the ego, is ready to become one with the "transcendent Deity". I had come to realize, therefore, that there is and can be no other way to mysticism than the way of personal experience and suffering.

Archers practice for years to hit the center disc of the target with their arrows. The ego strives desperately for perfection. But as long as the ego is in command we will not succeed. Success will follow only when the arrow is released with a smile on our face; a smile which follows from detachment from our ego.

Eugen Herrigel describes it wonderfully and pictorially, so that all of us who have not yet experienced this level of detachment can appreciate how it leads to success in all manner of sports.

> It is all so simple. You can learn from an ordinary bamboo leaf what matters. Through the weight of the snow, it will be pressed down. Suddenly the snow load slips off, although the leaf had not moved or resisted. Try to pause, similarly in archery. When the tension has reached its peak moment the arrow must fly and find its target.

Then the archer feels the Golden Wind. Each sport which we approach can be an experience leading us toward greater inner spiritual maturation.

3.2.3.5 Dance

Dancing has historically played an important role in the lives of people from every culture. It was once a dominant form of expression around the globe. It is unfortunate that dancing has been predominantly relegated to the young, largely disappearing as a universally expressive art form in much of modern society. When dancing, every single step requires a maximum of mindfulness. We find that the more we practice a dance the more that it is no longer ourselves who control the various steps; the dance takes over and we become one with the dance. This is another opportunity to open our awareness into receptivity. Only when we can let go and observe the flow of life as a non-doer, without binding expectations, are we openly receptive to receiving from the Cosmos. Every dance can be meditative just as any activity can be meditative. It depends upon our receptivity to being open to the unknown. We must not be distracted by focusing upon purpose and control, but rather simply practice trust while embracing mindfulness.

3.2.3.6 Religion

Religion is of great importance in that it serves to give orientation and support to many of us through all stages of our life. The importance of religion lies in the opportunity for growth which will lead us to the experience of God. It is preferable that our religious studies are guided by a master who has had direct experiences of God. Unfortunately, most priests or ministers are only able to ask us to *believe* in GOD. This is a serious limitation which ultimately leads to our disillusionment for contemporary Christian religions. It is perfectly reasonable that many of us are not willing to simply blindly believe.

3.2.3.7 Meeting People

Meaningful encounters with wonderful people who are secure in their individuality is a joyful opportunity for increasing our personal awareness. Earlier in this book Hans-Peter Dürr spoke about how important this personal interaction was for him. In the process of gaining maturity, we experience our own being in others, which leads to many benefits, including an honest appraisal of our own spiritual integrity. In both planned and unexpected encounters, if we remain open and receptive we are able to experience and observe our ability to remain mindful in our interactions with others.

Meeting others is an opportunity to step outside of our ego centeredness and listen to others with utmost awareness and compassion, those qualities which create the energetic atmosphere which connects all of us, one to the other. It is a great time to manifest the trust that *the other person is going to reach out and meet me!* Due to our competitive conditioning we are accustomed to being the initiating force in all conversations. When we lack empathy and trust we miss out on the true essence of shared companionship and conversation. But when we remain a critical listener we are able to extract value from both the beautiful and the less than beautiful influences in our lives. We have all asked another, "How are you?" and then not waiting for a reply have allowed our ego to power us along in a long monologue. If we truly care about how another feels we will ensure that we allow the time and space for their considered response, and we will trust that the same respect will be reciprocated. If we offer another our hand it creates an opportunity for a brief meeting to also become a meditation. Especially if we begin with a brief silence and then continue with a *loving dialogue*, such as Hans-Peter Dürr spoke about.

A meeting may not always be a dialogue with words. There are powerful meetings embracing total silence, meetings which are filled with a very special quality. I participated in Zen sessions conducted in complete silence during which I felt a great connectedness with all of the other participants. This was a most wonderful dialogue in stillness. Sometimes we also have encounters with difficult people with whom we do not feel connected due to their egocentricity. While admittedly difficult such encounters are excellent opportunities to practice empathy and compassion. We are inextricably altered in each and every moment, and altered the most by interactions with each and every person we encounter.

3.2.3.8 Illness and Suffering

Each disease has its own specific character and challenge for our lifelong process of learning. We need to "decode" the meaning of it at the time the hand is dealt to us. Illness and disease stretch us to examine to what extent we are able to let go, to step back from our "control center" and to give up our ego centeredness.

Suffering is a call for increased awareness and an opportunity for growth. When we find ourselves at dis-ease, the practice of mindfulness is both demanded and required, moment by moment. Hans-Peter Dürr advises that we need not exclusively deliver ourselves to medical practitioners, but rather also to the Cooperative Background Field. In times of illness it is increasingly important that we allow our awareness to recognize that this field exists behind, around and beyond us at all times. There is no break in it, there never has been and there never will be. It extends both backwards and forwards into infinity. When we are in perfect health, active, busy and doing well, too often we do not make time for consideration of our condition of being.

There are always two sides to any coin. The human condition consists of both health and disease. Maybe it is better to speak of ease (healthy lightness) and dis-ease (burdensome heaviness). When we are not in touch with the Cooperative Background Field, that field which includes perfect health, we get into trouble. Christians may call this field God, but many people today given the revelations possible though quantum physics speak rather of the *original essence, of energy with immortal nature and being.*

To trust in our concept of God and to have faith and confidence in our conception is quite ordered. As long as we are healthy we practice prayers, rituals or Christian contemplation, or we embrace mindfulness through an assortment of opportunities as previously discussed. These activities are a necessary preparation for successfully facing future illnesses and death, which is the ultimate form of letting go. Our presence, our living fully in the here and now is the best possible prescription for every phase of our lives. Only through our complete mindfulness does our self-healing attitude have an opportunity to be manifested. Hans-Peter Dürr states: "We are all co-creators of creation: God is within us, not apart from us."

How can we achieve the awareness of that *oneness* of which we are all a part? We must be completely present and receptive in order for this experience to be able to envelope us. Entering into a mindful experience of work, nature, music, dance, art or any other chosen endeavor is optional. However entering into the realm of experiencing illness and death is compulsory. If we are wise we will allow both to assist us in our quest toward greater personal awareness.

In the experiencing of illness and ultimately death we are confronted with the intuitive knowledge that we must relinquish control. When we finally do so we open to the spiritual dimension of our humanity, leaving behind our psychoso-matic trappings. As a patient, especially when we are hospitalized, we often feel lonely, distant from our friends, family members and all that is familiar to us. These feelings originate from our ego's separation from our Divine origin. Allevia-tion of those fears that come with a life-threatening disease is only possible when we reconnect ourselves to our inner source of being, our essential spiritual center. In any situation where we are distraught with anxieties and fears and feel alone it is wise to try to make our loneliness meaningful. To be alone does not have to feel like isolation, it can propel us toward the liberating, expansive feeling of being *one with all.*

When we make the effort through stillness and reflection, while letting go of all expectations, to connect with all that is we experience cosmic, unconditional love and the healing that accompanies it. When we consciously alter our negatively charged thoughts or words into positive ones and expressly ask that all negativity, including that which may be directed at us by others or even by our own subconscious be transformed into positive energy, which can then be released into the cosmos to assist others who are in greater need than ourselves, we access a transformative and empowering manifestation.

It is only through experiencing being one with all that we are able to create, as Walter Schwery says, a positive, healing impact on our body, soul and spirit. If our maturation is not yet sufficiently advanced we have no other choice but to undergo somatic, psychological or psychosomatic medical care by doctors. This is not a bad thing but it is a very limited form of healing, at best. While fully recognizing the achievements of modern allopathic medicine and research it is wise to also remain cognizant of the limitations of this practice of medicine, including all of its inherent hazards and inevitable side effects. It is always important to recognize that there are costs for any "cure", one of which may be an inhibiting of our ability to access real inner satisfaction, balance, harmony and peace of mind. In the case of any illness our system is disturbed somatically, mentally and spiritually. Every disease is a man-ifestation of a reality, one which we do not fully understand and thus cannot express precisely. This limitation does not detract from the reality which we are able to fully comprehend at a level beyond language. For Willigis Jaeger a disease is a space in time and experience which offers the opportunity to get in contact with our essence. When I told him of my cancer diagnosis he replied: "This supra-temporal Being, its essence and transcendence, is manifesting in all our aspects of your life, be it health or disease."

Since disease is a powerful learning opportunity which can lead us to an experience of the Cooperative Background Field as put forth by Hans-Peter Dürr, should we fight against a disease with which we are diagnosed? Our body is not a battlefield. We need to make peace with all of our cells, both the healthy ones and the diseased ones. The most effective healing process is created by an inner peace contract and agreement, one in which we lovingly welcome all of the cells in our body. Illness and disease are always opportunities for growth, a doorway into the larger circle of the *cosmic holon*, as Hans-Peter Dürr used to say. Frank Kinslow (Kinslow, Frank (2008)) describes in his book *The Secret of Instant Healing*, meditation exercises which assist us in getting in contact with the *zero-field*. Illness can provide an excellent opportunity for accelerating our learning processes. It allows for and encourages a great deal of self-reflection. Once recovered we may find that our commitment to ethical and moral attitudes and practices may be considerably strengthened.

3.2.3.9 Daily Life

There are a myriad of opportunities in our daily life for allowing our consciousness to mature. If we live each moment with full awareness and mindfulness then each moment encourages and supports our inner growth. All activities, things like waking up, brushing our teeth, washing our face, sitting, walking, standing, writing, reading, shopping, driving, waiting, looking, hearing, smelling, tasting, feeling, putting on our shoes, greeting people and shaking hands can all enhance our personal growth if done consciously, with the recognition of joyful purposefulness. It is entirely up to us whether we move through all these moments automatically without conscious attention, or with meditative awareness. Is it not prudent to avail ourselves of the opportunity to turn these necessary tasks into growth experiences? Not surprisingly, mindfulness is the necessary condition for creating serenity, cheerfulness, humor and compassion. Activities performed without deliberate attention may lead to tension, stress, anxiety, anger and sadness. When we separate ourselves *from* our Self we risk losing compassion for others, fostering isolation and loneliness.

Growth implies change. A metamorphose is essential in order for a caterpillar to be transformed into a butterfly. **We alone can make the decision to continue our life as a caterpillar or to become a butterfly!** We begin to change when we begin to be present in each and every moment. Day by day our daily activities are waiting for us. We begin anew each day. There is no past and there is no future. There is only our presence in the moment. Both the totality of *all* life and that of *our* life proceed in each moment that we are alive. Whether we limit the experience of living to one of mere mechanical repetition, or enrich the experience of living with mindful awareness is entirely under our control. When we choose the latter the result is a life full of equanimity, serenity, humor, compassion, harmony, humanity and love for others.

3.3 Growth by Quantum Physics

Inspired by my conversations with Hans-Peter Dürr and by the wisdom contained within his books, I felt compelled to ask myself whether one may grow within oneself without any meditation and individuation practice. The experience of truth, or more accurately of reality, can be approached by realizations from the field of quantum physics, the path followed by Professor Dürr. The findings arising from research in quantum physics direct us to new ways of thinking and experiencing the Self, as well as the Divine both within us and around us.

Hans-Peter Dürr calls it: *The Cooperative Background Field* or *The Permanent Acting Process of Life*, but he also speaks of:

Love, Spirit and Life.

I had the following great conversation with him:

Hans-Peter Dürr: I am an "atheist". But in the Sanskrit language the prefix "a" does not imply a negation, but only imparts that the objective of the question is invalid. In other words, for me God cannot be expressed in proper terms or in any way quantified, because God refers to the totality of Oneness, namely *Advaita*, the indivisible. Thus, I am not an atheist in the sense of one who does not believe; personally I do not have any doubt that there are connections beyond our comprehension. There most certainly exists a unique structure of interconnectedness that has many names, all of which are simply metaphors.

We can call it Spirit or Love. Love is the term which best expresses for me the unity of everything being "one" resulting from universal interconnectedness, which also enables us to experience, empathetically in a deeply personal yet expansive, validating fashion, the ever changing form of a spiritually engendered cosmos ...

Modern physics has now come to this startling realization: Matter is not composed of matter. If we reduce matter to almost nothing, hoping to find the smallest, formless, pure matter at the end of the process nothing is left which reminds us of matter. No substance remains, only form, shape, symmetry and relationship. This knowledge was, and certainly remains very confusing from our traditional "structural" point of view of reality. If matter is not composed of matter, then it means that the primacy of matter is of only minor importance. Relationship is primary, matter is secondary. Perhaps we could also say that when we reduce all matter as far as possible, then *the world of spirituality, holism, openness ... in fact ... life is revealed ... potentiality is the possibility of a probable realization.*

Matter is merely a convenient by-product of this spirit; separable, distinguishable, determinate, which we perceive as a reality. In the field of potentiality there are no clear cause and effect relationships. The future is much more open. At every moment the world is newly created, nothing is previously determined, nothing can be predicted, but our expectations can, and must shape creation.

The reason we cannot see into the future is that it does not yet exist.

The old potentiality in its entirety gives birth to new shapes and new realizations, but that which is newly defined remains fluid. Everyone and everything is involved in this never ending process of creation. The interaction follows certain rules. Physically, it is described by a super positioning of complex waves, which can variably strengthen and then weaken. It is a zero-sum, or win/win game in which cooperation leads to common growth. It is true creation, the transformation of potential into reality; a material/energetic manifestation of the possible. This may be disappointing for egoists who are bent on manipulating nature to serve their own selfish interests. We cannot know exactly what will happen in the future under any given circumstances as it remains indeterminate. It is perhaps wise to use verbs rather than too many nouns which, by implying the determinate, limit the fluid expansiveness of our life. For example, we may speak of to live, to love, to feel, to empathize and to act, rather than life, love, feeling, empathy and activity.

Reality, the result of the Permanent Acting Process, is pure potentiality and connectedness. This fundamental connectedness means that the entire world is one undifferentiated unity … It would serve us well to consider how the revolutionary insights of quantum physics may substantially expand our ways of thinking, and fundamentally examine our current beliefs and our behavior that these beliefs engender. No one is isolated in this world. *We are all one, interconnected into a single unity.* It is important to realize that in this unity our individual actions affect not only all of the constructs of society, of actions taken or not taken by other individuals and societies, but as a consequence also direct the constantly changing dynamic potentiality of living reality. Thus, the uniqueness of each individual's contribution is a vital constituent of our common cultural evolutionary process … We need to let go of narrow, static, mechanistic strategic patterns which limit, and reduce and replace them with expansiveness, mobility, openness and empathy to allow for a dynamic interplay, balancing the creation of real wealth and the support of humanity to realize their deepest form of wholeness, of oneness. A new world picture is visibly emanating from empathic people …

Have we all considered and learned from the latest available knowledge, and as a consequence changed our attitudes toward an ethical and moral work and private life? It would appear that we have not, no more than we have availed ourselves of the insights of mystics from centuries past.

Hans-Peter Dürr concurs:

It is amazing that this profound change in our understanding of reality has not yet been philosophically and epistemologically comprehended, after more than one hundred years since the paradoxical findings of the physicists Max Planck and Albert Einstein, and the great scientific insights twenty five years later by Niels Bohr and Werner Heisenberg.

This wisdom certainly has not yet taken root in the world of economy. It can hardly be expected, when not even scientists or scholars in all fields of the arts and humanities have yet to embrace this knowledge. Medical doctors who we like to think of as the "leading edge", at least in the healing arts, are still committed to attempting to explain and cure diseases with their mechanical, materialistic models. Those who espouse methods which arise from an understanding and acceptance of the "new reality" are being phenomenally successful, but they are few and far between. I am a chemist, whose education and training was entirely based upon a materialistic worldview, one quite in opposition to that which the details of quantum physics would dictate. But as a manager in the chemical industry who was blessed with mentors who encouraged me through a process of maturation, the knowledge and wisdom of Hans-Peter Dürr resonates deeply within me.

No matter what path we choose, in order to have meaning our experiences must lead to direct, immediate consequences in our daily activities. We all need to decide whether our chosen career will eventually become a loving profession, and if so how to facilitate this change so as to co-create an individual masterpiece from our life's work. Physicists and chemists certainly share a collective reputation. Some build atomic bombs, some produce gas for wars and other similarly unconscionable methods of destruction. Once we have travelled the inner path, have studied and comprehended the new physics and the interconnectedness and unity which it reveals, we cannot participate in a world of economy where people, nature or any part of creation is harmed, as by harming any of the parts of the whole, of which we are a part, we realize that we are harming ourselves. Separation is a mere illusion.

Hans-Peter Dürr completed his doctorate under Edward Teller (1908–2003) at the University of Berkeley in California, but he distanced himself from his mentor after it became known that Teller was the father of the hydrogen bomb. Hans-Peter has fought for many years with all of his means for world peace and harmony. He proposes a revolutionary energy plan which assumes more economical consumption, necessitating fewer new power plants. He advocates for decentralized, clean energy. He considers the unresolved question of the disposal of nuclear waste as a major threat to nature, and he takes a firm position against the future use of nuclear power. He always reminds people in his lectures of Hiroshima, Nagasaki, Chernobyl and Fukushima. Chemists enthusiastically mix and move around atoms and molecules, synthesizing all that is possible. When an experiment does produce the desired results they adopt new reaction methods such as those promoted by catalysts without reflecting upon whether the result will be for the benefit or to the detriment of the environment. It is unfortunate that questioning whether the resulting products serve the common good or promote evil intentions is not widespread in the industry. In chemistry there are products that are only evil, such as poisonous gas. There are also products that are only for the good, such as products for improved nutrition and health. There are also products that can be used for both good and evil. How these products are used is the decision of the users, the promoters and the marketplace. Even such seemingly harmless products as water, salt or air can be used to kill others. We are always wise to ask ourselves whether we are operating with a caring consideration for our natural resources.

Even without prior knowledge of the findings from the area of quantum physics, I have always tried to apply all I have learned from my mentors, and from my mindful reflections during my years in the chemical industry. When we all feel connected one to the other then the association with each other is one of caring, sympathy, empathy, love, understanding, challenging and always promoting and empowering. The results from leading and guiding in such a fashion will not only generate success, but also pleasure and joy at work. Re-born, due to an inner maturity, I now feel confirmed, validated by the wisdom of the new physics. Only the person who runs a business in accordance with the laws of nature can enjoy long-term success. Only those companies managed compassionately will survive. There is no future for a winner/loser game anymore.

True entrepreneurial achievements result from a very slow build-up of a company, with each change being considered in the light of its consequences. As a chemist I may have an advantage, since chemistry is always a step by step process. The development of the whole chemical industry underwent that continuous process and thereby achieved its success. Large investments in research, development and application techniques, pilot plants and huge production units, marketing strategies, controlling and coordinating all activities and balancing supply and demand together form the quality of a perfectly managed company. Sometimes as managers we may incorporate and integrate new aspects from science and wisdom and let them grow. The understanding of the new physics is very helpful and encouraging in this context. The future of a company and the nature of its daily work are always being re-born, as quantum physics tells us. The experience of the reality, the background field, the Permanent Acting Process has the potential to invisibly manifest itself in the company. There are always various options, choices and opportunities, including chance events, which determine a company's future. The key question is how we, as business leaders, can best influence these opportunities so as to manifest a desired reality.

3.3.1 Practicing the Loving Dialogue

Hans-Peter Dürr followed his own unique pathway toward the enhancement of his inner growth. It was influenced by his knowledge and experience of quantum physics. He was not a practitioner of any spiritual way, and he never entered into individuation by Depth Psychology or embraced any other psychological discipline. But there is no doubt that his inner growth was admirable. To listen to him was to be compelled by his conversation and of his desire to help others in the expansion of their inner growth. He lives his belief that it is all about "Making Living More Lively" for everyone.
Dürr stated in interview with me:

> I have never meditated but I reflect upon my life as one well-lived as I have tried to practice the loving dialogue. It is easier for me to explore new terrain with someone else rather than alone. I need to combine the "cautious" and the "spontaneous" and I cannot do it alone. When spontaneity simply goes dancing without knowing with whom it will dance or how, that's wonderful. That is when communication is also communion. Suddenly opening before you is a whole reservoir of images that are waiting for expression! It only takes a pulse, the energy of compassionate encouragement such as is found in dialogues such as these.

To practice openness in dialogue is of great importance. Dürckheim called it transparency, for Dürr it is the loving dialogue. It is the practice of opening, of inclusion, because it incorporates not only awareness but also spontaneity, trust and faith. This attitude is crucial in our business discussions. And when we speak to the sick and dying, a loving dialogue contributes to making their crisis tolerable. The acceptance of misery and the release of needing to be in control by "doing", and exchanging it for letting go and simply "being" is initially a very difficult exercise, but one very much worth the effort. When we rest in "being", relinquishing the control implicit in "doing", rewards will inevitably manifest. When we conduct a loving dialogue we are able to find love in every encounter.

> Love is the blueprint and the basis upon which the universe unfolds. Transcendence is another word for it. Love is transcendence because it breaks up the ego boundaries and overcomes separation. It is the source of all forms, the experience from which all life originates and in which all life interconnects … (Jäger 2009)

3.3.2 Business Ethics through Quantum Physics

It was very important for me to discuss the issue of economic activity as seen from the vantage point of the latest knowledge gleaned from observations in the field of quantum physics, with Hans-Peter Dürr, a quantum physicist and in addition winner of the *Alternative Nobel Prize 1987 and of the Nobel Peace Prize* 1995 (together with Pugwash). On October 29, 2010 we had the following remarkable dialogue in Munich.

> Erhard: "Hans-Peter, what can we learn about corporate management in view of what you understand about and have experienced from quantum physics? What would be your guidelines for people who are in the world of economics wishing to work for the benefit of our society and the world?"

> Hans-Peter: "It is the realization that life is the essential background for what we always try to express in a frozen snapshot. The essence of life is expressed as a kind of game. Two things that seem to contradict themselves must now work together as one. One insight is that I am different from you, everyone is unique in the sense that no one is the same. The other realization is that you do what you have chosen, or what has been laid out for your greater development. The pre-requisite for this development is the mutual desire and ability to initiate a game with each another. Take the example of walking. When shifting our weight from one leg to the other we are constantly 'falling down' at the moment of the shift. So, how do our feet and legs cooperate? The left leg should not say to the right one that it must do what the left leg wants because it had the idea first. Rather, it must say to do exactly the opposite. Then we see something that we did not have before, movement. We need no longer stay in one spot but rather we are able to move forward. This is great progress arising from co-operation."

> Erhard: "In your understanding the 'otherness' of the other is recognized when one cooperates with others to do business in partnership for the successful benefit of both. Much can only be achieved by working together. This principle should therefore be clear in the relationships of all participants in the economic process, should it not? So your advice is to play a 'plus-sum game' and not, as often observed, a 'zero-sum game' in which one gains at the expense of the other."

> Hans-Peter: "Exactly, that's it. But many consider that this principle is an unachievable utopia. They tell me that I should consider how difficult it is for many people to live together peacefully and cooperatively. The problem is that we are too often seeking enlightenment in the wrong places. Our society encourages us to look outside rather than within. The example of a successful and fulfilling marriage of many years duration is evidence that this peaceful cooperation is readily attainable. We may occasionally forget to open ourselves to accepting the shared light which is continuously being beamed to all of us, but we do have this knowledge and can recall it at will through simple meditative practices which allow us to re-establish our center, gratefully

accepting this Divine gift and living and sharing in unity. Even when we do not get along with some particular others we should just let it go, let it be, as difficult as that is for our ego to accept. Remember that everything is always present. Deep inside we long to bridge all separation and to open ourselves to the new dimension which cooperation with others offers. As we are all one, all connected, any dissention or conflict is dissention or conflict with ourselves. When united as one, no one loses, everyone wins and grows together. Moral decisions and ethical behavior are the result."

Erhard: "Is there still a role for competition in our society?"

Hans-Peter: "Competition will always be there. Consider how two waves when flowing against each other will cancel each other out, but will reinforce each other when they flow together. I will not be rewarded for simply co-operating but rather for my unique contribution towards the creation of a new dimension."

Erhard: "But what happens if a supplier's strategy is to capture another supplier's customers, as is common practice?"

Hans-Peter: "This is a derailment in the world of reality."

Erhard: "If the seller no longer cares about the customers of the competitor the end is inevitable is it not? Eventually the final customer will be captured and one company will face insolvency. Then a friendly merger could occur, but through this practice the existence of at least one of the companies would be at risk."

Hans-Peter: "If you do not act with mindfulness you will find yourself outside of the development wheel of life. You will be sitting on a rotten branch, so to speak. In the evolution of life again and again we see things exiting the stage as they complete their useful purpose. Their activities no longer serve the good of all. The world is full of such materially dead waste."

Erhard: "That is what we can see in the economy. Companies have reached a frozen state where they are no longer creating products or services of value to their customers. Then, even the development of sophisticated competitive strategies can only delay their inevitable demise. Would it not be wiser to play an innovative, creative and co-operative game, one in which long term viability can be maintained? It is important, as you said before, that it is the differences between employees, suppliers and customers that together will lead them through cooperation to a higher dimension. This ensures economic success, one which is consistent with all of nature. From my perspective and experience all of our efforts in our chosen profession should be of service to our entire life, it must have purpose and utility otherwise we will have failed. Companies generally plan for no more than five years into the future. This does not allow for sufficient flexibility in viewing the future, but it does allow for a consideration of probabilities. What you have termed the Cooperative Background Field has the potential to reveal itself as a reality in the future. Surely this applies equally to the reality of a company's viability in the marketplace. It must be possible to plan for a successful future for a company based upon what you have said about the new quantum physics, or is it not possible to plan anything at all?"

Hans-Peter: "You can certainly make a statement with regard to the future. Look at nature. The one hundred million different species which co-exist are all winners. This means that there are one hundred million different solutions! Ultimately it is not the competition which is all important. One can find many solutions all of which lead to survival."

Erhard: "With the proper guidance of employees a good manager can improve the probability of survival so that a company will have a better future."

Hans-Peter: "What is better?"

Erhard: "Better is a product portfolio with long term benefits for both the customers and the employees so that all stakeholders of the company can be satisfied. As a company manager I must be able to visualize a positive future otherwise I will not be able to make a case for the provision of necessary resources."

Hans-Peter: "That is easy. Decentralization is the solution for survival. Nature has taught us this. One should work with what is within reach. There is no reason to include the whole world. Plants successfully competing for a habitat in Europe do not question what is currently happening in Africa."

Erhard: "I had always preferred the model of decentralization and my success has proven it to be a viable strategy. When I compete as a company with one thousand decentralized units I always win. When I reorganized Hüls AG, the media wrote '*From an Aircraft Carrier into many Speedy Frigates.*' It was important that these decentralized units in the relevant marketplace maintained their leadership positions in the fields of products, services, costs, innovation and creativity, as well as in the qualification of employees. We had distanced ourselves from the disadvantages and attitudes of a large group. We grew into a great team with a spirit of enthusiasm and success."

It is clear that quantum physics offers a useful metaphor for business ethics in the economy, emphasizing that management should attach greater importance to interconnectedness, creativity, non-duality and nonlinearity.

3.4 Integral Consciousness

Before concluding a discussion of approaches leading toward an integral ethic, I would like to refer to the important experiences of Jean Gebser and Ken Wilber. Both the unconscious and consciousness are important concepts which are worth further exploration. For Gebser human consciousness is always in transition, not continuously but as a sort of progression of "mutations". One evolves from the other with the previous still operating within that which follows. When one becomes deficient, another supersedes it. Gebser introduced the following ages of consciousness of mankind (Gebser 1986):

– Archaic
– Magical
– Mythical
– Mental

We are now in the age of mental consciousness with all its deficiencies, and we are heading for the integral, a more mystical level which is evolving out of the previous ages of consciousness. It corresponds with Jung's vision that the new religion, most probably a mystical one, is not yet here but is imminent. What are the main orientations of the previous ages?

The following is extracted from Wikipedia:

In the magical structure events, objects and persons are magically related. Symbols and statues do not just *represent* those events, objects and persons, but rather *are* those same objects and persons.

In the mythical structure events, objects and persons are woven together in stories. Mythologies give coherence to consciousness. The soul and its visual world, the dream, both individual dreams and the myths of the people which are in a sense the collective dreams of humanity, are related to each other and above all they are on the one hand human, and on the other hand seen individually as expressions of mythical consciousness … The mythical man is already a man of dream consciousness. Instead of the single unity in which the "magical" man exists, the mythical man embraces the complementation of both polarities … For the first time the human gets a reflexive consciousness of the nature of time. He accepts a greater responsibility for his consciousness than does the magically inclined man, at least in the cosmic and natural flow of time … The mythical man's ego was not yet awakened. He lived in the "we".

In the mental structure events, objects and persons are appropriated by the use of logic. Gebser called this deficient form of the mental structure the "rational" structure. The rational structure of awareness seeks to deny the other structures with its claim that humans are *exclusively* rational.

Influenced by quantum physics as discussed previously, the integral consciousness was made evident by a new relationship to space and time. Dürr mentioned that "Being" gives way more and more to transparency. This is *Dürckheim's transparency for immanent transcendence.* All psychological and spiritual practices for mindfulness try to improve this transparency. If we succeed so that our mindfulness is integral in spite of our ego mind, then we experience time as an indivisible *whole*, not as a past, present or future. Then, awareness becomes integral. The more we practice awareness and mindfulness the more we experience the "whole".

3.5 Integral Spirituality

Based on Jean Gebser's philosophy Ken Wilber formulated an integral approach to spirituality, one which integrates spiritual wisdom, religion, science and culture. These key components all have something to contribute to a more integral spirituality. He describes how the wisdom of the East and the West can lead us to a higher level of consciousness through a developmental and psychodynamic psychology. Sri Aurobindo was the first to use the word "integral" in connection with spirituality. His work is described as Integral Vedanta and Integral Psychology. He influenced many other authors to use the word "integral" in connection with philosophy and psychology. These well-recognized sources make a strong case for using "integral" in connection with ethics.

The new Integral Business Ethic 3.0 emerges from an Integral Consciousness, while the Old Ethic has its foundation in a purely Mental Consciousness, one which as a result of it advocating the suppression and repression of the dark side, in conjunction with the psychological and spiritual immaturity of much of humanity, has serious functional limitations. What remained a unity in our Mythical Consciousness was separated by our Mental Consciousness and now must come together once again in Integral Consciousness.

3.6 Transpersonal Psychotherapy

Transpersonal psychology and Transpersonal Psychotherapy, which is based upon it, expand classical psychology and psychotherapy to include philosophical, religious and spiritual aspects. Transpersonal psychology evolved from other psychological schools such as psychoanalysis, behaviorism and humanistic psychology. It attempts to describe spiritual experiences and to integrate them into existent modern psychological theory. These experiences include mysticism and epiphany, along with altered states of consciousness and trance, among others. For a long time Western psychology tended to ignore the spiritual dimension of the human psyche, but with the powerful and compelling influence of Jung this is no longer possible.

The term transpersonal psychology was coined in the late 1960s by representatives of humanistic psychology in the USA. Significant founders and theorists of this discipline are Stanislav Grof, Anthony Sutich, Frances Vaughan, Roger Walsh, Abraham Maslow, Ronald D. Laing, Charles Tart, Roberto Assagioli and Ken Wilber. In Europe elements of the analytical psychology of Carl Gustav Jung, and the Initiatic Therapy of Karlfried Graf Dürckheim were also integrated into Transpersonal Psychology.

3.7 Psychology and Spirituality

When reflecting upon psychology and spirituality we must confront the question of whether it is possible to combine the ways of psychotherapy and spiritual realization, and if so whether it is a fruitful pathway to follow. Psychotherapy and spiritual paths are very different worlds. The representatives of each have concerns and prejudices about the other. Psychotherapists fear that by concentrating on the "Beyond", one's relationship with reality in *this* world is lost, that "love and work", along with social and political commitment are no longer possible, or at least marginalized. They fear a retreat from the real world of business. Dismissal of the ego could lead to a loss of self-responsibility and self-reliance; and the loss of conscious, deliberate control may open chaotic and psychotic flood gates. This is a misunderstanding and misrepresentation of the situation. It is not the ego which must be dismissed but rather exclusive egocentricity. That is a big difference!

Representatives of Spirituality fear the converse in psychotherapy, that our "essence", our divine principle, is not considered; our pursuit of becoming *one* with the Numinous. When we are having difficulties in our pursuit of a spiritual pathway and seek therapy there is a danger that a therapist who is not sensitive to spirituality will not recognize and acknowledge the nature of our issues, instead relegating them to simply personal psychodynamics. This can result in the severing of our personal, spiritual development, often with fatal consequences.

In spite of the apparent discrepancies between the two forms of practice there remains much common ground. The advantages afforded by a combination of Depth Psychology and Spirituality are both considerable and important. They are mutually supportive and it is through their unity of purpose that we may arrive at a New Integral Ethic.

3.8 Integral Business Ethics 3.0

As previously introduced, Integral Business Ethics 3.0 is "Integral" to all that we have experienced, learned and integrated thus far. It incorporates REASON instead of simply the ego mind, numerous philosophical directions following upon the Aristotelian approach, theological considerations of many different religions and the depth psychology and spirituality of the Doctrines of Wisdom. As Gebser pointed out, one evolves from the other and continues to exist in each subsequent ethical formulation. For anyone to successfully apply the essential wisdom contained within Integral Ethics to Business Ethics 3.0 a precondition is an excellent education and considerable experience in business management. Without practical experience people working in the economy sector may become enamored by theoretical statements but lack the necessary judgment to apply them appropriately, increasing the risk of compensating with self-serving, unethical practices. Thanks to the internet we have unprecedented access to an understanding of all of the aspects which constitute Business Ethics 3.0. It is the ideal *New Ethic* for today's digitalized and globalized economy.

3.9 An Integrative Business Ethic

Integral Business Ethics has in addition a very important, active and deliberate "integrative" approach. Unlike previous tactics this ethical approach does not separate and divide, but rather integrates and merges. It is inclusive of light and dark, good and evil, subject and object, masculine and feminine, young and old, ego and self, ego mind and reason, suppliers and customers, companies and shareholders along with managers and employees. All of these apparent opposites are merely polarities of *THE ONE REALITY* which cannot be described, only experienced. The experience of inter-connectedness which has been advanced and enhanced recently by modern quantum physics, along with mystics for thousands of years, integrates the apparent opposites into a single unity. This uniting process is what Jung refers to as Individuation and the *Coincidentia Oppositorum*, which lead naturally and seamlessly to moral decisions and ethical practices.

> The coincidence of the opposites is one of the fundamental organizing principles in Jung's thoughts. Key concepts such as the Self, the God image, the Collective Unconscious, Wholeness and Synchronicity are said to be instances of the coincidence of the opposites. (Henderson 2010)

There is an ever-present danger that Integral and Integrative Business ethics can be disturbed by diversions and distractions, or even derailed by severe blockages of our individuation. Let us now consider these possibilities.

3.10 Diversions

Diversions are an enticing fork in our life's path, offering the false promise of a shortcut to bliss. They beckon to us, appearing more and more attractive as our life becomes more and more stressful and overwhelming. They entice us with the promise of releasing our stress and fulfilling our desires. But they are imposters, they need to be unmasked and disenfranchised. They need not *necessarily* keep us from arriving at our destination, but they *will* make our trip longer and more arduous. Radio, television, computer games, mobile phones, e-mails, Facebook, Twitter and even exotic holidays, which promise us an escape from drudgery to nirvana, all entice us away from the genuine search for inner peace. Unlike virtual reality the genuine search for inner peace in our *real life* cannot be clicked on or off, or purchased for the price of an airline ticket to some exotic paradise. It is our life's journey. By unknowingly following diversions we regress into our shadow whose tentacles then gain an even firmer grip upon us, as with encouragement from our ego we venture further and further into denial. We risk losing sight of our spiritual center which in turn increases the ease with which we can continue to be diverted from our ultimate destination: reunification with our Divine essence. We feel the symptoms in the endless progression of problems in our life, in our suffering and distress, which result from our ego's insatiable appetite for diversions. It is a dilemma.

Diversions which distance us from the serenity, cheerfulness, humor, joy and passion which we crave clearly make it increasingly difficult for those qualities to be manifested within us. Diversions are a drug to our ego, which now inflated locks us into our childhood ensuring that we never progress beyond emotional infancy, where we continue to feel victimized and respond with an aggressive, blaming, judgmental and easily offended attitude. We seek "noise" in conversation, in music, in what we read and watch and in our relationships. The silence, the stillness, the tranquility necessary for inner growth eludes us, and eventually *we are no longer available when our destination comes looking for us*. The solution is through mindfully living in the present moment of the here and now, knowing and recognizing when our choices are diverting us from our destination, and allowing this knowledge to inform our ego that we don't recognize its authority to direct us to lose our focus.

3.11 Distractions

If we agree that there is an urgent need based upon the experience of depth psychology to achieve stability through the development of personal inner growth, we must beware of distractions which can short-circuit our pathway to a greater awareness of our Divine potential. Being distracted is the opposite of being focused. We can enter into a distraction purposefully, or we can find ourselves unwittingly distracted by allowing someone else's intent to envelop us. Either way, the focus which we can achieve through the gateway of mindfulness and awareness is lost. The result is dissatisfaction and restlessness, which in turn hinder our ability to experience the divinity. Escape into distraction is typical of our times, a modern "dis-ease". We seem uncomfortable with mindful concentration. The art of conversation is lost. Too often we no longer listen to others, choosing instead to speak about ourselves. We feel powerless to remain focused.

The marketing of products for diversion, distraction and relaxation is an enormous industry. We are seduced by offers of entertainment and attractions accompanied by stimulating but empty promises that they will satisfy us. If we are scattered, searching for we know not what and receptive to anything we believe will bring us relief, we are unlikely to say NO! We are easy victims. How do we find our way through this confusing maze of possibilities? Simply ask yourself one question before initiating or accepting any distraction: "will this product, service or activity bring me peace?"

But beware! Our ego will resist. It does not wish to be limited in its exploration of new distractions. It wishes to rule! The dilemma here is that while we are the primary victims of our own ego, it is the nature of our ego's influence to disguise its domination. The ego wishes to convince us that we can achieve the entire spectrum of desirable qualities by following a path of doing, controlling and manipulating. But the qualities we value and desire to welcome into our life can often only be realized by *not* doing, by being, allowing them to find us as we rest in the present moment. We pay a considerable price for allowing our ego to dominate us. It is expressed in nervousness, meaninglessness, disorientation, anxiety, fear of loss, depression, burnout and fear of death. We then attempt to alleviate these trying conditions by indulging in idleness, by scattering our resources and stimulating ourselves with meaningless and too often harmful distractions, indulging in excessive consumerism and the abuse of drugs and alcohol. It is a great fallacy that once our profession is behind us in the third triad of our life that we can instantly rid ourselves of all the negative symptoms we have accumulated over a lifetime. Our work may be behind us but we not only carefully preserve and carry forward all the compensation mechanisms we previously developed in order to help us cope, but we expand upon and strengthen them as we struggle to make the transition to retirement. Well-being can seem to be an impossible goal, and then desolation sets in.

There is only one solution. We must open ourselves to the experience of the one reality in each and every moment of our lives. The revelation of this ultimate reality; our intimate interconnectedness and resonance with all of life fills us with bliss. If we truly wish to welcome peace, silence, balance, serenity, kindness, charity, compassion, perseverance, harmony and happiness into our life, mindfulness is the key. Living mindfully in the present, fully embracing the here and now, gives our life new meaning. It invites the Golden Wind into our life which in turn will guide us gently back to our original home in the universe. If we can quiet all the external and internal noise around and within us sufficiently that we can meditate, great! But if at this time in our life some of us lack the resolve and discipline to meditate, it will serve us well to seek out an assortment of the opportunities for expanding our consciousness which interest and fulfill us, ones in which we can practice entering into mindfulness. In time meditation will come calling, asking for a second chance!

3.12 Relaxation from Mindfulness

The great violinist Anne-Sophie Mutter will certainly never relax the strings of her Stradivarius because her instrument would lose its wonderful sound. The same principle applies to the human body. Excessive relaxation reduces our ability to be present. We need to seek a permanent balance of tensions; that center which exists between stress and relaxation. The longing for relaxation originates in the ego. Self-indulgence, misrepresented as wellness, has become a billion-dollar industry. The world is offered to us as a big party. All-inclusive holiday locations, cruises and specialty entertainment holiday clubs promise us nirvana; but what about after the holiday is over? Nothing has changed! The shallow game which has become our life, along with all of the false promises we pursue without ever finding true satisfaction begins all over again. Hours of daily television distract us from exploring our emptiness, but rather than true relaxation it is a prescription for dementia. Alcohol, nicotine and other psychoactive drugs are able to temporarily relax us but we know that they are ultimately destructive. It is tragic, because through their use we obstruct our inner growth process.

Compare these empty, sterile and destructive offerings with meditation in which, rather than the brain being turned off, it is activated in regions seldom used, regions which afford us a respite from thinking and feeling while opening us up to a focus on the background field and its potentiality. While the longing for relaxation is a significant factor in these hyperactive, stressful times, it is not to be confused with the true relaxation achieved through meditation in which, as we are released from thinking we relax into a state of elevated awareness. A holiday, a day in which we can regain our wholeness is also called a vacation. Vacation comes from the Latin verb *vacare*, *to become empty*. The original meaning long since usurped by commercial interests, applied only to those work-free days which were religious holidays, with the intent that on those days in which we were not occupied with our work we should study and worship, so as to more closely approach God. Spiritual vacations are the greatest vacation bargains available. Freeing ourselves from the stresses of our daily lives requires only consistent discipline with a focus upon expansion of our inner consciousness.

It is only natural for us to occasionally allow ourselves distractions, diversions and relaxations. Our accumulated tensions cry out for some *time out*. As long as we are aware of the dangers inherent in permanently relinquishing control over our ego and the self-destruction which could follow, we can consciously and cautiously embrace some time out, as long as we ensure that we have control over its nature and duration. What we want to avoid is allowing our process of inner growth, serenity, cheerfulness, humor and compassion to be compromised by the promise of short-term thrills. Rather let's honor ourselves with a life of inner peace and endless blissful moments.

3.13 Blockages of Individuation

Even when we follow a very intensive and disciplined spiritual path for many years, we occasionally experience unsettling symptoms which we do not expect after a prolonged period of meditative practices. The following "triggers" which many experience and describe are a phenomenon that while apparently common have received very little attention or examination. Meditation literature generally only speaks of the progress one achieves through meditation. *"Meditate and you'll be fine!"* Well, as lovely a thought as that is, it is not always the case. Despite all of our mindfulness and spiritual practices, when we engage in experiences through which we hope to gain greater awareness we may all of a sudden be triggered to experience fear when we:

- are angry
- argue
- are greedy
- want to be a hero or a heroine
- do not want to lose anything
- are afraid
- hurt others
- want to dominate others
- want to be right

In a conversation with Walter Schwery he related to me a story about a monk who approached him and said, "Mr. Schwery, I have a big problem." "What is your problem?" asked Walter. He said, "In spite of 30 years of Zen meditation I get angry easily and often, and do not know how to avoid it."

Many apparently highly spiritually advanced individuals are often involved in great conflicts, because their dark side is not sufficiently integrated. After the death of C.G. Jung his best friends fought for his inheritance, with several institutions to this day continuing to lay claim to it. There are countless other examples, leading us to ask, "How can scholars of great spiritual leaders and teachers, with a great heart for everyone and everything all of a sudden act in this fashion?"

And, of course we may ask ourselves, *how could I do this?* There are blockages and constraints which may short-circuit the process of individuation when despite all of our disciplined practices and enlightened experiences our ego manages to trigger non-compassionate thoughts, ones which do not hold love at their center. The path we must follow to achieve and maintain a healthy state of maturity is often necessarily long and arduous, but it is always worthwhile. According to my dear friend and teacher Walter Schwery there are three major situations which may block the process of individuation and inner growth, even in those who meditate daily. Walter kindly accepted my request to more fully explain what these situations are in a conversation which took place on November 1, 2013.

> Walter: "Let me describe our difficulties and tasks under the heading *The Cosmic Drama*. This drama occurs in three phases, the *Fall* the *Loss* and the *Return*."

3.13.1 The Fall

> We all want to be happy and we all want to avoid suffering. But the first noble truth of Buddha is very simple: life means suffering. The question of why we suffer is an essential religious and philosophical issue, as is the question of how we can end the suffering. Eastern philosophers imagine the beginning of suffering as a cosmic process with its origin in the "casting out" of the Divine One as a result of enquiring into the nature of "Self" which resulted in the recognition that "I am", or from a biblical point of view, "in the beginning was the Word." Astrophysicists tell us that in the beginning there was the "Big Bang." From this point on began the *Fall* of the wisdom or the creative power first into creation, then into matter which includes the dark side, the shadow of each human being.
>
> In Indian mythology Shiva is prior to the Fall, connected forever as a unity with the Shakti aspect of man. In the biblical story of the "Fall of Man," man is forever connected with the Divine. The Fall is the separation of Shakti from Shiva, who because of the separation becomes a dead body in the sense that as long as Shakti remains asleep trapped in matter, she is in a material, cultural prison. What do we mean by "sleeping?" Shakti is confined to our unconscious, suffering, and as she suffers we suffer with her. She is unredeemed, relegated to the darkness. It is the Kingdom of Maya, the kingdom of ignorance. This ignorance is the impediment which keeps man from recognizing his true nature, that of Divine Wisdom or the essence of Sophia, who now in turn suffers from her fall into Creation. Ignorance itself now begins to suffer due to its own ignorance, which begins to awaken Sophia, who is desperately searching for the way back to the source, to the *Light*.

3.13.2 The Loss

Sophia's attempt to return is blocked by the opposite of Light, the Dark Brother, the Shadow or biblically, Satan, the Devil. How can mankind assume mastery over his dark influence? The key is compassion. Not by binding him and throwing him into the abyss, as is related in the apocalypse, nor by psychologically repressing him as is our usual lazy practice, but rather by accepting him, embracing him in a loving attitude. To heal, to redeem in Jungian psychology always has the meaning of "being aware", of allowing to "enter into consciousness". Let us be clear that this means that we are not to condemn our dark side. We read in the bible, "Do not judge!" As long as we do not become aware of our shadow and fully accept it, we experience it as a blockage which affects both our inner and outer life. To embrace this process of consciousness which Eastern philosophy calls the elimination of ignorance or Maya, we do not need to invent new concepts or engage in more scientific studies. We do not need more "*Theoria*" but rather "*Experientia*", wisdom handed down to us by the Alchemists. But how do we achieve this particular awareness? How do we, in practical terms redeem the shadow? Our encounter with the shadow generally occurs as a result of a breakdown of our previously established identity. We experience it as a personal apocalypse, one which creates chaos in our life. In C.G. Jung's description of this state he says, "One is entirely at the mercy of external influences, without any orientation as in a rudderless ship where one is subject to the constant anger of the elements. The never ending suffering experienced in this situation is the encouragement for Sophia to search for a solution which will end the pain."

3.13.3 The Return

Eros, who includes a liberating aspect but who also far too often leads us into untold dangers, illuminates our escape route. Initially, Eros looks for the most comfortable and comforting solution. Men are attracted to younger, attractive women, and women to handsome heroes. But this frivolous external attempt at a solution is blocking Sophia whose path of salvation targets that which lies "within" us, not that which is "outside of us". C.G. Jung called this inside center the Anima. He often iterated that Anima is man's greatest problem. For women it is the Animus. The Anima, or sentiment is a powerful, greedy sexual energy, one which is bound to the body. According to the Alchemists, the water (of this sentiment) associated with the all-consuming, craving, yearning sexual desire for the "Babylonian whore" must be purified. If the water is purified then it will quench our thirst according to the Gospels, and will afford us eternal life. The task of life thus becomes the transformation of the erotic into an inner maturation process (Tantrism). Dürckheim emphasizes that lively erotic is quite different from pure sex, but sex belongs of course to the wholeness of human beings as well. C.G. Jung often stated that sex is the backside of spirituality. According to the Depth Psychology of C.G. Jung and of the Alchemists, reconciliation between the shadow and your Self is a necessary condition for a successful transformation. For C.G. Jung the Self is the symbol of our united opposites. According to the "*Tabula Smaragdina*", the Emerald Tablet, our life's mission is to "*Seek to be One with the Divine Sun!*" Only then is the "Work of the Sun" done. The "Work of the Sun" means the pure Gold, the Reality, The Golden Wind, as you have called it in your book: *Living in the Golden Wind*.

Erhard: "Thank you Walter for your comprehensive survey of blockages to individuation. There are not many who can describe these complex interdependencies so succinctly. Before your

explanations I was of the opinion that the following three blockages were three separate problems of mankind that had to be solved independently.
- The fall into the ego centered world of matter, mind, science, technology, and economy.
- The reconciliation with our Dark Brother.
- The Anima/Animus issue.

Now I see that the blockages are phases of what you so aptly refer to as the Cosmic Drama, which is running its course in each of us. Transformation is our life's task. Transformation is also the corner stone of this book. How appropriate that you now end your explanation with a reminder of our need for transformation.

Coming back to the fall of Sophia into matter, I remember that you told me of a statement of C.G. Jung which I mentioned earlier in this book. He said that he had never worked with a patient whose various manifestations of psychological problems were not ultimately the result of separation from the spiritual."

Walter: "You are absolutely correct. Jung expressed the fall of Sophia with different words. The fall into matter is the separation from God, from Divine Wisdom."

Erhard: "At the moment we can see how all levels of society, countries, economies, companies, churches and cultures which have been built upon patriarchy are disintegrating. Would it be fair to say that Sophia, the Divine Feminine Wisdom is breaking through these antiquated structures and that this breakthrough can only be achieved through chaotic means?"

Walter: "Yes. It is evident worldwide. It is the 'Zeitgeist' which is demanding a breakthrough. The tragedy is that most people are suffering without knowing why, or how to escape. They have no idea about the Cosmic Drama."

Erhard: "All the more reason for those of us who are aware and do understand to work diligently to ensure that both an explanation and guidance is offered to others."

3.13.4 Distractions Are Detrimental: C.G. Jung's Visions

After writing his *Red Book* C.G. Jung decided to ensure that the book was kept a secret for almost 100 years. He was convinced that people would not believe him and would call him crazy at the beginning of the twentieth century. It has now been published, first in the USA and following that in many languages including German. It was his hope that at the beginning of the twenty-first century people would be sufficiently mature to understand his concepts and to take actions accordingly. But we are obviously still far from being able to fulfill his vision. It is tragic that we have progressed so little in areas that really matter, areas which encompass greater humanity.

C.G. Jung describes in the *Red Book* (Jung 2009b, pp. 375–376). "The Three Prophecies" he has seen for our future through his imaginative conversation with his soul.

From the flooding darkness the Son of the Earth had brought, my soul imparted to me ancient things that pointed to the future. She gave me three things: The misery of war, the darkness of magic, and the gift of religion. If you are clever, you will understand that these three things belong together. These three mean the unleashing of chaos and its power, just as they also mean the binding of chaos. War is obvious and everybody sees it. Magic is dark and no one sees it. Religion is still to come, but it will become evident. Did you ever imagine that the horrors of such atrocious warfare would come over us? Did you know that magic existed? Did you contemplate the possibility of a new religion? I sat up for long nights and looked ahead at what was prophesized and I shuddered …

War and conflict we see everywhere, in units as small as families and as large as nations. War is of egocentric origin and thus separates one from the other, creating endless victims. There is no realistic hope that it will end until the total annihilation of mankind is complete. By magic, Jung was referring to "Black Magic" which is a viable, destructive force acting upon both the individual and the collective. Lance Owens, a scholar of Jung and his literature stated the following in his seminar about the *Red Book*:

> I think I know now what Jung was intending with his prophecy of "a darkness of magic". Consider the technological digital development during the last thirty years. The *Technos*, the creative human ability exploded and is growing exponentially. Computers, Smartphones, Laptops and the Internet are interwoven into the very fabric of human life. In the streets, in cars, trains, airports, even in what could be the solitude of nature, *everywhere* it is hustle, hustle, hustle with no time to stop and ponder, to contemplate, to meditate, to mindfully consider. We must hurry up and wait! People are having their mindful *attention, awareness, consideration and compassion* usurped by the vampire of "magic".

Our *mindful awareness* is being sucked out by the *vampire of magic.*

We read in *Die Zeit* March 26, 2015. "The smartphone as permanent entertainment prevents a highly productive state of mind." Silence and stillness, doing nothing, mindfully not doing, is absolutely necessary for intuitions and creativity. It is impossible to enter into this state when we remain permanently connected to our distractions.

3.13.5 The Tragedy of Modern Distractions

> According to a representative survey conducted by the polling institute YouGov, 44% of Germans automatically take their mobile phone out of their pocket when they have nothing else to do. In the 18 to 24 year old age group, it is as high as 73%. One who does this directs his attention outwards, although the brief moment in which the individual has no direct responsibility provides an excellent opportunity for reflecting inward. "These two forms of attention function like a switch", wrote the psychologist Daniel Willingham of the University of Virginia recently in the *New York Times*. When one is on, the other is off. His thesis is not that mobile phones make us stupid, but that they quench our "appetite for endless entertainment". As a result, time-outs for the brain disappear and thus also the opportunities for sudden intuitions and inspirations. It is especially in our phases of undirected thinking that psychologists see a source of creativity. Many people tell us that their best ideas come to them during routine activities like showering, driving, or gazing out of the window on the train. Unless we are a trained Zen Monk we cannot avoid the brain constantly fabricating new ideas during moments of mental relaxation. These may be very unproductive thoughts such as yesterday's confrontation with the boss, but they may equally well be intuitions that suddenly solve a problem upon which we have been cogitating for quite some time. (*Die Zeit* March 26, 2015)

Soren Gordhamer quotes Google Ventures partner Joe Kraus (Gordhamer 2013, p. 11).

> As a culture we have got a crisis of attention. We are becoming a distracted culture ... one that is disconnected from one another ... unable to pay attention to *anything* – our ideas, our line of thinking or each other. Insight, imagination and empathy with others, which are at the heart of creativity, suffer.

Soren Gordhamer describes this distraction (Gordhamer 2013, pp. 2–3):

> Studies suggest that up to three out of every four US workers now call their job stressful. In a recent National Sleep Foundation study, 63 percent of Americans say their sleep needs are not being met during the week. More people today feel increasingly hurried, overwhelmed and distracted, which has much to do with the pervasiveness of these same technologies. While once we could go home and get away from work, now it follows us through our cell phone and computer, so that we are always "at the office" and available for demands. The constant onslaught of messages and information leaves us feeling frazzled and unhinged, and it's damaging the quality of our work and our relationships ... In spite of my epiphany, I was not (and I am still not) willing to renounce my interest in or use of technology. These devices and services can be powerful tools for creating a freer and more open world. The truth is, that we can use just about any device either for benefit or harm. What matters is not that Twitter and Facebook exist. They are what they are. Whether we use them as means of distraction or gossip, or harness them to help us accomplish what is most important depends on us. I wrote this book (*Wisdom 2.0*) to help you learn to make conscious choices about how you use these tools, so that you may live in our constantly connected world in a way that is creative and aware, and where you are in the driver seat.

It is doubtful that most people are able to make wise decisions about their interaction with technology on a daily basis. Jung and Neumann explain clearly who is in the driver seat. It is our suppressed and repressed dark side.

Lance Owens comments,

> Twenty years ago people were speaking directly with each other and reading books. In an emergency room recently I observed numerous young adults with major, life threatening medical issues, all focused upon their smartphones. What else is distracting people today, demanding their attention? A lot more! Where does the Magic come from? It arises within us as humans, given life by the "Creative Fire" of the modern World. Magic is very dangerous. It denies us meditative time alone with our own psyche, from our inner voice, our intuition, our spiritual center. After a century of war we remain vulnerable. And now we are facing an even greater danger from this Magic.

Soren Gordhamer quotes Bill Keller in his book (Gordhamer 2013, p. 19):

> In a blog post titled "*The Twitter Trap*", Bill Keller, the executive editor of the New York Times, writes about the challenges of staying focused: "The most obvious drawback of social media is that they are aggressive distractions." He continued: "Every time my Tweet Deck shoots a new tweet to my desktop, I experience a little dopamine spritz that takes me away from .... from .... wait, what was I saying?"

Der Spiegel of August 14, 2015 contained the headline: "How Me Remains Me – Being Human in the Google Age." It is a good example of how digital dependency creates dissonance between the ego mind and objective REASON:

The human being just climbs a new stage of evolution; from reasoning beings to artificially reasoning beings. From *Homo sapiens* to Homo augmented. He benefits from the fact that the boundary between man and machine, between the smartphone and its owner visibly disappears. The capabilities of the machine are going to be faculties of man. He is more powerful, smarter and more sensible than ever. He finds solutions to problems that overwhelm him alone. In the digital revolution, as it is seen by optimists, every man is put in first place, in the position to take advantage of his freedom.

This is a good example that, following the spirit of the time, one has not understood the difference between mind and REASON. Access to knowledge and linking knowledge is indeed expanding and strengthening mental abilities, but this has nothing to do with REASON. The individual is increasingly destabilized, leaving REASON behind.

When we are constantly being torn from our center, from the mindfulness of the here and now, we become more and more removed from our soul. The soul is our guide to our unconscious and when our access to the unconscious is lost we undermine and weaken our consciousness. Once we lose our focus, our stability, our center and become easily manipulated, we are on our way to experiencing any of a host of diseases. In this state one cannot promote and *live* the New Ethic; not personally, not societally and certainly not as a ruling force in the economy.

Religion is still to come, but it will become evident! "A new religion is not yet established but it is on the horizon" (Jung 2009b, p. 376). There is progress on the individuation of countless individuals which is also beginning to be evidenced in the collective. A new epic of human consciousness can be seen to be evolving. This book about the New Ethic is giving testimony to that arising consciousness.

Germany recently held a *Cyber Security Conference*. Many speakers led the participants to the sobering realization that every day hundreds and thousands of attacks are being made on the "secure" networks of governments, banks, companies, nuclear power plants and the army. Protection programs are constantly being developed and employed to fend off the attacks, but to little avail. No one knows for sure that it will not result one day in a mass destruction of unimaginable magnitude and consequences.

Jung prophesized it all too clearly!

4 The Application

4.1 Applying and Sustaining Business Ethics 3.0 in the Economy

Hans-Peter Dürr (Dürr 2011) reported on a reunion of German scientists which took place in Auerbachs Keller, a historical restaurant in Leipzig, where an attempt was made to find a German term for sustainability. Up to that time in business, we always spoke of *sustainable development* and built this responsibility into our corporate goals, but we had no single German word for the concept. The scientists endorsed a proposal from colleagues in forestry who presented a concept of sustainability which already existed in the forestry industry. Dürr passionately opposed it because the concept of simply "planting a new tree to replace each one that is harvested" was insufficient for him. He was adamant that the approximate maintenance of the *status quo* is insufficient for real sustainability. Following further discussion, the following definition was adopted by the *World Commission on Environment and Development*. "Sustainability is development that meets the needs of the present generation without compromising the ability of future generations to meet their own needs and to choose their own lifestyle."

This is certainly a forward step, but is it perhaps still too liberal? Manemann (Manemann 2014) believes that since the concept of sustainability has become a marketing slogan for car manufacturers and other CO_2-intensive companies it has lost its critical essence. As previously presented, Dürr's benchmark for a new concept of sustainability is *Making Living more Lively*. When we engage in the "Wheel of Life," it is not sufficient that we simply maintain the *status quo*, we have an obligation to *improve* life. This can present a real challenge in its application and has the potential for enormous practical consequences when rigorously applied, but the positive personal, societal and economic results are well worth the effort. This forward looking concept of sustainability which endorses making living more lively is the main principle and driving force of Business Ethics 3.0.

In *Action Networks*, ethicist Peter Knauer (Knauer 2002) recognizes sustainability as a fundamental principle of ethics. Drawing upon Thomas Aquinas, he makes the observation that every action has two consequences: one desirable and one undesirable. A basic question of ethics is to consider and resolve which risks and side effects are acceptable. All the classic experiments exploring "off-set" demonstrate that collisions of values can never be perfectly resolved. Is economic growth more important than the environment, or vice versa? Knauer points out that the question itself is nonsensical. As we already know, we need not choose one exclusively over another, it is not a viable approach. We need rather to find a balance which results in a win/win solution. Knauer promotes the ethical demand that our actions allow the morality to which we aspire to grow and prosper in the long term, rather than compromising it for short-term gain.

This moral position must be universally formulated and applied. Not just *my* wealth, but *all* wealth. When we increase our wealth in a manner which also increases

https://doi.org/10.1515/9783110572292-004

everyone else's wealth, we are acting in a morally responsible fashion. When we seek to increase our wealth at the expense of others, we are acting in a morally reprehensible fashion due to our desire for over-exploitation. Knauer's conclusion allows us to rise above the fruitless debate over values. The values to which we subscribe, whether they be wealth, ecology, social awareness or self-determination, remain a personal decision; but in order for the actions arising from our decisions to be ethical, it is crucial that we multiply these values in their universal formulation and duration. When this wisdom is applied to the economy, it leads to a responsible approach, one which ensures sustainability in the sense which Dürr has adopted and is promoting.

To enshrine this combination of *Responsibility* and *Sustainability* as goals and practices within the framework of a new ethic for the economy would be tremendously beneficial at both an individual and societal level. This unity has the potential to empower individuals and companies to make decisions which will be of personal benefit as well as being environmentally and societally sound. Unfortunately, as Andreas Ackermann observed, most companies are limited in their vision of their employees; viewing them simply as an isolated expense must be mitigated (Ackermann 2004).

4.1.1 Sustainable Personal Responsibility

My experience leads me to the conclusion that for leadership to be able to effectively promote individual responsibility, it must recognize five vectors. The first four are directed at ourselves, our boss, our team and our colleagues:
- within ourselves
- below ourselves
- above ourselves
- adjacent to ourselves

The final vector is directed toward all outside stakeholders, such as customers, suppliers, competitors, stockholders and the community at large:
- outside of the company

If we are serious about applying the New Ethic, we must assume responsibility for these five developmental programs.

4.1.2 Developing Ourselves

There are two very important questions to be considered when interacting with others:
1) What is my dark side, my shadow, which I have to integrate in order to avoid having others feel hurt?
2) What is the "living" in the other person which I can make "livelier"?

Of primary importance is our own personal development.

In 1999, I wrote a paper entitled "The Leadership of the Person in Times of Change" (Meyer-Galow 1999), which I will summarize: When we consider leadership most of us expect a few detailed accounts about how to lead others. Here is one however, which is almost always overlooked: How can we lead others if we cannot find our own way? Those who have made the effort to do so are few and far between! My thesis is therefore: leadership always begins with assuming responsibility for the leadership of ourselves.

After birth we can only truly call ourselves holistic for about our first three years. Then begin the distinctions of *me* and *you*, of *mine* and *yours*. With these distinctions our "wholeness" is shattered by the development of our ego. As parents we have an enormous responsibility. We shape our children by rewarding them for what we consider to be good behavior; that which leads to success, to joy, to love and so on, until their ego becomes strongly developed and independently ambitious. Then they may study, go to work and attain more success in the advancement of their career. They are living a life of *acquiring* and *ego fulfillment*. Sometime later negative experiences and crises arise, often with their first leadership or other demanding responsibilities, or after several years in an intimate partnership. Too often they are unprepared and thus entirely incapable of navigating their way through these early crises in a fashion which ensures a successful resolution for everyone concerned, because they lack the leadership skills which can *only* result from the development of their self-awareness. We *must* all become self-aware before we can successfully guide others toward their self-awareness. Or in the words of Horst-Eberhard Richter: "Only he who is reconciled within himself can work with others in a caring way!" We must always lead *as we are* and not as we have been trained to be, or as others expect of us, because patchwork behaviors that are not anchored in our own personality inevitably have a disappointingly short life span. The development of oneself *as a whole person* is a crucial task in our life, one which becomes the innermost dimension, the cornerstone of leadership.

It is now 19 years since I published that paper and I believe equally fervently today that we must undertake the essential work necessary to develop our inner self, our self-awareness, in order to embrace the essence of the New Sustainability in a contributory fashion. Assuming responsibility for allowing and encouraging our inner growth to develop is an essential prerequisite for anyone who is contemplating a leadership position.

We achieve an essential step in becoming a fully functional adult, one who is able to *live* the new ethic, when we stop blaming others for our fate and assume responsibility for it ourselves. As a holistic, accomplished and self-aware person, we are at peace with ourselves, able to embrace a balance of good and evil, spiritual and secular, masculine and feminine with everyone and everything. We exude inner peace. We are full of energy and focused upon the here and now. When fully present with ourselves and our surroundings like a Samurai or a Shaolin, we feel empathy and congruence with the outside world. Ethical rules or guidelines are no longer necessary. Inner growth is an ongoing, lifelong journey to be initiated and continued, not a final destination at which we may expect to arrive. The powerful, empowering and self-affirming determinations that we internalize along the way ensure that the necessary knowledge and expertise which we seek out and achieve will be sufficient to ensure that nothing will stand in the way of our successful career.

4.1.3 Assisting Others in Their Development

The real challenge for all of us in executive positions is to demonstrate effective leadership by helping those for whom we are responsible to move toward the New Sustainability. It is universally advantageous to promote our employee's personal development. The nature of our leadership and the degree to which it can be expected to be effective is crucially dependent upon the status of our internal development. Each individual employee is the key to a new consciousness. Managers know from experience that when individuals are not valued, their consciousness is likely to be directed against the company. Interestingly, what many do not realize is that psychological harm creates the same impulse in the brain as if it were physical harm. According to brain researcher Gerald Huether, if we abuse someone psychologically, it is as if we have physically injured them.

> Slights, experienced by murderous competition do hurt, social rejections make one desolate, as do the emotions resulting from having been treated unfairly. All this leaves a distinct mark in the brain ... That is why we need more mutual support. The most appropriate form of support arises from small communities ... in which people encourage each other to grow beyond themselves, and to help each other to rediscover their common desire to create. (Hüther 2015)

Recently epigenetics research took Huether's findings one step further in the discovery that the experience of a severe trauma results in the modification of a genome. A methyl group is added which hinders our ability to be resilient in subsequent stressful situations. The changed genome is even passed on from the parents' generation to their children's generation. While we are still at the beginning of this exciting, groundbreaking research, it has already produced findings which explain many previously puzzling recurring behavior patterns across generations.

In January 2015, it was reported on German TV that a well-known German car manufacturing company was not paying the full amount of an agreed upon bonus to employees whose productive and innovative ideas were adopted. This *does not* motivate other employees to explore other possible profitable innovations! Also, in a well-known German steel company, retirees did not receive the increase to which they were entitled. The company was taken to court and the retirees won the case. This was *not good* for the motivation of the people still active within the company! It is of paramount importance that those who assume responsibility for others set an example by being a whole, self-realized person. Too often this developmental task is not undertaken by managers who do not understand that establishing and maintaining a profitable enterprise depends upon the development of their employees.

I am in agreement with the former Executive Director of Telekom AG, Thomas Sattelberger, who is critical of the macho culture rampant in the boardrooms of German enterprises. Those who have power must also be able to wield it compassionately, and the lack of this ability all too often results in serious problems. Frequently, German companies are much too focused on a flawed concept of efficiency which leaves no opportunity for employees to consider new, innovative ideas. Sattelberger predicted that companies which refuse to accept the changing values of society do not have a rosy future, as the young workforce continue to become less and less tolerant of the old practices.

It is reassuring however that there is a powerful and encouraging trend occurring. It is estimated that almost 30% of the young generation (20–35 years of age), the so-called Millennials, expect to live very differently than did their parents. They value a work/life balance, flexibility and freedom, community and cooperation, opportunity and gender equality, participation, integrity and transparence, self-realization and social responsibility and sustainability along with authenticity and diversity. This shift is changing the basis of responsibility in the economy dramatically. Many companies in the so-called Old Economy are experiencing difficulties in keeping up.

Zynga, PayPal, Google, Microsoft, LinkedIn and Cisco are among those companies that initiated the first *Wisdom 2.0* conference in Mountain View, California, with great success. Subsequent conferences followed with the number of participants increasing each time. I participated in the *Wisdom 2.0* conference in Dublin at the Google Headquarter in September, 2014. The topic was "Mindfulness and Compassion in the Digital Age." Mindfulness is the entrance way into spiritual development. It has been demonstrated to change employee's mindsets in a most positive and welcome fashion. The previously mentioned companies are now supporting the inner growth of their employees with great success. There is an intense desire by those of the younger generation to work within a company that takes their values seriously. Those companies which accommodate this desire are the winners. They attract the most talented employees.

Assuming responsibility for our employees pays dividends on numerous fronts. It is an example of Clark's equation that "economic responsibility" working optimally equates to "profitability." Companies practicing mindfulness and compassion are on their way to becoming leading "Caring Companies." Their employees appreciate being appreciated, and have great allegiance to their employers. The New Ethic is growing and taking form inside these companies. Their employees are supportive and more productive. But, ultimately, the spiritual pathway *must* lead to liberation and freedom for each individual, so we must be careful not to become totally dependent upon places of employment for spiritual enlightenment any more than we would expect to find enlightened liberation in a political party or even a church. True spiritual maturity is necessarily a lonely, personal quest, as each of us begins from our own unique initial evolutionary position and must follow the correspondingly unique pathway, which will lead us to fulfillment of our individual potential.

4.1.4 What We Can Learn from Social Entrepreneurs

Antonio Vaccaro (Vaccaro 2015) stated:

Social enterprises do not seek profit, but want to alleviate social problems. Even profit oriented companies can learn a lot from them. In its annual list of the 30 under 30 social entrepreneurs Forbes celebrates the amazing success that these young people achieve with their charitable work around the globe. However, the term "social entrepreneurship" seems to have diminished in importance among economists recently, who state that every business tries to serve unmet needs and begin their companies precisely in order to close this gap. They argue that the distinction between social entrepreneurs and other entrepreneurs is no longer necessary. Although it is true that classical, profit oriented companies (a central pillar of our economy) make many important contributions to the welfare of our society, this nevertheless is different from social entrepreneurship. Social entrepreneurs have completely different goals and motivations. And this fact in turn has a fundamental impact on their start-ups. The good news is that both sides can learn from each other.

He continues, and points out the main issues:

Ambitious goals and high motivation: Social entrepreneurs are first of all interested in doing a better job of tackling major core issues of our society – such as poverty, health, education and equality. This encourages them to set high goals. The awareness that their work is for an important cause is additional motivation for both individuals and the team.

Markets are the means, not the goal: Social Entrepreneurs initially see the problem, and then use the markets to solve it; not the other way around.

People are the focus: This is probably the most important discovery that every entrepreneur and every manager in his company would do well to implement. Those who work in a social enterprise recognize very quickly that people and their needs are crucial to the business success of the company. This also means that both in-house and business activities must have the goal of improving the lives of people: not just the lives of customers but also those of employees or stakeholders. Although this view is not new, it is the *sine qua non* in order to secure the success of businesses in the long term.

Economic sustainability: This must be recognized as an indicator of financial sustainability. Only generating a profit ultimately guarantees the success of the social objective. Every company should operate sustainably, but profit should never detract from the social mission of a company. Both classical, profit-oriented entrepreneurs and social entrepreneurs would benefit from this mutual learning process. There are also forums where entrepreneurs of both can share their experiences (a good example is the annual "Doing Good and Doing Well Conference" of The International IESE Business School).

"Such conferences support economic sustainability: Profits are important for social entrepreneurs, but so are initiatives and bringing together experts from different sectors. Participants can then learn in "Best Practice" sessions. Such approaches in the pursuit of sustainability have so far been very successful.

Our society suffers from the reality that corporate activities of entrepreneurs and managers are often designed only to further financial interests, rather than the interests of society as well. All people have a right to live in dignity and to develop freely. It is time for a change. It is time that we enrich those entrepreneurs who hold both the individual and the society to be of equal importance.

Antonio Vaccaro is Professor of Business Ethics at the IESE Business School International (Munich / Barcelona), where he heads the *Centre for Business in Society*. He conducts research, in particular on the subject of fighting corruption and economic crime, as well as social innovation and social entrepreneurship.

While writing a previous book entitled *Living in the Golden Wind* (Meyer-Galow 2014), I received a phone call from my son Philipp, who is working for Evonik Industries, which was formed by the merger of Hüls AG and Degussa AG. He said,

Hi dad, a colleague who was with Hüls in the "90s" asked me about you. I told him that you are writing an English version of your new book. He said that he still has an impressive letter from you in his files, which to this day remains a guideline for him.

You will find in the following 20-year-old letter that even then an important basic understanding of the characteristics necessary for "Sustainable Personal Leadership" was not significantly different from my current understanding:

Dear Colleagues,

I encourage all leaders to commit themselves to the following attitudes:
- Positive thinking: hold positive intentions for all others.
- Reliability: Be consistent in:
    - What you say and what you do.
    - What you teach and how you live.
    - What you promise and what you deliver.

- Hospitality: Offer and receive hospitality as an enduring connection with others.
- Compassion: Choose your words carefully. Develop compassion for everybody.
- Do not be hurtful.
- Be a good listener.
- Precision: Project a clear, precise message with your words.
- Conscious awareness: Continue learning day by day.
- Engage in trial and error learning. Mistakes launch learning.
- Love: Practice unconditional love for all others.
- Respect: Each individual is unique. Treat them accordingly.
- Alertness: Recognize results from the chain of actions which begin with your words and actions.
- Attention: Be aware of details. Something of an apparently minor nature can be very important.
- Liberating: Facilitate others in the use of their creative energies.
- Empowering: Encourage co-operative enterprises between others.
- Proactive: Be aware of any issues which hinder the free flow of energy and resolve them.

With kind regards and best wishes for our bright future.

Professor Dr. Erhard Meyer-Galow
Chief Executive Officer, Hüls AG

At present, this paradigm shift is occurring only *inside* companies, the true measure of its success will be whether it has an influence on the larger market place. Companies based upon the old economy must follow or they will fall hopelessly behind in a competitive world. Even if they simply begin to offer training in mindfulness because it is "in," without the maturity to realize that the intention is to open the door to inner growth, it will be only a step in the right direction. Ideally this step will lead to an increased awareness of the benefits of employee empowerment, including greater concentration, increased efficiency and more desirable results.

Sustainable Leadership must always be oriented toward those we are leading by taking into consideration their individual situations. Therefore there is no one "leadership style." Individuals make the difference. In my first years of business I tried a very democratic participatory style. This was what everyone was teaching and learning at the time. Once I tried to convince a colleague to change what he was doing. I talked and talked and talked to him. Then he said: "Do not talk so much. Just tell me what to do. I know what that means, because I was soldier in the army!" From this moment on I understood that the *Art of Leadership* is based upon the recognition and treatment of each individual as an individual.

4.1.5 New Sustainable Relationships with Our Supervisors

When a supervisor progresses along the path of inner development, cooperation, contentment and productivity benefit. If supervisors are inflexible, adhering to a "top down" management style, enlightened employees are at risk because supervisors see their inner strength as a potential threat. In this situation, progress will be slow and frustrating for both employees and supervisors. Patience is paramount. Improvement in the development of mutual respect and tolerance will be an ongoing task. It is not an easy issue to resolve, and its resolution must involve the desire and dedication of both employees and employers.

4.1.6 New Sustainable Relationships with Our Colleagues

In any group of employees, there will be a considerable mix of progression toward ethical maturity. The common ground between all of the employees must of course be to contribute to the success of the company. This is best accomplished within the state of serenity and compassion which arises from successfully developing a "team spirit," where inclusion and mutual support are priorities, as opposed to exclusion and competition.

A leader who has progressed in inner growth becomes the ideal partner for engaging with customers, suppliers, shareholders, analysts, politicians, union members and all other direct and indirect stakeholders in the company. The individuals who make up all of these factions will understand that this manager is something special, different from others they know. They will observe this leader making "living more lively" for everyone within a wide sphere, and in time they begin to understand the powerful influence that is wielded by a leader who embraces sustainability, and will be impressed by how effectively this leader can move a business forward.

4.2 Sustainable Corporate Responsibility (SCR)

In addition to the classic instruments for publishing annual reports, such as the *International Financial Reporting Standards* (IFRS), which are generally confusing due to the tendency to artificially inflate good news and play down the bad, the reporting of companies on *Sustainability* and *Corporate Social Responsibility* (CSR) has risen sharply in recent years. The *FAZ* 07/20/15 reported:

> We read in the literature of incantations such as Value, Business, Intangible Assets, Risk, Corporate Governance, Corporate Social Responsibility and more recently, Integrated Reporting in the same breath. The negative experience of the last financial crisis of 2008/09 shows that the quality of the balance sheet figures according to the information oriented IFRS ("fair value") is insufficient information for the short term shareholder. This quality gap must be closed by innovative reporting formats ("soft formats") that deal with various non-financial performance indicators. At the forefront of this is the reporting of corporate management and supervision (Corporate Governance) ... No less controversial are the developments in sustainability and integrated reporting. CSR reports are demanded following the financial crisis, as a commitment from sustainably minded companies to their stakeholder groups ... The EU Directive 2014/95/EU also provides a non-financial statement for PIEs with an average of more than 500 employees which reports on environmental, social and employee matters, respect for human rights and combating corruption and bribery ... the EU directive which is analogous to the Corporate Governance reporting does not require a substantive assessment of the information by the auditors.

Clearly the reporting formats which are primarily used as marketing tools do not afford a true picture of a company. Appeals and rules similar to ethical guidelines do not lead to impeccable moral attitudes or ethical behavior, but too often to even more suppression and repression of the truth. "Sustainable Corporate Responsibility" (SCR) must be much more than CSR, it must become our responsibility to ensure that "living is made more lively" in all of our corporation's areas of influence.

Soren Gordhamer (Gordhamer 2013, p. 11) quotes Biz Stone, the co-founder of Twitter:

Whatever your role is in the company you work for – whether you're an executive with many reports, or an individual contributor on a team – practicing regular daily mindfulness and compassion will make you a healthier, more productive person. Additionally, the people you work with are going to respond better and do better work. The outcome is going to be a superior product or service, a happier user or client, and in the best case, have a positive global impact.

Yes! A positive global impact results from adherence to ethical practices!

The responsibility in this sense is experienced at the level of the collective, the sum of the individuals within a corporation and works top down from the CEO, down to the board of directors and so on through all levels of employment. Like individuals, a company also has an identity and a mask; the persona and the shadow. On the outside, trying always to create a good impression the mask reflects empathy and competence, while everything unpleasant, irresponsible or deceptive is forced into the shadow. For some the shadow is integrated and controlled, but not for many. More often the company behaves like it is stuck in a state of childlike socialization; self-centered and inflexible. Just like an egocentric individual. Of course there are responsible managers working ethically who maintain their style even under duress. But these are few and far between, and infrequently encountered. More often encountered are the many who freely live out their dark side, following reckless, irresponsible business practices and making ego-centered decisions. Balance sheets are manipulated, supervisory bodies are either not informed or misinformed and discussions are undertaken with competitors regarding pricing, market shares and distribution of customers. The markets are being manipulated. At the extreme, bribery, perjury, deception, lies and corruption are employed, often causing personal and environmental harm, all for personal gain at the expense of the company, and all too often without a guilty conscience due to the lack of a moral compass. Sadly, as mentioned earlier, in the last 20 years ruthlessness has increased appallingly. Mutual trust has disappeared and the differences and difficulties that inevitably result are now more often dealt with by the courts.

In July 2015, the media reported on a scandal concerning Toshiba in Japan. The scandal came to light in April resulting in dire consequences for the top management of the company. A review by external auditors indicates that in the past the company had, through false accounting totaling more than 170 billion yen (about 1.3 billion euros), shown too much profit – more than three times as much as Toshiba actually made. According to insiders, the experts assume a cause of the balance scandal might be that the group's management, after the nuclear disaster in Fukushima, Japan, in 2011, demanded excessively ambitious targets for other divisions. This could have led managers to exaggerate the revenue and underestimate the costs. The inspectors questioned whether the top management encouraged the managers in this deception.

An aggregate amount of $130 billion was paid to reach settlements between investment banks and the Ministry of Justice for malfeasance in connection with the sale of mortgage bonds just prior to the financial crisis (FAZ 9/2015).

According to a report of Ernst &Young in 2016, the major US and European banks together were fined $ 21.1 billion because of violations of stock exchange rules and state sanctions, manipulation of exchange rates and controversial mortgage practices (FAZ March 13, 2017).

In the same context, junk papers were given AAA credit rating by the rating agencies. One leading agency had to pay $1.3 billion in a settlement. Why are bank managers not being personally sued for their decisions? It is surprising that this is not yet been done. These managers and entrepreneurs damage the reputation of the entire economic enterprise.

What has happened?

New banking specialists, especially at Wall Street (creative investment bankers), created financial products that no one else understood. They underwrote building and other loans to people without sufficient income, and relying upon the high reputation of their bank sold the loans to the financial markets in the US and Europe for a considerable profit. The specialists knew very well that what they were selling was unconscionably speculative, but the buyers, including banks and private and institutional investors who trusted the sellers from Wall Street, did not know that the papers were worthless. They had faith that the mortgages and other securities underwritten by respected banks were safe investments. The bank specialists made huge profits, were paid enormous bonuses and were able, through deception, to get rid of risky assets.

Financial rating agencies unwittingly assisted in the deception due to a completely incomprehensible ranking system, one which ranked the issuing banks rather than their products. When the US housing market collapsed because owners could no longer service their loans due to unemployment resulting from the recession, the crisis exploded. It began with the Lehman Brothers, with numerous other banks following. The banks involved in initiating the crisis acted with immoral intentions, without a commitment to ethical considerations.

Herbert Prantl (Prantl 2011) wrote an indictment against the financial market capitalism under the title, *We are Many*:

> "Ostensibly, the protest movement against banks, financial markets and social degradation is a negative move, because it just seems to make no difference. But their continuing refusal to change is fueling the search for a positive way to proceed; for a better perspective and for meaningful guidelines which can become enacted policy. In a globalized world protestors everywhere are demanding that their governments ensure a certain degree of decency and grace. That's not unreasonable, it helps to establish stability, a primary, fundamental responsibility of States and the European Union."

Prantl's expression of the longing for stability is very much justified. Because of their own personal, ongoing suffering, people are no longer willing to accept the loss of societal morality and the reflected unethical practices.

Is Islamic Banking more ethical and less immoral? I am not certain, but it is worth considering Islamic Banking as an alternative model with promising ethical standards. Asia is the place with the greatest potential for Private Banking, especially Islamic Banking. Malaysian banks are at the forefront of Sharia compliant financial products with high net worth. The Sharia bans the payment of interest and bans speculation. Therefore Islamic Banks do not get involved in the money markets and would not have considered sub-prime. They rule out highly leveraged debt, derivatives for speculation, insurance and gambling. Asset-backed securities are acceptable because they are based on real, tangible assets. Islamic finance is more akin to asset finance. The banks do not make loans but serve their customers by buying their assets and selling them later with a markup. The underlying concept is one of sharing, "sharing of the risk" with the attendant sharing of the profit. This sounds very promising and ethically sound, but as I have not had any direct experience with this type of banking, I cannot speak to any possible "downside" that it may have.

From what has the recent ruthlessness in economic activity resulted? Wolfgang Berger (Berger 2013), economist and philosopher, argues in his book *Business Reframing* that Max Weber developed the theory of the Protestant Ethic, and comes to the realization that today's industrialization would not have been possible without Calvin. Berger describes the opposite positions taken by Luther and Calvin. Calvin was an ascetic, taxonomist and organizer, who had organ music and singing banished from the church, encouraged the destruction of valuable religious paintings and had critics executed. On the other hand, Luther declared that God is a God of love, goodness and mercy who also forgives sins, thus a God to whom we can entrust ourselves. Calvin's God is a God of omnipotence, omniscience of glory and power who calls for unquestioning obedience and the merciless destruction of his enemies. It is from this *Calvinistic* attitude that greed and commercialism under the guise of piety resulted. Wealth was worshipped, as if surrounded by a halo.

Berger believes that under the influence of the Roman Catholic Church and the Lutheran Church, industrialization of the magnitude witnessed today would have been impossible, just as it is absent in Islam, Hinduism and Buddhism, as the fertile soil for its development would not be present. Over time a winner/looser game evolved among managers in the economy. The strategy for such a game is clear. Our genetic code, in accordance with the reality that our biography becomes our biology, retains a memory of the struggle over thousands of years. We still behave as if confronted by predators. Management vocabulary is rich in war terminology and analogies. Morality and ethical practices fell by the wayside. If we are not successful in altering our course, we have set the stage for our collective suicide.

Berger asks, as does Clark, for a new definition of responsibility in management of our society, one in which it is required that managers accept personal responsibility for their decisions and activities. For Berger, taking responsibility means accepting personal responsibility for *causing* results as well as responsibility *for* the results. Berger emphasized that *integrity* derives from the Latin word "*integer*," to be *whole*, as a supreme principle. A lack of integrity separates us from the "whole" and plunges us into ruin. Wolfgang Berger's belief that integrity is the only gateway to success corresponds perfectly with Clark's statement, "Be responsible: be profitable."

4.3 Moral vs Morality

To prevent any misunderstanding when discussing important ethical issues, it is important that we are clear about the meaning of the terms "moral," which involves having an admirably high personal standard and involves both our motives and our behavior, such as is implied in the Golden Rule, and "morality," which involves being able to *distinguish* between right and wrong.

Moral arises out of our mind, and *morality* out of our spirit, our inner dimension. Whether we focus upon "moral" or "morality" as the initiator of a particular action is dependent upon our respective maturity and attitude of consciousness. "Moral" comes from our very limited ego consciousness, and "morality" from our unlimited self-consciousness.

4.4 Measuring the Return on Character

When we hear about unethical executives whose careers and companies have gone down in flames, it's sadly not surprising. Hubris and greed have a way of catching up with people who then lose the power and wealth they've so fervently pursued. But is the opposite also true? Do highly principled leaders and their organizations perform especially well?

They do, according to a new study by KRW International, a Minneapolis-based leadership consultancy. The researchers found that CEOs whose employees gave them high marks for character had an average return on assets of 9.35% over a two-year period. That's nearly five times as much as what those with low character ratings had, whose ROA averaged only 1.93%.

Character is a subjective trait that might seem to defy quantification. To measure it, KRW cofounder Fred Kiel and his colleagues began by sifting through anthropologist Donald Brown's classic inventory of about 500 behaviors and characteristics that are recognized and displayed in all human societies. Drawing on that list, they identified four moral principles: integrity, responsibility, forgiveness and compassion as universal. Then they sent anonymous surveys to employees at 84 US companies and nonprofit organizations, asking among other things how consistently their CEOs and management teams embodied the four principles. They also interviewed many of the executives and analyzed the organizations' financial results. When financial data was unavailable, leaders' results were excluded.

At one end of the spectrum are the ten executives Kiel calls "virtuoso CEOs" – those whose employees gave them and their management team high ratings on all four principles. People reported that these leaders frequently engaged in behaviors that reveal strong character – for instance, standing up for what's right, expressing concern for the common good, letting go of mistakes, both their own and others' and showing empathy.

At the other end of the spectrum, the ten lowest scorers – Kiel calls them "self-focused CEOs" (although ego-focused may be a more accurate expression) – were often described as warping the truth for personal gain and caring mostly about themselves and their own financial security, no matter the cost to others. This group includes the CEO of a public high tech manufacturing firm, the CEO of a global NGO and an entrepreneur who heads a professional services firm. Employees said that the ego-focused CEOs told the truth "slightly more than half the time," couldn't be trusted to keep promises, often passed off blame to others, frequently punished well-intentioned people for making mistakes and were especially bad at caring for people.

Early in the project, the researchers expected to find a relatively weak relationship between strength of character and business performance. "I was unprepared to discover how robust the connection really is," Kiel says. In addition to outperforming the ego-focused CEOs on financial metrics, the virtuosos received higher employee ratings for vision and strategy, focus, accountability and executive team character.

Do leaders who need to work on their character know it? In most cases no, they're pretty deluded. When asked to rate themselves on the four moral principles, the ego-focused CEOs gave themselves much higher marks than their employees did. (The CEOs who got high ratings from employees actually gave themselves slightly lower scores, which is a sign of their humility and further evidence of strong character.) Fortunately, Kiel points out, leaders can increase their self-awareness through objective feedback from the people they live and work with. But they have to be receptive to that feedback, and those with the biggest character deficiencies tend to be the least receptive, often in denial.

How can such leaders get past their denial and overcome their character deficits? Seeking guidance from trusted mentors and advisers helps a great deal, Kiel says. He discovered that first hand early in his own career. After earning a PhD in psychology, he built two large clinical practices and briefly served as the CEO of a publicly held company. Back then, he says, he was more like the ego-focused CEOs than the virtuosos. "While I never engaged in any illegal behavior, I'm sure many of my colleagues in those days felt that I was more than willing to throw them under the bus if it meant success for me." As Kiel reached middle age, though, he began to feel a sense of moral and spiritual emptiness, and he knew he needed to change. It was a long, difficult process. After all, he was trying to undo deeply ingrained habits. But with practice and counsel, he succeeded and became inspired to help other business leaders do the same.

If Kiel's experience and that of his clients is any indication, character isn't just something you're born with. You can cultivate it and continue to hone it as you lead, act and decide. The people who work for you will benefit from the tone you set. And now there's compelling evidence that your company will too (Kiel 2015).

4.5 Power and the Abuse of Power

CEO's have a great deal of power. They must ask themselves from time to time whether they use this power in accordance with sustainable leadership, and they must also ensure that they do not abuse this power.

On July 16, 2013, I had an interview with the psychologist and business coach Dr. Barbara Schmidt, the outcome of which she used in her book *Erfolgreich führen mit Innerer Macht* (Successful Leadership by Using Inner Power) (Schmidt 2015) . I was invited to first make some introductory remarks concerning "inner power," which for clarity I am calling internal power, with its opposite being external power, following which are some edited excerpts from the interview.

"Let me begin by speaking about the polarity of 'internal power' and 'external power'. *External* power is the effect of power or strength against individuals or groups. But is *internal* power actually power? What is at stake if I have it or not? If I do not promote inner growth but rather remain on the ego trip I began as a three year old, then my only development is one of expanding my knowledge in an effort to try to learn as much as possible. That's all fine, a necessary condition for establishing a stable career. But if I'm not aware that I had left inner growth behind during my development, then it is only my ego which develops and I will become ego centered and limited to activities which satisfy my ego. As a consequence my dark side, my 'dark brother' or shadow potential that I have accumulated as a result of my ego-centric behavior, which is frequently rewarded by promotions in the company and praise from my managers, takes over as the director of my life . The dark brother demands that we be greedy, that we strive for more, that we exercise our power and instigate a win/lose situation in which *we* will be the winner. Without internal power we follow his advice, we have no control. We must have the inner strength to be able to dictate to our dark brother, "OK, you are an integral part of me, but I play the game of life and not you!" This is only successful if our bright, positive side is powerfully developed. It can be achieved through years of practice in meditation or other spiritual pathways, but only through the exercise of great discipline. Only then will we have the fortitude to confront the dark brother as an equal partner, with the strength to say No! And mean it. In Buddhism one contemplates the following:

"I have this greed, but I'm not the greed"

"I have this arrogance or vanity, but I'm not it"

"I have the dark brother in me, but I'm not him."

"I am something else. I am the manifested divine spark as a human being in this world. This is me. And the other one, the dark side, I simply have."

Internal power is primarily power over the dark side. The fight, however, is too often a suppression or repression and it ends up in the shadow. The point is to prevent the dark brother from manifesting. Then, without the negative influence, I have power over both the dark and the bright side of myself, my external power. Power always means to be able to make decisions without being influenced by others, and without internal confusion. I may at any time decide freely for myself, strengthened through my spiritual training. I can decide to expand my knowledge and improve my job performance. I am now free to engage in creative activity and interactions and to concentrate fully in the moment with mindfulness and compassion. So, we have to be aware of the dark side. If this is not done, the dark side gains power. Of course, we have to be aware that we can decide freely, without being influenced by others. "Now I run this company, now I take over this project, I will not let myself be deterred by anything, not even by others. I've decided that I will do it my way, relying upon my inner resources. Then I have power over the dark and the bright side. It is very important that we are able to keep them apart.

> Question: What impact does the development of this internal power in executives have in business? From your experience and perspective how important is it that managers are able to make the distinction between internal and external power?

The impact is felt by managers when their boss, exercising external power, clearly tells you what is, or is not to be tolerated because of environmental considerations, because of its potential harm to customers, because it is ego-centered or fraudulent or any other number of practices concerning evolving policies.

Managers will inevitably spend a portion of their early career under control of the dark side. The potential energy contributed by the dark shadow is considerable; greed being a powerful motivator, activating immense energy which can initially stimulate the economic sector. It would be counterproductive to eliminate all corporate greed. It would sacrifice the economic drive. Control by the dark side is a necessary step toward the development of the ego in the young who are striving to succeed, to be promoted, to make more money and to be recognized. These desires in those with developing egos help to position the company favorably in the economic sector.

However, those appointed to positions of management must be more advanced in their inner maturity, they must be individuals who can and will make decisions for the company based upon moral and ethical principles. These supervisors must ensure that their employees keep their dark side under control. Questions such as the following must be addressed: Are your proposals contributing to inner peace for yourself and myself? Are they morally and ethically sound for our company? Do they avoid harming others and contribute to protecting the environment?

Many psychologists, coaches and trainers advocate that only those consistently operating from their "good side" are of value in the economy. This is an illusion. I suspect that if a company's only employees were those who had accomplished considerable inner growth that the company would go broke as a result of not being competitive. The dark energy potential is essential for economic survival. The challenge is for the leaders of the company to integrate the dark potential energy in such a manner as to result in a positive corporate outcome for everyone associated, both directly and indirectly, with the company. That is the task of leadership. Awareness. An even greater challenge is to ensure that young employees are aware that their manager understands where they are in the process of their spiritual development, and through dialogue and the promotion of self-awareness exercises guide them to the realization that there is another, brighter dimension, and while they may not yet have fully entered into it, that during their inner journey customers must not be cheated.

> Question: What is for you the dark side, "the dark brother" who has a place, and where is the limit beyond which it becomes destructive to the climate and the culture in a project team?

The boundary must be the age and maturity of the managers. If I have young leaders who behave like the "dark brother" I know that their ego-centered practices and bad habits can be facilitated to evolve over time. But if someone over the age of 45 retains these egocentric vices and demonstrates them in his leadership performance, then he must be dismissed before he can destroy more positive energy than I can replace.

> Question: Does this mean that these executives over 40 would be a kind of coach for the young professionals in addressing the controlling and integrating of the "dark brother?"

Yes, by clearly stating and demonstrating what is acceptable and what is not. In this way the future of the company is secured by only moving those executives up who are fully aware and accepting of the expectations placed upon them. A supervisor's action is quite transparent in so far as how he does, and does not do business, who he promotes and who he does not. This transparency allows all employees to become better aware of the managers' vision of how to develop a positive corporate culture. As a CEO we must promote executives who at the very least have a big heart, demonstrate empathy and an understanding that we are all connected and thus all capable of empowering others. The more of this type of leader we can encourage to develop and then promote, the less work we will have ourselves. It is important to realize that this type of personnel decision making will be closely observed from the bottom upward, which helps to ensure that both our direct and our more subtle messages will help to form the desired corporate environment.

> Question: Project groups that are central to the company's development must have many young people in them but they cannot be allowed to disintegrate into power games. What is the situation with project groups?

Project groups are formed because it is hoped that the results of a project at the end are more than the sum of the performance of the individuals. We begin a project group in the assumption that significant progress results from the cooperative effort. The greatest achievement of the project is stimulating others with new ideas, intuitions and innovations. To block project groups' power players who are hindering the transfer of momentum, we have to separate them from the rest of the group. The most valuable players are those who through listening, speaking and gesturing with a positive attitude and spirit are able to stimulate others with new ideas. The entire company is ultimately a project group.

There are people who can do this naturally and there are those who cannot. Some individuals are wrongly socialized by parents or superiors or an influential segment of society. They believe success will come to them only by cheating others. And then we are faced with the question, do we play a zero-sum game, one in which I win and you lose, or do we play a plus-sum game, one in which $1 + 1 = 3$, which is the game that must be played, one in which parties together provide more than the sum of each separately. The more people in a group project who think this way, the better the result. And the more each of us has power over our "dark brother" or "dark sister" and can thus follow our spiritual leader, the more the bright side leads us through life and the better we all succeed in both the project work and in leadership. Management development programs must develop these types of potentials so that they can unfold in the company, in the market place and in the entire outside world. Then the company is light years ahead of competitors who have not effected these changes in their employees. That's not a theory. I did it and proved that it is possible. There is nothing more credible than success. It adds authenticity to theory.

> Question: In retrospect, what are the key points in this change process based upon the theme of power and social behavior, of dealing with each other, collaboration and leadership? Why do you think that you were eventually so successful?

It is probably best expressed in the way I learned it from Dürr and his concept of sustainability. I chose to not only speak about it but to live it emphatically. It was necessary that I engage myself with others in a supportive fashion so as to also receive their support, as I could not make the changes alone. We can recognize those who are receptive to inner growth and sustainable productivity by their actions. They are *making living livelier* for everyone over whom they have influence. They have left behind the power games which are played out in most board rooms. Everyone who left my office after a conversation left "empowered." The result has been the creation of a company with a culture for living fully and productively.

> Question: That is to say it was like a chain reaction, because your direct subordinates having personally experienced positive experiences then passed them on to others?

My employee's lives are connected with mine. That is the divine spark; the divine network. It is essential that we find people with whom we can develop this connection. We all have it within ourselves. It simply needs to be activated, to be set in motion. Then we have achieved a workforce that does not operate mechanically, rather one which transforms their work into a great opus. When we design something through ourselves, through our spark of life, then it has an *inner dimension*. This work then becomes a manifestation of the cooperative background field, of God manifesting as reality. We create an ever-changing new reality with positive content. One which replicates itself, with ever-increasing positive realities created out of the initial one.

Question: What about layoffs and other confrontations?

There will always be confrontations whenever you're in a situation where you have to say "no" to someone, or to tell them that they must make a change. The question is how to go about it? Sometimes, with someone who is stuck in "power play" mode, it is essential that we confront them head on. It is all that they understand. To ask them to "please sit on this mat and meditate" is not going to get the job done! Confrontation is necessary. But it is important that the confrontation does not arise from an emotional state. There must be a recognition that we are using our power to establish who is in control and who will set the rules, not to belittle or bully another.

Question: What are the obstacles that you have experienced in this process?

The worst obstacle is of course always a supervisor who has greater power than you due to his position. He may block your way without regard for the success you are achieving, simply because he can. A supervisor who says, "I expect you to do it my way," even when you realize it is nonsense or will cause damage, is a formidable obstacle. Other obstacles are employees who see no need for a change to sustainable leadership. They have no sense of urgency for change because the company's success will ensure that they will be rewarded even if they remain permanently on their ego trip. The change process must be slow, deliberate, calculated and consistent. It will then become obvious that those individuals who are experiencing inner growth are making a positive difference. Mindfulness and compassion will follow. Others will both recognize the benefits and get on board, or they will leave, realizing that they no longer fit with the new culture. While it is preferable that all employees will see the light, and embark upon an inner journey toward realization of their Self, it is unreasonable to expect that everyone will. It is best for all concerned that recalcitrant individuals leave the company."

Hermann Hesse professed that managers lacked a spiritual dimension. He should have said that the artist's lack of a profitability mind set corresponds with a lack of spiritual dimension for the antipodes, entrepreneurs and managers.

That is rather drastic. One hopes that it is not that black and white. In today's digital age almost everything is transparent, and that has positive aspects. So, concerning the question of morality or immorality there is probably a *Gaussian* distribution for the spiritual quality of managers. Without a doubt there are a few who behave morally whether or not laws exist to govern their behavior, a great many with all gradations of behavior between moral and immoral, and some really black sheep. There is an urgent need for a New Ethic!

Robert C. Solomon about *Cooperation and Integrity in Business:*

> The following is an abstract of the book:
>
> The Greek philosopher Aristotle, writing over two thousand years before Wall Street, called people who engaged in activities which did not contribute to society "parasites." In his latest work, renowned scholar Robert C. Solomon asserts that "though capitalism may require capital, but it does not require, much less should it be defined by the parasites it inevitably attracts". Capitalism has succeeded not with brute strength or because it has made people rich, but because it has produced responsible citizens and – however unevenly – prosperous communities. It cannot tolerate a conception of business that focuses solely on income and vulgarity while ignoring traditional virtues of responsibility, community, and integrity. Many feel that there is too much lip service and not enough understanding of the importance of cooperation and integrity in corporate life. This book rejects the myths and metaphors of war-like competition that cloud business thinking and develops an "Aristotelean" theory of business. The author's approach emphasizes several core concepts: the corporation as community, the search for excellence, the importance of integrity and sound judgment, as well as a more cooperative and humane vision of business. Solomon stresses the virtues of honesty, trust, fairness, and compassion in the competitive business world, and confronts the problem of "moral mazes" positing as its solution, moral courage. (Solomon 1992).

A very important focus of SCR is that management has to take responsibility for all products manufactured and for all manufacturing processes. They have to fulfill the obligation that nobody is damaged and that the environment is protected. What should *not* occur are deliveries of products that are used by customers, with the explicit knowledge of the manufacturer and supplier, to produce hazardous substances that cause damage to humans, animals or to the environment. This blatantly immoral practice is commonplace. Greed results in the casting aside of any previously held ethical principles. As an example, *Der Spiegel* in May of 2015 reported that the German Government has documents that suggest that for decades German companies have helped Syria to produce chemical weapons.

4.6 Disruption and Ethics

A new buzzword is making the rounds: "Disruptive Innovation." Any discussion of Business Ethics must consider whether the "disruption" is promoting or hindering ethical practices. We know that 100 years ago, along with the statements of John Maurice Clark and C.G. Jung, Joseph Schumpeter coined the term "creative destruction." In the past because the pace of change, of destroying and building anew was slow, it often took decades before evolving companies crumbled.

"According to Schumpeter, those involved with the disruptions that accompanied change were content to observe the "creative destruction" that was occurring. They were interested in initiating change, they wanted to be the ones to "scoop" with new inventions. They were in love with success.

Schumpeter wrote of the "joy of creating." The digital revolution has changed that. Everything is more globally connected and occurs more quickly and brutally. Old business models are destroyed by new ones and sometimes replaced in months. Uber and Airbnb are two examples. 3-D printers, the self-propelled car, algorithms for decentralized financial transactions, the smart grid and digital home management are others. It seems that our lives, our work, even the way we think is changing with unprecedented speed. Machines are networking and communicating with each other, eliminating many jobs. There are no opportunities for the displaced workers in the new business models. They fall to the bottom of the social ladder. For many people this "creative destruction" is clearly and understandably frightening.

With Kalanick (Uber) and his followers, the destruction is deliberate. It's not just about having better ideas than others, or being in love with success, it's about destroying something else. Not "I want to play also", but rather "I am going to play and in so doing eliminate all others." For those who were previously established in the market and have had their niche destroyed, "there is often no place left for them in the market" (Edited from Süddeutsche Zeitung April 6, 2015).

Where does that leave moral and ethical considerations?

The inventors of the digital revolution and of all disruptive innovations are ruthless. The new technologies will prevail regardless of any intrinsic values held, or not held, by the inventors. Their innovations will not be held back just because they are harmful to many people who remain in the old economy. The promoters will point out how advantageous the innovations are for many others. The victims will complain, but their voices will not halt the rapidly developing process. One cannot blame the inventors. Innovations are not immoral but the way that they are brought to market and promoted may be immoral. It brings to mind the term "apocalypse," which C.G Jung used when asked about his vision for the next few centuries.

Business Ethics 3.0 also applies to the new players in these newly evolving business models. Society will have to confront the question of whether they create more good than harm for mankind. These new players must be scrutinized and evaluated. Given the current situation, it is of considerable concern that a great wave of "Disruption of Ethics" is inevitable. We are certain to experience an increase in immoral decisions and unethical behavior in the economy both from those whose businesses are destroyed and from those who will do the destroying.

Even though disruptive innovations are unstoppable, a new integral ethic can assist those who are victimized to find the stability necessary to allow them to move forward and discover or invent a new niche for themselves. There is hope in that, as described in the Wisdom 2.0 movement, young professionals are committed to mindfulness and compassion and that the young generation insist upon greater attention to the meaning of life; demanding a good life balance for both themselves and others.

4.7 Organization and Structure

Before considering sustainability it is important to look at some basic ideas and definitions in business. We can position all businesses in a portfolio matrix to make it clear that each business has to be managed differently according to its unique position in the matrix. In managing the economy, these findings are often not taken into consideration, especially when deciding which managers should run which business according to their specific talents and experience.

Wikipedia states: "*The growth–share matrix* is a chart that was created by Bruce Henderson for the Boston Consulting Group in 1970 to help corporations to analyze their business units, that is, their product lines. This helps the company allocate resources and is used as an analytical tool in brand marketing, product management, strategic management, and portfolio analysis. Analysis of market performance by firms using its principles has recently called its usefulness into question. To use the chart, analysts plot a scatter graph to rank the business units (or products) on the basis of their relative market shares and growth rates.

- *Cash cows* are companies with high market share in a slow growing industry. These units typically generate cash in excess of the amount of cash needed to maintain the business. They are regarded as staid and boring in a 'mature' market, yet corporations value owning them due to their cash-generating qualities. They are to be 'milked' continuously with as little investment as possible, since such investment would be wasted in an industry with low growth.
- *Dogs*, more charitably called *pets*, are units with low market share in a mature, slow-growing industry. These units typically 'break even,' generating barely enough cash to maintain the business's market share. Though owning a break-even unit provides the social benefit of providing jobs and possible synergies that assist other business units, from an accounting point of view such a unit is worthless as it is not generating cash for the company. They depress a profitable company's return on assets ratio, used by many investors to judge how well a company is being managed. Dogs, it is thought, should be sold off.
- *Question marks* (also known as *problem children*) are businesses operating in a high market growth, but having a low market share. They are a starting point for most businesses. Question marks have a potential to gain market share and become stars, and eventually cash cows when market growth slows. If question marks do not succeed in becoming a market leader, then after perhaps years of cash consumption they will degenerate into dogs when market growth declines. Question marks must be analyzed carefully in order to determine whether they are worth the investment required to grow market share.
- *Stars* are units with a high market share in a fast-growing industry. They are graduated question marks with a market or niche leading trajectory, for example: amongst market share front runners in a high growth sector, and/or having a monopolistic or increasingly dominant USP with burgeoning /fortuitous proposition drive(s) from: novelty, fashion/promotion, customer loyalty, goodwill and so on. The hope is that stars will become the next cash cows. Stars require high funding to fight competitions and maintain a growth rate. When industry growth slows, if they remain a niche leader or are amongst market leaders and have been able to maintain their category of leadership stars, then they become cash cows, otherwise they become dogs due to low relative market share.

As a particular industry matures and its growth slows, all business units become either *cash cows* or *dogs*. The natural cycle for most business units is that they start as *question marks*, then turn into *stars*. Eventually the market stops growing thus the business unit becomes a *cash cow*. At the end of the cycle, the *cash cow* turns into a *dog*.

As BCG stated in 1970:

Only a diversified company with a balanced portfolio can use its strengths to truly capitalize on its growth opportunities. The balanced portfolio has:
- stars whose high share and high growth assure the future;
- cash cows that supply funds for that future growth; and
- question marks to be converted into stars with the added funds."

In any organization, there are individuals who are introverts and others who are extroverts. The following characteristics of psychological types (see Table 4.1) were developed by C. G. Jung (Jung 1971).

Leaders must select the correct person for each different portfolio position from these eight types. In doing so, we must also consider the progress that each person has made on developing their internal growth as previously described. The effort necessary to do this is easily offset by the increased quality of the personal decisions which result.

Even in a modern and democratic society many structures and processes remain inspired by the military. Many individuals are promoted as visionaries after the business they manage demonstrates success, without ever considering how this success has been generated. Even though leadership style is taken into account, evaluators often rated others based upon their own style which does not necessarily fit with modern practices. The end result is that success and high performance are too often justifying bad habits! To ensure a sustainable organization, we must distinguish between technical and substantive expertise, the "rank" and "level." The rank is the hierarchical position in the organization and the level refers to Dürckheim's concept of individual maturity, be it in accordance with Jung's individuation, Christian character or spiritual maturity. Promotions must result in accordance with competence, the rank, *and* the level of maturity of the individual.

The higher we climb in rank and the older we get, hopefully the greater the progression of our maturation, especially from mid-life onward. The highest rank is the Chairman of the Board who ideally will have the highest level, the greatest maturity. If that is the case, the Chairman will hire people with high levels of

Table 4.1: Characteristics of psychological types by C. G. Jung.

Function/type	Extrovert	Introvert
Thinking Type	Objective, Productive	Creative, Critical, Unrealistic
Feeling Type	Sociable, Adapted, Conventional	Silent, Inaccessable, Profound
Sensation Type	Realistic, Uncritical, Pleasure oriented	Closed, Passive
Intuition Type	Speculative, Inspiring	Visionary, Artistic

wisdom and maturity for the Executive Board. The Executive Board members will then fill leading positions with people who are "essential," with highly developed inner growth. Of course it is difficult at present to hire sufficient numbers of spiritual and individuated people who can also manage. But it's enough if those who lead can win the hearts of the people by being congruent and empathic, with a high degree of authenticity, perhaps simply because they follow Christian principles and deal with others compassionately. Or perhaps they just manage with soul! Employees who are set upon a path of maturation during their professional career will change slowly but steadily. It is a top management task and responsibility to facilitate this growth.

4.8 Wise Leaders

The recent collapse of the global financial system is evidence of the lack of wise leadership. With major institutions failing and market leaders filing for bankruptcy, the need for mature leadership has never been greater, and never have we had greater reason to be disappointed. Failure on the part of CEOs cannot be blamed entirely upon uncertainty in the global market place. The prevalence of selfish attitudes which is presently endemic at every level of the workforce predictably leads to unethical and who can lead us out of this dead end approach are in desperately short supply.

Nonaka and Takeuchi published an interesting paper about a wise leader from their point of view (Nonaka and Takeuchi 2011, p. 2):

> It isn't uncertainty alone that has paralyzed CEOs today. Many find it difficult to reinvent their corporations rapidly enough to cope with new technologies, demographic shifts, and consumption trends. ... Above all, leaders find it tough to ensure that their people adhere to values and ethics. The prevailing principle in Business seems to be, "What's in it for me?" ... The purpose of business, executives still believe, is business, and greed is good as long as the SEC doesn't find out.

There's a philosophical tendency in the West, following Plato, to conclude that if a theory isn't working, there must be something wrong with reality. People behave less ethically when they are a part of organizations. As Bent Flyvbjerg (Flyvberg 2001) pointed out, instead of trying to emulate the natural sciences we must ensure that management asks questions such as: "Where are we going? Who gains, who loses, and by which mechanisms of power? Is this development desirable? What should we do about it?"

Wise leadership recognizes that knowledge is more critical than ever before, and realizes that unless companies create social as well as economic value they will fail. Several decades of studies clearly indicate that CEOs must, through the integration of lessons learned through personal experiences, acquire the practical wisdom that leads them toward prudent, moral decisions.

From knowledge to wisdom:

Nonaka and Takeuchi (2011, p. 4):

> The origin of practical wisdom lies in the concept of phronesis, one of the three forms of knowledge identified by Aristotle ... Practical wisdom ... is experiential knowledge that enables people to make ethically sound judgments. ...They (the companies) would do better to pursue the common good, not because it's right or fashionable, but because it will ensure their sustainability. ...
>
> **The six abilities of wise leaders:**
> 1. *Wise Leaders can judge Goodness* ....Without a foundation of personal values executives can't decide what is good or bad ... Eiji Toyoda, Toyota's former president, always said, 'Do what you believe is right. Do what you believe is good. Doing the right things, when required, " The origin of practical wisdom..." to " which is why they must turn the dual quest for knowledge and practical wisdom into a way of life." is a calling from on high ....' At Honda, the question most frequently asked is "What do *you* think?" It encourages employees to reflect deeply about their *own* values in relation to those of Honda and society. Tadashi Yanai, the CEO of Fast Retailing which owns Japan's fastest growing apparel brand Uniqlo, states: "Not only does a company have to live in harmony with society, but to be accepted, it must contribute to society (pp. 6–7) ... Managers must make judgments for the common good", not exclusively for profits or competitive advantage. Thinking only about the company will ultimately result in failure."
> 2. *Wise leaders Can Grasp the Essence.* (p. 7): Before making judgment calls, wise leaders project a vision of the future" and decide upon the action needed to realize that vision ... It is also important that leaders grasp universal truth from the particular and the details. This requires continual interaction between subjective intuition and objective knowledge ... It involves recognizing that employees who interact directly with customers are frequently better equipped to determine the particulars of the goods or services to be provided, than is someone in headquarters.
> 3. *Wise Leaders Create Shared Contexts.* Phronetic leaders constantly create opportunities for senior executives and employees to learn from one another. This may involve the dissemi-nation of information through the building of short-term relationships which encourage new perspectives, and/or facilitating intense interactions between colleagues with a shared sense of purpose, so that participants may better understand their relationship with others through an interpersonal understanding of their views and values. It is like a "shared context in motion," with participants coming and going, relationships changing, and contexts shifting over time.
> 4. *Wise Leaders Communicate the Essence.* Phronetic leaders are able to communicate in a way that everyone can understand. The essence of a situation is often difficult to express, so they must use stories, metaphors and other figurative language. This allows for individuals groun-ded in different contexts and with different experiences to grasp things intuitively ... (CEO) Tadashi Yanai's favorite is: "In baseball, teams with a large number of stolen bases have a high number of attempted steals. You can't run if you're thinking only about not being tagged. The same could be said of management." ... At Mitsui, storytelling became an important part of the review process under Utsuda. In 2002, he changed the corporate performance criteria, putting much more emphasis on qualitative results than quantitative ones. The process for achieving results thus became more important than revenues or profits.

5. *Wise Leaders Exercise Political Power.* Phronetic leaders must bring people together and spur them to act, combining and synthesizing everyone's knowledge and efforts in the single-minded pursuit of their goal .... Wise leaders exercise political judgment by understanding the viewpoints and emotions of others, gleaned through everyday verbal and nonverbal communication. They carefully consider timing, such as when to make a move or to discuss issues. ... Phronetic leaders also strive to understand all the contradictions in human nature – good and bad, civility and incivility, optimism and pessimism, diligence and laziness – and synthesize them as they arise ... they engage in dialectical thinking, which enables them to deal with contradictions, opposites, and paradoxes by moving to a higher level. By thinking in terms of "both and" rather than "either or." Phronetic leaders can make the decision best suited to a situation without losing sight of the goodness to be achieved.

6. *Wise Leaders Foster Practical Wisdom in Others.* Practical wisdom ... must be distributed as much as possible throughout the organization ... Employees at all levels can be trained in its use. Fostering distributed leadership is therefore one of the wise leader's greatest responsibilities ... People can often learn about practical wisdom by observing an exemplar's behavior. At Honda the company's founder is still the dominant exemplar. Takeo Fukui, a former company president, told us, "It is important for Honda to create many Soichiro Hondas." That doesn't mean Honda workers should imitate the founder; the situations they face are often different from those he faced when he was alive. Rather, it means that when a judgment call is necessary, a worker should ask himself or herself: "If I were Soichiro Honda, what would I do?

Today's knowledge-creating company ... must metamorphose into the wisdom-practicing company of tomorrow. That demands a new kind of leader – a CEO who is many things at the same time. Including:
- a philosopher who grasps the essence of a problem and draws general conclusions from random observations;
- a master craftsman who understands the key issues of the moment and acts on them immediately;
- an idealist who will do what he or she believes is right and good for the company and society;
- a politician who can spur people to action;
- a novelist who uses metaphors, stories, and rhetoric;
- a teacher with good values and strong principles, from whom others want to learn.

... Companies have to create new futures in order to survive. Those futures can no longer be extensions of the past; they must be leaps of faith into tomorrow. CEOs cannot be content to analyze situations using empirical data and deductive reasoning; they must also make inductive jumps according to their ideals and dreams. If they aren't idealistic, they simply can't create new futures. Being idealistic isn't enough, though. Leaders must also be pragmatic – looking reality in the eye, grasping the essence of a situation and envisioning how it relates to the larger context ... CEOs have to become idealistic pragmatists, which is why they must turn the dual quest for knowledge and practical wisdom into a way of life."

One need not look to Japan to find wise and moral managers. You can find a few, along with the undeveloped and immoral ones, everywhere.

Among board members and executives there is of course always competition for better results and greater recognition by the supervisory board. A manager even operating at a low "level" with intense ego-centered dynamics can still generate good short-term results utilizing suspicious, questionable methods. While this occurs, in today's climate it is not long until the imposter is detected. The manager at a higher "level," with substantial inner growth will always win in the long run. By his tolerance and serenity, he has an advantage over his lower-level competitors. Today quarterly results and one-year results are important, but increasingly, however, the question of *how* these results were achieved *and was it in a sustainable fashion* must more and more be the focus of evaluation. The promotion of immature managers of low levels to high ranks has catastrophic consequences. One of the catastrophic consequences is that immature managers lose their employees. Many leave the company and others stay with "inner resignation."

This is not necessarily an impetus to find new employment, rather just a resignation that if we keep our head down and put in our hours we will hopefully remain un-noticed and un-hassled each day. Because when we "shut down" internally, we are keen not to draw attention to ourselves, we become largely invisible. We cancel the "psychological contract," the unspoken expectations, hopes and wishes that a healthy employee/employer relationship includes. Colleagues and supervisors often do not notice what is going on.

Ralf Brinkmann (Brinkmann 2008), a Heidelberg Economic and Industrial psychologist who teaches at the University of Applied Sciences, the phenomenon of internal termination and states:"

> Internally dismissed persons no longer have any interest in arguments with supervisors and colleagues. They are no longer ready, even against the majority, to express their opinion. They do not contribute any new ideas, suggestions or criticisms.

What causes this distancing between employees and their company? What is meant by "inner resignation?" Psychologists define it as the decision of an employee to "shut down" dedication and commitment to the company. The psychologist Ralf Brinkmann (Brinkmann and Stapf 2005) considered several factors that contribute to this "mental resignation":

–   Bad leadership style

Needs are ignored, proposals and ideas are not taken seriously or rejected and the work of the employees is not valued.

–   A Culture of Distrust – a lot of control and little freedom of choice

Employees are assumed from the outset to be lazy and need to be given guidance and objectives in order to do their job. This is enforced with arbitrary and excessive control.

–   Expectations are illusionary

There are few or no opportunities to be promoted, or worse, individuals are ignored during promotions. Employees are poorly paid and undervalued.

–   There is no sense to the work

All work has a deeper meaning. It is tremendously important to see meaning in our work.

–   Attachment to the company is missing

When there is no motivation to introduce our own ideas into the company, valuable innovations are lost.

–   Mobbing at work

"Ganging up" on a colleague can be exercised by colleagues or initiated and condoned by a supervisor. The person affected has the feeling that he has been "internally terminated" from the outside.

–   Distancing ourselves from our work: "I only work to earn money."

Work should be fun. But many of us fail to "find the fun" in our employment. We work to earn money. Work becomes a necessary evil. This is especially the case in those companies that do not value and promote a work/life balance. When we are affected in this way, we resign ourselves to our work and focus our lives only upon our free time and family life.

–   Organizational changes

We often feel threatened when our familiar work and organizational structure is altered.

–   Transition to retirement

Many workers emotionally abandon their employment long before they actually retire. They remain in the company but have given up. As far as continuing to contribute to any "team effort," they are already retired.

The description of organization and structure would be incomplete if the adoption of a New Ethic was only demanded of managers. The current behavior of employees must also be critically examined. In *Süddeutsche Zeitung* (a South German Newspaper), it was reported on May 17, 2010:

> The relationship between workers and their company has long been unsatisfactory in Germany ... Market researchers wanted to know about the workers, whether they regularly hear praise, feel encouraged to express their views, bring in new ideas or consider their place of employment to be a good friend. The devastating statistic is that only thirteen percent of German employees feel a genuine commitment to their businesses and are dedicated to their work. Twenty percent have already inwardly resigned. They have no further expectation of satisfaction. The remaining are only slightly emotionally tied to their company. They generally simply punch in on the time clock and punch out exactly at quitting time. No commitment. Even worse, the trend in Germany unequivocally shows that the situation is deteriorating. When market researchers surveyed German workers in 2001, sixteen percent had a strong emotional bond to their work, with only fifteen percent having inwardly resigned themselves to the drudgery of their job. World – wide this places Germany a little lower than average in terms of dedicated employees. The leader is India with forty-four percent of the work force being very dedicated, and in the United States around twenty-nine percent.

When will we finally realize that employees are a company's most important resource? The status of an enterprise can be easily determined by listening to how employees speak about their own companies. Wolfgang Berger (Berger 2013) astutely stated that the hardest reality in a company are not the figures on the balance sheet indicating profit and loss, not fixed assets, licenses and patents or market share, but the hardest reality is what the employees think and say about "their own" companies.

4.9 Integration of the Dark Side in Organizations

Under the Old Ethic, management "ordered" employees to be "good." Under the New Ethic, it is recognized that the *dark side* must *not* be isolated and shunned, but rather must be integrated and controlled. We cannot perform well without the enormous energies of the dark side in the economic process. One does not hear this stated in discussions of the economy, but from the point of view of Depth Psychology it makes perfect sense. It's perfectly fine that young people continue, even into their mid-life, with the development of their ego consciousness. These ego-centered, knowledge- and performance-oriented, eager for recognition, success, greed and material wealth young adults are driving the economic process, keeping it going. The attributes previously cited by John Steinbeck – evil cunning, greed, deceit, meanness, egotism and selfishness – are specifically intended to damage others, and therefore cannot be accepted as an engine for the economy. Other properties which are a necessary consequence of the gradual maturation of the individual do not necessarily harm their fellow human beings. These driving forces are not *a priori* bad. This is the standard for the determination of which personal attributes are acceptable in the economy.

The ethicist Peter Knauer wisely observed:

> *"Bad is only bad when it damages others."*

Or as Jung stated:

> *"To be only good is bad!"*

The recognition here is that when we suppress and repress the "not good," it has a way of emerging suddenly and unexpectedly from the shadows.

What *is* essential is that there are supervisors who limit the bad habits expressed by the ego of the younger employees. If this occurs in a top down fashion, there will be a limitation imposed upon those egocentric behaviors which are detrimental to the enterprise and to society at large. It is the responsibility of the managers at the higher tiers to let the good and the evil, the light and shadow of the employees to unfold in a way that is to the benefit, and not to the detriment of the environment, the company, the employees themselves or any other stakeholders. My experience has taught me that it is essential that we first must be aware of *our own* Dark Brother and have learned how best to handle him. We must be able to detect when the dark brother wants to take over as the director and never agree to his enticements to do so.

4.10 Strategies: Mergers and Acquisitions, Divestitures and Investments

John Maurice Clark wrote in his famous dissertation almost 100 years ago:

> The modern prayer is not so much for strength as for wisdom. In the economic world this issue is presented more clearly perhaps than anywhere else. We have inherited an economics of irresponsibility. We are in an economy of control with which our intellectual inheritance fits but awkwardly. To make control really tolerable we need something more; something which is still in its infancy. We need an economics of responsibility, developed and embodied in our working business ethic.

Unbelievably this is still true today. Wisdom is sadly lacking in our economic decisions. We are still in urgent need of an economics of responsibility, developed and embodied in our working business ethic. Wherever and whenever you read the daily newspaper, the results of an economics of irresponsibility remains the focus of the media. The authors of the book *The Power of Ethics,* Pete Geissler and Bill O'Rourke (Geissler and O'Rourke 2015) hold both optimistic and pessimistic positions: they are optimistic in that they see considerable interest and renewed vigor in teaching ethical behavior in our business and professional colleges, and pessimistic in that they do not see our popular media either willing or able to change from reporting unethical behavior to reporting ethical behavior.

Under the heading *Raw material corporations are Destroyer of Cash,* the *FAZ* (*Frankfurter Allgemeine Zeitung*) on 6th March 2015 reported that 90% of mergers and acquisitions failed:

> The world champions in the take-over business have largely failed: The five largest raw material companies have depreciated around 90% of all their multi-billion dollar acquisitions and take overs since 2007. Thus has been destroyed ... through wrong decisions of their boards, a capital worth a total of around 85 billion dollars (investigated by Citibank).

As decisions around these actions have a major impact on companies, they must not be born out of the egocentrism of individual Board members, but rather be decided upon and implemented in accordance with the new ethic, with an important criteria being whether they are value enhancing and life enhancing. It is foolish to blindly follow the proposals of management consultants and investment bankers whose primary interest is their *own* bottom line. Investments can fail, and by then the "experts" are long gone. Fifty percent of acquisitions and mergers fail to pay dividends. It is a very risky adventure. When they fail many people suffer. Examples are rampant, world-wide.

Too often companies invest in businesses which are not in alignment with the purpose and competence of the investing company. Mergers too often result in new organizations which do not honor the ongoing transactions, promises and bonuses previously agreed upon. Morality is adversely affected by greed for greater profits. Considerable expertise and inner maturity is necessary to decide upon whether to accept or reject what other "experts" propose. Examples in the markets are numerous.

Employees and taxpayers are too often the ones who ultimately pay the price for irresponsible corporate decisions.

On occasion a decision is made to sell off certain responsibilities of which a company wishes to divest itself. In this case, some of the business and the employees attached to the transferred business will become the responsibility of the new owner. The selection of a purchaser must be very carefully done, with the interests of the employees always considered. The responsibility must remain, at least until a state of stabilization is created under the new owners, with the original company. There is an opportunity here for consideration of the new ethic in a forward looking fashion.

Splitting's and divestitures of assets lead to a loss of identity within the workforce. If promises are broken, there is the unfortunate opportunity for a lot of previous good will to be lost and considerable damage to be done. Management can lose a positive reputation which it may have taken years to develop. Trust can be lost. The motivation of the remaining employees can plummet as they begin to fear that they too may be sold off without regard for advances established and promises made.

Here is a prime example. In 1993, financial analysts proposed to the Board of ICI that the company should divide ICI into the pharmaceutical company Zeneca and the chemical company ICI. The rational was that the value of ICI would increase after the division. The board complied and Zeneca went on a growth path with a high rating, while ICI was sold in increments to financial investors. I asked a colleague who worked for ICI what he thought of the decision to split the company. "I am no longer loyal to my company, I am only loyal to my contract." His identity with the company and subsequently his motivation were lost, replaced simply by a contract. He has been reduced, in Ernst Jünger's vocabulary, to a "fellah." We can presently observe a similar situation occurring in many companies. Deciding upon ethical actions in cases such as these is difficult.

Individual sectors of a company are often sold off for too low a price because they are no longer considered core business, and have become a diversion of which the company wishes to divest itself. The selling company and its stakeholders are harmed by not demanding and receiving a fair return for the sale. The sectors sold to a financial investor are then promoted and perhaps turned into a core enterprise, which expands and prospers on the stock market, rewarding the new investors and stakeholders, or the financial investor sells it off at a profit without consideration for the employees and stakeholders and then disappears.

Following are a few other cases that demonstrate a lack of responsibility. In the German energy sector, we can currently observe how large depreciations of unsuccessful acquisitions, or in some cases lack of sufficient revenues from the sale of businesses, are reducing their market value dramatically. The all-time high market value of EON AG of roughly € 130 billion has been reduced to € 30 billion. The market value of Evonik (previously the chemical part of EON) is €15 billion and that of Brenntag AG (a subsidiary of Stinnes AG and the Chemical Distribution part) is €8.6 billion. These two divestitures are now close to the value of the company which spun off these activities. If you add the total value of all activities sold off, it is far above EON's value. The political decision on a change of energy production in Germany of course had an influence, but it is not the only reason by far. With its focus on its core energy business, EON realized far too late that the existing business model is no longer valid. Decentralized units and higher production of green electricity will be the future. Thousands of employees are to be dismissed. On December 1, 2014, EON announced its focus on green energy and the spin-off of nuclear, coal and gas power plants.

RWE, a pure energy company, following the advice of consultants and analysts, acquired waste disposal and water companies to diversify like VEBA – now EON. It was a disaster because there was no fit with the existing business. They paid too high a price and received in return low performance. Ultimately, they sold the acquisitions and wrote off the costs of this misadventure. Now their reserves are gone.

FAZ dated July 9, 2015 reports on the failures of EON/RWE and Microsoft: *The Caprioles of the Energy-loser.* "The two energy companies EON and RWE simplify the situation when trying to explain their decline as a result of energy transition and the nuclear phase out. The cause was a result of a mixture of management failure and hubris." Microsoft explains the Nokia acquisition fiasco: "Microsoft paid 9.4 billion dollars for Nokia and has now written off 7.6 billion dollars. 7800 employees will be dismissed ...."

In both cases, great damage has been done. Even if we take into account that the companies have followed all the laws, the question we have to ask is whether in these and similar examples the executives and the supervisory boards acted morally and ethically. The most forgiving answer would be that their actions were "within the law," but morally and ethically indefensible.

The public that is following the results of these actions upon the economy is concerned about the irresponsibility and incompetence of the executives, along with the callous approvals of the supervisory boards. One CEO is on the acquisition track ... applause! Afterward another one is on the track for divestitures and concentration on the core business ... applause! The investment bankers, the consultants and the executives involved have earned a lot of money, but no one is holding them liable for their decisions. Of course, all of these companies have no shortage of written ethical guidelines!

4.11 Taxation of International Groups

It has become common to transfer income from subsidiaries into a holding company in a country where taxes are low, such as Luxembourg or Ireland. Taxes on income are then not paid in the country in which the production and sales were made. This results in a significant loss of revenue for that country. Even if the entire procedure is lawful under the taxation legislation, if the criteria of the new ethic is applied, this procedure is immoral. It may be permissible under existing guidelines, but it is never "ethically acceptable."

Especially when considering ethics in business, it is of importance to distinguish between "permissible" and "ethically acceptable." Peter Knauer's example bears repeating.

> He who does not steal in a self-service store because he is afraid of being caught is in a sense "ethically right" in that one cannot accuse him of a bad action. However, his action is far from being "good". It would only be good if he would not only *de facto*, but also *in principle* not steal, even if there would be no risk of being caught.

Business ethics expert Prof. Bernd Irlenbush comments (FAZ November 22nd 2014):

> The social consensus seems to have shifted. Milton Friedman's statement that the only duty of companies is to maximize their profits within the law is no longer fully accepted. It is expected that companies act responsibly and pay taxes in the jurisdiction where they make use of the infrastructure and have their customers. Again, I see elements of "moral licensing", both Starbucks and Ikea launched comprehensive corporate responsibility programs.

4.12 Sustainable Supply Chain Responsibility

The flow of raw materials, products and services into a company is called a supply chain. A single company can influence the entire supply chain. Modern supply chains and value chains are highly complex and interconnected, and will become even more so with the ever-expanding globalization of the marketplace. The supply chain is like an octopus with tentacles which can extend over the entire world. The conditions of production undertaken by the suppliers along with the entire chain leading back to the factory needs to be guided by the New Ethic. All parties must be on board. When companies are guided by ethical practices concerning sustainability and personnel, the opportunity to get the suppliers into the sustainability boat as well is greatly enhanced. The power within these chains is vested in the largest players, especially the ones who dominate certain industries, materials or applications.

This power brings with it an increased responsibility for these companies and their management. We are frequently reminded of this when scandals around supply sources are exposed by the main stream media. An example is the company KIK, a low-cost apparel retailer, which was recently publicly accused of neglecting to establish and ensure responsible safety and working conditions for some of their suppliers, resulting in accidents which included many casualties. KIK attempted the defense that they did not even know the company in which the accidents occurred. They were just a sub-contractor of a sub-contractor. This is a common excuse when unsustainable and unethical behavior is exposed, but it is evident from the reaction of the public and the media that this flawed argument is no longer going to be accepted. Tim Cook, CEO of Apple Inc., stated: "We don't let anyone cut corners on safety. If there is a production process that can be made safer, we seek out the foremost authorities in the world, then cut in a new standard and apply it to the entire supply chain."

According to the New Ethic, it is required and expected that companies, especially the dominant ones, take proactive responsibility for their supply chains in a holistic sense. They are obliged to enforce transparency and tackle unethical, unsustainable and unsafe conditions head on, in an open and honest manner. Business models can no longer be built upon the exploitation of human and natural resources which do not ensure the delicate balance necessary for sustainability. The unsustainable approach, as the word itself implies, will eliminate itself much more quickly than was previously the case. This is the result of the global transparency which results from the internet and other modern technologies. Ethical leaders will expand their organizations from within, powered by people who will not tolerate unsustainable, hence unethical practices.

What does the Ethical Corporation community have to say about this? Liam Dowd spokesperson for the Ethical Corporation presented the following summary on July 20, 2015:

> *Top global supply chain sustainability trends.* Following are some trends and opportunities as identified by four hundred and fifteen members of the Ethical Corporation community. As part of the build up to the 10th Annual Sustainable Supply Chain Summit, we wanted to gauge the top trends and issues, both those which are current and looking forward into 2016. We reached out to our global community to get an understanding of the global patterns, and here are some of our key findings:
>
> 1. *Eliminating supply chain risks is the main driver:* Over 32% of executives polled said their incentive lies in eliminating supply chain risks.
> 2. *Industry collaboration is the biggest opportunity in 2015/2016:* Just over 24% of respondents stated that industry collaboration is the single most exciting opportunity in relation to supply chains' sustainability. The second most exciting is creating a circular economy and third is customer/consumer awareness, at 16% and 11% respectively.
> 3. *Traceability and environmental concerns are the biggest issues to watch out for in 2015/2016:* Nearly 30% of the community stated that traceability and environmental improvements will be key issues in the coming years.
>
> When breaking the responses down by regions, the primary issues differ. European respondents favored traceability, North Americans preferred eliminating dependency on unsustainable raw materials and Asian Pacific respondents focused upon environmental concerns. The Ethical Corporation helps businesses around the globe do the right thing for their customers and the world. They believe this is not only how to guarantee a future for all, but that it also makes good business sense. They serve CSR, compliance, risk and governance communities with topical and insightful business intelligence and meeting places. They provide business intelligence to more than three thousand multinational companies every year. The customers are also NGOs, think tanks, academia, governments and consultancies.

4.13 Sustainable Customer Bonding

H.E. Richter's earlier statement may be modified to state: "Only the company which is itself in ethical balance can properly handle caring for its customers."

Marketers and sellers who follow Steinbeck's vision of kindness, generosity, openness, honesty, understanding and empathy are extremely successful in the marketplace, as evidenced by numerous satisfied customers. A corporate effort to focus upon the customers, enhancing their experience by "making their lives livelier," is the royal road to business success, ensuring that customers will remain loyal and be reluctant to switch to a new vendor for whom the New Ethic is a foreign concept. The secret of many successfully innovative companies is maintaining their proximity to customers. Marketing being my expertise, I must say that the digital world destroys client relationships. Portals rely increasingly on customer interface. Established value chains are destroyed. It's all about saving costs in the name of "efficiency" in order to make greater profits at the expense of customer loyalty. That's very destructive to customer relations.

4.14 Sustainable Competitor Relations

We do not have to love our competitors, but neither should we be antagonistic toward them. Without competition our development is stymied. Competition is the engine driving innovative improvements. It is far better and more productive to reflect upon our own strengths than dispersing our efforts by trying to weaken the competition. The manner in which we treat our competitors is always a test for how well we are applying practices endorsed by the new ethic.

4.15 Ethical Consumerism

A discussion of SCR would be incomplete without addressing the importance of the attitude of consumers. They are part of the economy and a book about Business Ethics would not be complete without the framework of Ethical Consumerism. A moral consumer will have an influence on the morality of suppliers and an immoral consumer will support the immorality of suppliers.

Ethical consumerism, alternatively called *ethical consumption, ethical purchasing, moral purchasing, ethical sourcing, ethical shopping or green consumerism,* is a type of consumer activism that is based upon the concept of "dollar voting." It is practiced through "positive buying" or a "moral boycott" when ethical products are favored.

> "The term 'ethical consumer', now used generically, was first popularized by the UK magazine the *Ethical Consumer*, first published in 1989. *Ethical Consumer* magazine's key innovation was to produce 'ratings tables', inspired by the criteria-based approach of the then emerging

ethical investment movement. Ethical Consumer's ratings tables initially awarded companies negative marks (and from 2005 overall scores) across a range of ethical and environmental categories such as... 'animal rights', 'human rights' and 'pollution and toxins', empowering consumers to make ethically informed consumption choices and providing campaigners with reliable information on corporate behavior. Such criteria-based "The term 'ethical consumer', now used generically, was first.... This change reflects an increasing awareness of ethical issues and corporate identity amongst mainstream consumers." (Adapted from Wikipedia)" ethical and environmental ratings have subsequently become commonplace both in providing consumer information and in business-to- business corporate social responsibility and sustainability ratings, such as those provided by Innovest, Calvert, Domini, IRRC, TIAA-CREF and KLD Analytics. Today, Bloomberg and Reuters even provide 'environmental, social and governance' ratings direct to the financial data screens of hundreds of thousands of stock market traders. The not-for-profit Ethical Consumer Research Association continues to publish *Ethical Consumer* magazine and its associated website which provides free access to ethical rating tables.

In *The Global Markets as an Ethical System*, John McMurtry argues that no purchasing decision exists that does not itself imply some moral choice, and that there is no purchasing that is not ultimately moral in nature (McMurthy 1998). The central study by McMurtry, entitled *What is Good, What is Bad? The Value of All Values Across Time, Place and Theories*, is an encompassing in-depth critical study of known world philosophies and disciplines to explain the inner logic of each canon and school in relationship to world problems across languages and eras, including the method of life value onto axiology which is deployed to excavate, explain and resolve life-blind presuppositions of the world's major thought systems, from the ancient East and West to modern and contemporary philosophy.

Some trust criteria, for example credit worthiness or implied warranty, are considered to be part of any purchasing or sourcing decision. However, these terms refer to broader systems of guidance that would, ideally, cause any purchasing decision to disqualify offered products or services based on non-price criteria that affect the moral rather than the functional liabilities of the entire production process. ... Often moral criteria are part of a much broader shift away from commodity markets towards a deeper service economy where all activities, from growing to harvesting to processing and delivery, are considered part of a value chain for which consumers are 'responsible'. In an effort by churches to advocate moral and ethical consumerism, many have become involved in the Fair Trade Movement.

As large corporations have tried to position themselves as moral, principled or ethical organizations, the definition of ethical consumerism has become wider and has come to mean different things to different groups of people. For example, McDonald's started to sell salads which are considered a health-conscious choice, and has a corporate social responsibility blog. Ethical Consumerism can be seen as a movement in marketing, which may or may not reflect actual changes in the practices of businesses. Particular areas of interest for large businesses are environmental impact and the treatment of those workers who are at the bottom of the organizational hierarchy. This change reflects an increasing awareness of ethical issues and corporate identity amongst mainstream consumers" (Adapted from Wikipedia).

When considering "moral spending," it is clearly valid to apply all moral attitudes and ethical practices which we demand from the responsible representatives of the economy to consumers as well. There is plenty of guilt to be shared around, especially concerning the absence of personal growth by both sides. "Greed is cool" has for many years been the slogan of the electronics chain Saturn in Germany. This practice has been extended to numerous other manufacturers over time, which focuses upon those consumers whose primary consideration is to buy as cheaply as possible, with no concern for the conditions under which the product was manufactured.

Intelligent adolescents aged 12 to 19 know an amazing amount about ethical problems in the manufacture of clothing; however, that makes very little difference to their purchasing practices. According to a study by Greenpeace, 96% of young people know that the workers in the fashion industry often have to work under inhumane conditions, and that chemicals used in their manufacture are harmful to the environment. But only 13% pay attention to a quality seal such as FAIR TRADE. They simply ignore the problem and choose to buy their fashion ware as cheaply as possible (Amann 2015).

The Dark Side of their behavior is suppressed. They are aware of their irresponsible conduct and feel badly about it when confronted. But it is also the case that many eco labels are unfamiliar, since the known brands promote their goods with tremendously positive advertising campaigns.

4.15.1 Sustainable Ethical Consumerism

There are numerous opportunities to change the world through "ethical purchasing," which involves the selection of products and services produced in a way that minimizes social and/or environmental damage, and avoiding products and services deemed to have a negative impact on society or the environment. The market for ethical products and services includes the following sectors:
- Ethical food and drink
- The green home
- Eco-travel and transport
- Ethical personal products
- Ethical finance
  (See ethicalconsumption.org)

What does Ethical Consumption mean?

Tanja Lewis (Lewis 2012) gives us answers: "During the past couple of decades, the concept of ethical consumption has gained increasing prominence in wealthy capitalist nations around the world, more recently attaining mainstream appeal."

A 2009 issue of *Time* magazine ran with the banner *The rise of the ethical consumer* and featured *The responsibility revolution* article reporting that, in their poll of 1,003 Americans, "nearly 40% said they purchased a product in 2009 because they liked the social or political values of the company that produced it".

As both Littler (Littler 2011) and Humphrey (Humphrey 2011) have noted, however, the term "ethical consumption" does not refer to a clearly defined set of practices but rather has become a convenient umbrella term covering a wide range of concerns from animal welfare, labor standards and human rights to questions of health and well-being and environmental and community sustainability.

Ethical Consumption in practice: The rise of ethical consumption thus connects to a broader popular critique focused on a range of concerns around environmentalism, anti-materialism and unsustainable lifestyles. ... A poll by Global Market Insite (GMI 2005) across 17 countries, including the USA, Australia, Japan, China, India and various European countries, found that 54% of online consumers would be prepared to pay more for organic, environmentally friendly, or Fair Trade products.

What are the politics of consuming ethically?

Such paradoxical practices point to the gap between people's professed values and beliefs and the realities of their everyday life routines and habits... Critics point to the limitations of a politics defined by and through the logics of the market. The UK environmental commentator George Monbiot (2007) has little time for what he sees as the superficial platitudes of ethical consumption which, to his mind, encourages people to continue consuming while simply replacing less "caring" products with others. It raises the question of whether market-driven societies have the ethical capacity to develop a sustainable consumer culture.

Where ethical consumption becomes potentially much more interesting and challenging as a cultural force is not through its ability to challenge market culture but in the questions it poses more broadly around ways of living and the fashioning of new ethical/political realities. As such, I would suggest that our obligation to consume ethically should not be glossed over as a mere marketing ploy or status trend for the progressive middle classes. Instead, it asks to be approached through a broader political frame linked to key questions around the ongoing sustainability of existing social and economic structures in the global North.

Are we actually progressing toward more ethical purchasing and consumption? "The idea is impressive. With ethical consumption, consumers could change the world. But the project has made little progress. Do ethical purchasing practices really make people feel better?" Claudia Langer, founder of an Internet portal for ethical consumption with the poetic name Utopia, once believed that customers could save the planet with their choice of purchases, but her frequent and direct observations of blatantly selfish, thoughtless and unethical purchasing have resulted in her reluctantly admitting that we are losing the battle. (Amann 2015)

4.16 Sustainable Environmental Responsibility

For HH The Dalai Lama, true religion embraces *transcendence – a recognition* of the wholeness and the perfection of all of creation. He often speaks compassionately about our world; its ecology, the need for sustainability and, sadly, our lack of environmental awareness. Compassion refers not only to our fellow human beings but encompasses our responsibility to all of creation. In the rapid pace of modern life, including our rush to employ technological advances regardless of the consequences, we have lost our connection to nature with the resulting loss not only of a major source of joy in our lives but also of our future livelihood.

Hans-Peter Dürr, as previously discussed, not only understood this transcendence but also experienced it though revelations resulting from a study of quantum physics. In conversations with him I always recognized his deep understanding of love as the source of the universe. His commitment to the Pugwash Group and his stand against nuclear power and nuclear weapons was an indication of his love of humanity, and of his tireless efforts to promote peace and a sustainable environment. Hans-Peter was adamant that anyone engaged in activities which impact the environment has a responsibility to do it no harm. He also considered maintenance of the *status quo* to be insufficient, insisting that our duty is always to improve the environment, leaving it in a better state than it was prior to our intervention.

The following is taken from Wikipedia.

> "Formally known as the *World Commission on Environment and Development* (WCED), the *Brundtland Commission's* mission is to unite countries to pursue sustainable development together. The Chairman of the Commission, Gro Harlem Brundtland, was appointed by Javier Pérez de Cuéllar, former Secretary General of the United Nations, in December 1983. At the time, the UN General Assembly realized that there was a heavy deterioration of the human environment and natural resources. To rally countries to work and pursue sustainable development together, the UN decided to establish the *Brundtland Commission*. Gro Harlem Brundtland was the former Prime Minister of Norway and was chosen due to her strong background in the sciences and public health. The *Brundtland Commission* officially dissolved in December 1987 after releasing *Our Common Future*, also known as the *Brundtland Report*, in October 1987, a document which coined, and defined the meaning of the term 'Sustainable Development'. *Our Common Future* won the University of Louisville Grawemeyer Award in 1991. The Center for Our Common Future organization was started in April 1988 to take the place of the Commission."

Hans-Peter Dürr defined sustainability in terms of its ability to *make living livelier.* The source for this initiative came from his experience of transcendence. If we rely solely upon our ego to decide upon and create environmental guidelines, then morality and ethics as applied to environmental protection will be insufficient to ensure sustainability. Evidence of this is all around us, and is increasing each and every day.

Article 6 of the "Manifesto Global Economic Ethic" (Küng et al. 2010, p. 159) as quoted below is an important and laudable directive.

> Sustainable treatment of the natural environment on the part of all participants in economic life is an uppermost value norm for economic activity. The waste of natural resources and the pollution of the environment must be minimized by resource conserving procedures and by environmentally friendly technologies. Sustainable clean energy (with renewable energy sources as far as possible), clean water, and clean air are elementary conditions for life. Every human being on this planet must have access to them.

The results of recent World Climate Conferences are rather sobering and completely unsatisfactory in their inability to effect results. Countries such as China and India, to name only two, wish to first raise their standard of living to match that of more industrialized nations before committing to any binding climate targets. The production of baby formula in China is an example which illustrates the immoral attitudes and unethical practices which continue.

> The Chinese government disclosed that one of the country's biggest dairy producers had been watering down formula and adding melamine, an industrial compound used in manufacturing plastics and adhesives. Six children died of kidney failure, 53 000 were hospitalized with kidney damage or other illnesses, and an estimated 300 000 were sickened. (USA Today, August 31, 2015)

The recent decisions of the Communist Party Congress in October 2017 are an indication that China *may* be beginning to take environmental issues more seriously.

It is a tragedy that at the same time in the USA that the Trump administration wants to cancel its participation in the *Paris Accord* which promoted increased environmental protection. For Trump, the immediate economic interest of the USA is of greater importance than ensuring that the environment is protected for future generations.

The Climate Change Conference in Bonn in November 2017 has taken some steps toward the implementation of the Paris Climate Agreement. In addition to direct negotiations, voluntary actions were also launched. In the coming year, this will create a workable rulebook for the climate agreement of Paris so that the efforts of all countries can be measured on a uniform scale. However, the text draft for the reduction of greenhouse gases covers 180 pages. The rulebook will be adopted at the upcoming climate conference in Kattowice, Poland. It is difficult to imagine that this conference is going to result in the type or magnitude of changes that are essential and urgent.

In fairness, good examples may also be found. Data illustrates that the ban on fluorochlorinated hydrocarbons which contribute to the depletion of the ozone layer is a success.

Both the Dalai Lama and Hans-Peter Dürr consider sustainable environmental responsibility to include not only the protection of the environment but also its enhancement. Dürr's appeal to help *make living livelier* may be restated as an appeal in relation to the environment to:

Help Nature Remain Natural.

The dual action principle of ethics previously espoused by Knauer applies equally when engaging in the environment. Any intervention has two or more effects that must be considered and weighed. One must be aware of this double effect and create a positive balance. When raw materials are exploited, with the exception of renewable resources, they are irreplaceable. Gentle, minimally intrusive harvesting is a basic requirement. A core consideration must always be whether or not the final products made from the resources are urgently needed for the greater benefit of mankind. Only if they are can an argument be made that their use is justifiable.

Following are some examples.

If one takes salt from the Earth, the harm is minimal because of the abundance of salt. Its use allows for the production of chemical compounds through chloral-kali electrolysis, compounds which are of great value to our society. Therefore this is acceptable. But for a complete environmental review, we must also take the high energy consumption of electrolysis into consideration.

Likewise, if one takes sand from the Earth, the damage is negligible and the advantage is the production of silicon wafers for the electronics industry. This also creates benefits for our society.

If one takes coal, gas and oil from the Earth, the balance between benefit and harm is not quite so simple to calculate. Power generation in coal power plants has come under criticism because of the resulting carbon dioxide emissions and the resulting negative impact on our climate. This technology in industrialized countries is on the decline, but in developing countries there are often very few viable alternate options. As coal power plants fell into disrepute, energy production from oil and gas increased. But gas plants were barely operational in some countries, such as Germany, before they became unprofitable due to advances in the technology allowing for inexpensive electrical generation from solar and wind power. It is difficult to justify the use of oil and gas for power generation. They are better off left unexploited as raw chemical materials for future generations.

The production of energy from nuclear power has long been considered as environmentally friendly and cost effective, but the environmental risks have been purposely underestimated. The Fukushima accident following on the heels of the Chernobyl melt-down changed everything. Environmental risks are now recognized as significant. The cost of treating and/or disposing of the residues resulting from nuclear power production from a variety of sources have received too little attention. Balancing the desire for modern, clean, cost-effective power production with the caveat that it must be sustainable is a formidable challenge.

There are electronic components that can only be produced with rare earth elements, which are in very limited supply. As the deposits continue to decline, the research for replacement must be significantly strengthened. We must also ask whether, on balance, all of the digital electronic components being produced are essential for the benefit of humanity.

4.16.1 The Volkswagen Scandal

Eleven million cars were sold with diesel engines which were unable to meet the legally required values for NO_2 emissions. Eleven million buyers were deceived, and countless millions of others who unknowingly breathe in toxic exhaust gases have been victimized.

With reference to *CSR*, public response has been to call VW's corporate behavior *Corporate Social Irresponsibility*. The concept was to develop a diesel engine which consumes very little diesel fuel, with this low fuel consumption serving as a powerful marketing tool. To market this concept, the resulting pollution was accepted by VW as a consequence, and software was developed and installed which would control and manipulate the emission levels during testing so as to give lower than actual emission values.

After all the evidence is gathered and considered, it is the job of the responsible authorities to pass judgement. Meanwhile, VW is now the large projection screen onto which everyone can project their similar dark activities in order to divert attention away from themselves. Can there be a stronger argument for replacing the old ethical approaches with a New Integral Ethic? Volkswagen, like no other automaker, is intricately intertwined with the German government in an authoritarian union. It is a tightly knit, hierarchical company with aspirations of becoming the largest automaker in the world. Apparently, adhering to moral principles and ethically defensible practices are not as important as fulfillment of sales expectations and greater profits.

In a talk with the Magazine *Cicero* on October 11, 2015 in Berlin about "Power and Morality," the previous German Chancellor Gerhard Schröder and Klaus Engel, ex-CEO of Evonik Industries AG, discussed the Volkswagen scandal. Schröder stressed that the worst part of the exhaust gas scandal was the loss of confidence by customers, shareholders and society at large. VW had committed clear breaches of the law, but the responsibility should not be borne by the "workers on the assembly line." A general "VW bashing" is not appropriate, fair or constructive. Rather, the "top level management team" must assume ultimate responsibility, with responsible lower level managers also bearing their share of the damage claims.

Did only a very few people at VW know of the exhaust emissions test manipulation? A behavioral scientist suspects something quite different. How did such serious, ongoing fraud occur over years in a reputable company such as Volkswagen? These questions are important not only for prosecutors, politicians and VW customers; even researchers are looking for answers. "In the present case many among the staff and in the management must have known of the manipulation," says Bernd Irlenbusch, Professor of Corporate Development and Business Ethics at the University of Cologne. This contradicts the statements of VW CEO Matthias Müller, who, in the FAZ, had stated only a few days after his appointment that, according to current knowledge, only a few employees were involved. If Irlenbusch is correct, all the more urgent is the question of why in the giant company not a single manager has vociferously objected to the fraud imposed upon customers and authorities. Ethnologist Irlenbusch, who through many empirical studies, has examined the moral behavior of people provides for a number of conditions that could have favored the misconduct. It is possible that the employees are advised on a morally "inclined plane," with any one individual not being in possession of all of the facts. There are many small steps along the way which could allow emission levels in the test to appear particularly advantageous. "The problem is that you hardly notice such small steps taken by yourself or others, allowing them to be justified," explains Irlenbusch. "The use of software for manipulating the exhaust emissions is in a way only one small step further."

Volkswagen's "Mr. Clean" image led to moral distortion. In addition, the researchers observed a number of distortions in the organization that could have favored the deception. "VW has itself always been the image of the very clean car manufacturer," says Irlenbusch. What actually appears positive can become a problem. Studies with volunteers have shown that people who are convinced of their moral behavior may justify their occasional misstep more than they would someone else's. Irlenbusch speaks of a "moral license." Even more systematic distortions in moral behavior, "such as conformity, obedience in hierarchies or peer pressure appear to lie in the nature of man," says the economist. Given these findings, failings in organizations cannot be explained solely by reference to individual members.

> Companies and their compliance departments need to work together to find innovative ways with the scientific community so that conditions can be created which reduce such systematic distortion of moral behavior in members of an organization. (An edited extract from Irlenbusch, October 15, 2015, John Pennekamp in the FAZ October 15, 2015)

In October 2015, the media reported that in talks in Brussels the German government attempted to prevent the adoption of stricter limits on pollutant emissions from cars. In a debate on one of the EU Commission's proposals for new limits, the representatives from Germany were subsequently criticized by VW for not pushing for *less* stringent requirements. It was as if the scandal over manipulating emission levels never existed! The other "VW States" with representatives from the Czech Republic and Slovakia reportedly lobbied against the Commission's proposals (FAZ October 13, 2015).

In so far as whether Volkswagen's Executive Board was informed of the manipulation software, in my experiences in similar authoritarian corporate cultures, the Board usually knows everything and controls everything, and the pressure the workforce feels from above can lead to misconduct. What is not allowed is suppressed and repressed into the shadow until the dark potential can no longer hold it. The Dark then ultimately breaks free with everything being exposed. The public is shocked.

The counter current, in accordance with Gaede's earlier explanation, began to take effect in an imperceptible fashion long before the unethical actions manifested. This was a result of the members of the Board and the executives continuing to operate from the level of the mind, rather than elevating their decision making up to the level of REASON. The mind is always responsible for the creation of things that are intended to increase profits. The individual accommodates this by taking refuge in suppression and sometimes even in repression.

At VW, the dark shadow forces seem to express themselves about every ten years. In 1996, Ferdinand Piëch had to dismiss VW's purchasing chief Lopez, whom he had previously lured away from General Motors, in order to settle a deal with them. What had happened?

In early 1993, the industry was awash in rumors that Lopez was interested in joining VW. Ferdinand Piëch, VW group's chairman had noticed Lopez and sent top lieutenant Jens Neumann, then a VW board member, to woo the Spaniard. VW was Europe's sales leader, but it also was the auto maker with the highest costs. Piëch wanted Lopez to rectify that problem. To land him, Piëch promised that VW would build a car plant in the Basque region of Spain, which was a dream of Lopez's. He also promised that VW would install Lopez's Plateau 8 lean production system at its main plant in Wolfsburg, and assemble a new city car that required only seven hours of labor to complete.

Under the Lopez system suppliers were to provide component modules for assembly in the factory and remain responsible for the unit through final quality checks and delivery. The clash pitted two giants, VW and GM, against each other over charges of document theft, corporate espionage and patent infringement. Criminal charges and civil suits were filed in Germany and the United States. Personal and professional relationships were shattered. In 1997, after years of hurling toxic insults and accusations at one another, the exhausted companies agreed to settle their civil suits. The following year, the criminal case in Germany was dropped. A US criminal case has been shelved, but not formally dropped. (Extracted from Diana T. Kurylko & James R. Crate in Automotive News Europe, February 20, 2006)

In 2005, the next scandal broke out of the shadow when the worker's council was bribed with sex parties.

Car giant Volkswagen seems headed for the corporate scrapheap, dragging with it the reputation of the Made in Germany marque beloved around the globe…The world's biggest car maker has been mired in controversy, corruption, sleaze and sex scandals for the past three decades. Industry experts say the 'Wolfsburg Fortress Mentality' – the town where the company has its headquarters – made arrogant bosses feel invincible in the face of competition and regulation….Prostitutes, Viagra fueled sex parties … How latest emissions scandal shows VW has learned nothing from its murky past. (Extracted from the *Daily Mail*, September 24, 2015)

With the present scandal still unravelling in late 2017, the question is whether CEO Matthias Müller can expect to remain. The call for his dismissal is common in such crises. If he knew about the manipulation, the dismissal is justified, and if he did not know about it, then he does not know what was happening in the company, and therefore needs to be fired. In addition, a company requires a CEO as a sacrifice. This is a common, long-running ritual. Müller was dismissed in April 2018. In the lower ranks, some experts who supposedly concocted the whole thing alone will be dismissed as well. Then it's all about limiting the damage and starting anew. VW wishes to give the impression that as an institution it is always ready to take the moral high road, with only a few rogue employees who have acted criminally. The reality is that in every large organization there are many suppressed and repressed dark sides which inevitably result in unethical practices. The challenge is always how to handle that reality. When there is a lack of "wise leadership," then the dark will always find a way to manifest itself.

VW will survive. Sales figures in 2017 are good. As stated in the chapter "Ethical Consumerism," for the consumer "stinginess is awesome." Consumers will continue to buy VWs if they are better and cheaper than other cars, no matter what comes out of the exhaust. The consumer suppresses the misconduct.

Of course, VW has ethical guidelines:

> The Volkswagen Group has always considered itself bound by more than just legal and internal regulations. We also see voluntary commitments and ethical principles as an integral component of our corporate culture, providing a frame of reference we can use to guide our decision making. It is our conviction that sustainable economic success can only be safeguarded by following rules and standards. In our daily business we advocate honorable and honest behavior that complies with the rules. We ensure that rules in our organization are obeyed, and raise awareness among employees through suitable preventive measures and their integration into the existing management system. We are, however, aware that it is not possible to entirely exclude the risk of individual misconduct. We have created a compliance network throughout the Volkswagen Group which brings together the expertise of compliance officers in the brands and companies and of various Group bodies. *Definition of compliance*: Observing statutory provisions, internal company policies and ethical principles. *The Volkswagen Group Code of Conduct*: Lawful action is the basis for sustained economic success. The Volkswagen Group Code of Conduct contains essential basic principles, provides orientation and thereby fosters correct behavior on the part of all employees in their daily work.

Hans Dieter Pötsch, chairman of the Board, has recently confirmed that they have made substantial mistakes. Tremendous damage has resulted from the immoral decisions and unethical practices. A fine of €25.5 billon was accrued for the years 2015–17 of which €17.5 billon has already been paid. Several executives are accused in the USA. One, who was in charge of environmental issues of VW in America, has been sentenced to prison (WAZ December 9, 2017).

As I have experienced in practice many times, ethical guidelines are developed by a consortium of PR consultancies on behalf of the Management Board, and are then approved by the Board, to a certain extent as a PR measure. They are not "intrinsic" to the inner constitution of the Board or to the company and therefore are not "owned" by those to whom they apply.

Obviously it is not only VW which manipulated the data in the automotive industry. Other national and international car makers are similarly accused.

> In 2016, the scandal widened to include incorrect fuel consumption tests by Mitsubishi Motors. The company admitted ... to having used different test methods than those prescribed in Japan for 25 years. ... "Customers bought our vehicles based on false fuel consumption data," said President Tetsuro Aikawa ... "I can't help but apologize." (FAZ April 27, 2016)

Ethical guidelines have not saved VW from disaster. Any institution that requires its employees' unquestioning obedience and performance must assume responsibility for the lack of meaningful, effective moral attitudes and ethical practices. The previously described Milgram experiment clearly illustrated that if a manager asks a subordinate to act in a fraudulent manner, it will be carried out, often with no sense of guilt, especially when other colleagues are also complying. When mindfulness and compassion are missing, inner maturity cannot occur; neither at the personal nor at the institutional level.

What is the way forward? Is it not also likely that there are other products knowingly manufactured, for example in the German chemical industry, with risks exceeding legal limits? One must always be receptive to rapidly emerging new information and realizations. Our entire culture must gradually change to ensure that top managers have already completed, or at least embarked upon, an inner growth process; be it Christian, spiritual or the study of Depth psychology.

4.16.2 The Chemical Industry

My perspective, based upon my 50 years of experience in the Chemical Industry, is that it would be unimaginable that any German chemical company has been operating for any amount of time outside of existing environmental and safety regulations. There are undeniably examples from the more distant past, but the mentality has changed. As it is in the chemical industry that I have spent my career, including as CEO of HÜLS AG and as Past President of the GDCh (Gesellschaft Deutscher Chemiker/ German Chemical Society), it is fitting that as closure to this chapter I comment on sustainable environmental responsibility in this industry.

When I was working in the early 1970s in the Titanium dioxide industry, it was a common occurrence that the waste sulfuric acid from the manufacturing process of titanium dioxide was dumped into the Baltic Sea using special ships. The production manager who was in charge joked onboard the ship: "The fish like it. They swim after the ship and drink it." As this practice was allowed by the authorities, I didn't question whether it was unethical behavior, unacceptable for ethical managers. I had no specific ethical training. The situation changed many years ago. Now the waste acid is recycled, but at greater expense.

For many people, chemistry is still difficult to understand, and therefore frightening. We all need the products produced by this industry, but due to poor communication and accidents which receive global attention, the chemical industry has acquired a bad reputation. Numerous positive innovations have improved our lives but when an unfortunate, dramatic incident occurs, the benefits are temporarily forgotten. In the early 1920s, an explosion destroyed the chemical plant BASF Oppau killing 561 people. Even worse hit were the people in Bhopal/India in 1982, when a pesticide plant belonging to Union Carbide exploded. Thousands died, and many survivors are burdened with life- long health issues. Prior to this human tragedy, Seveso had already shaken up the Chemical Industry in 1976. *Time Magazine* reported:

On July 10, 1976, an explosion at a northern Italian chemical plant released a thick, white cloud of dioxin that quickly settled on the town of Seveso, north of Milan. First, animals began to die, as TIME wrote about a month after the incident. One farmer saw his cat keel over, and when he went to pick up the body, the tail fell off. When authorities dug the cat up for examination two days later, said the farmer, all that was left was its skull. It was four days before people began to feel ill effects – including nausea, blurred vision and, especially among children, the disfiguring sores of a skin disease known as 'chloric acne' – and weeks before the town itself was evacuated. Residents eventually returned to the town, and today a large park sits above two giant tanks that hold the remains of hundreds of slaughtered animals, the destroyed factory and the soil that received the largest doses of dioxin.

Following are further details taken from: (http://www.getipm.com/articles/seveso-italy.htm, by Mick Corliss, staff writer).

A valve broke at the Industrie Chimiche Meda Societa Azionaria chemical plant in Meda near Milan, releasing a cloud of chemicals containing dioxin that wafted an estimated 50 meters into the sky. Carried southeast by the wind, the toxic cloud enshrouded the municipality of Seveso and other communities in the area. About 3,000 kg of chemicals were released into the air, according to some researchers. Among them was 2.4.5 trichlorophenol, used in the manufacture of herbicides, and anywhere from about 100 grams to 20 kg of dioxin. The first sign of health problems, burn-like skin lesions, appeared on children a few hours after the accident. Beginning in September of that year, chloric acne, a severe skin disorder usually associated with dioxin, broke out on some of the people who were most exposed to the cloud. In the first seven years after the accident an incredibly high proportion of females were born to parents who were exposed to the chemical cloud: 46 females compared to only 28 males. Usually, the proportion is roughly equal. This was the first time a chemical had been observed to change the sex ratio," Mocarelli, the chemist in charge of the investigation stated, "There is no other molecule known to induce change in the sex ratio," he said, adding that this implicates dioxin as a hormone disrupter.

Victims of the Seveso accident also reported symptoms of other afflictions – immune system and neurological disorders as well as spontaneous abortions – but studies found no link to dioxin. However, minor increases in some forms of cancer were found in one exposed group, suggesting a possible link between dioxin and cancer.

While *Time* magazine reported that Seveso is one of the severest environmental accidents, it also carried articles about Chernobyl, Kuwaiti Oil Fire, Exxon Valdez, Tokai-mura Nuclear Plant, as well as two others which follow.

4.16.2.1 Minamata Disease

For years residents of Minamata, a town located on Kyushu, Japan's most southwesterly island, had observed odd behavior among animals, particularly household cats. The felines would suddenly convulse and sometimes leap into the sea to their deaths – townspeople referred to the behavior as "cat dancing disease." In 1956, the first human patient of what soon became known as Minamata disease was identified. Symptoms included convulsions, slurred speech, loss of motor functions and uncontrollable limb movements. Three years later, an investigation concluded that the affliction was a result of industrial poisoning of Minamata Bay by the Chisso Corporation, which had long been one of the port town's biggest employers. As a result of waste water pollution by the plastic manufacturer, large amounts of mercury and other heavy metals found their way into the fish and shellfish which comprised a large part of the local diet. Thousands of residents have slowly suffered over the decades and died from the disease. Many never received any compensation from the offending Chisso Corporation.

4.16.2.2 Three Mile Island

"Nuclear Nightmare" screamed the April 9, 1979 cover of *Time* magazine. On 28 March, the Three Mile Island nuclear reactor near Harrisburg, Pa. partially melted down. Coming two weeks after the release of the Jane Fonda film *The China Syndrome*, the Three Mile Island incident became the natural outlet for fears about the nuclear power industry. The ironic thing is that while it has become known as one of America's worst nuclear accidents, nothing much really happened. No one died, and the facility itself is still going strong. While the near melt down is often cited as the reason, no new nuclear plant has been built in America in the past 35 years, the industry had actually begun to slow down construction before Three Mile Island ever happened.

How do we do it better?

In too many instances, production, profit and performance are more important than a consideration of moral responsibility and ethical practices. When one is responsible for a chemical company, the question of whether that also entails responsibility for the chemical products that it produces inevitably arises. As CEO of HÜLS AG, I was faced with the question of the toxicity of nonylphenol. Nonylphenol and similar compounds are used in manufacturing antioxidants, lubricating oil additives, laundry and dish detergents, emulsifiers, and solubilizers. This is a huge market. These compounds are also precursors to the commercially important nonionic surfactants alkylphenol ethoxylates and nonylphenol ethoxylates, which are used in detergents, paints, pesticides, personal care products and plastics.

If octylphenol is produced according to safety standards which take into account the protection of the environment, there is no objection to its production. The effect of this chemical in the environment depends essentially on how it is used. If products made from it allow octylphenol to be released into the environment, then the production and marketing is a problem. The manufacturer of these compounds must then decide who must assume responsibility for the products application. If octylphenol is utilized in the formation of compounds which ultimately preclude octylphenol from entering the environment, the application is acceptable. Nonylphenol and octylphenol belong to the group of alkylphenols, which it has been suggested interfere with the hormonal balance in fish. The chemical structure is responsible for disrupting their endocrine system. The substances bind to an estrogen receptor site in vertebrate hormonal systems, blocking its intended functioning. This receptor, for example, is also activated by 17-beta-estradiol in human birth control pills. In fish, exposure to estrogen-like substances leads to deformities in the sexual organs, negatively influencing their reproductive ability. At higher concentrations, they can also cause growth in male fish to be stunted.

On February 22, 1993, after a chemical accident at Hoechst AG in Frankfurt involving ten tons of chemicals including o-nitroanisole, which is a suspected carcinogen, those of us in the Chemical Industry in Germany realized that all production facilities must operate in a much safer manner. Thus far, the very strict conditions we ultimately adopted indicate that we are on the right track toward taking responsibility to ensure safe, sustainable production. Chemicals are not inherently bad, it is the manner in which man uses them which determines whether they are harmful or beneficial for people, animals and the environment. For example, chlorine which is used as a raw material in the production of countless extremely useful products was also used a hundred years ago as a chemical weapon in the First World War against the French.

Following that inhumane practice, chemists have developed even more efficient chemical weapons.

The responsibility of the Chemical Industry goes far beyond production. Chemists must recognize, through their various organizations, their moral obligation in weapons. EuCheMS (European Chemical Sciences) reported in the September issue:

> 100 years after the first use, on 21 April 2015, ambassadors to the Organization for the Prohibition of Chemical Weapons (OPCW) gathered in Ypres to commemorate those who have died as a result of these awful agents, to present a commemorative plaque to the town of Ypres, to initiate a new declaration on chemical weapons, the Ypres Declaration, and to review progress in eliminating these weapons. Chemists were represented by Thomas Geelhaar (President of the Gesellschaft Deutscher Chemiker/ German Chemical Society), David Phillips (a past President of the Royal Society of Chemistry) and David Cole-Hamilton (President of EuCheMS). They jointly called for a complete world –wide ban on chemical weapons and promoted the policy that no chemist was to take part in their development or deployment.

Along with other chemists, I welcome the adoption of the code of ethics which denounced all chemical weapons. It was declared in September 2015 by the OPCW in The Hague, with substantial support from the German Chemical Society, represented by my dear colleague Professor Dr. Henning Hopf, also a Past President of the German Chemical Society.

4.16.2.3 The Hague Code of Ethics

> "The responsible practice of chemistry improves the quality of life of humankind and the environment. Through their many peaceful uses, such as in research and industry, chemicals play an essential role in this improvement. However, some chemicals can also be used as chemical

weapons, or to create them, and these weapons are among the most horrific in the world. The 1993 Chemical Weapons Convention (CWC) embodies the powerful international norm against chemical weapons, requiring its States Parties "never under any circumstances:
(a) To develop, produce, otherwise acquire, stockpile or retain chemical weapons, or transfer, directly or indirectly, chemical weapons to anyone;
(b) To use chemical weapons;
(c) To engage in any military preparations to use chemical weapons;
(d) To assist, encourage or induce, in any way, anyone to engage in any activity prohibited by a State Party under this Convention."

The task of destroying the world's declared stockpiles of chemical weapons is ongoing, but the threats that the use of chemicals as weapons pose to global security have not yet been eliminated.

As destruction of the remaining chemical weapons continues, a concerted effort is needed to prevent their reemergence. This includes training and raising awareness among chemistry practitioners; defined as anyone trained in chemistry as well as others dealing with or handling chemicals. Their support is needed so that production and use of chemicals are accompanied... by recognition of the responsibility of ensuring that they are applied solely for peaceful and beneficial purposes. Fortunately, ethical standards established by the global chemistry community already provide a foundation. Building on that foundation, a group of experts from 24 countries from all regions of the world convened to define and harmonize key elements of ethical guidelines as they relate to chemical weapons, based upon existing codes.

"Code" is used as a general term and includes the full range of such documents, from aspirational statements such as the Hippocratic Oath to codes that are enforceable, for example as part of a practitioner's terms of employment. Such codes are primary ways through which the community's ethical standards are addressed. The key elements presented in this text should be incorporated into new and existing codes in order to align with the provisions of the CWC. A code need not mention chemical weapons or the CWC to support its basic goals, and provisions may need to be tailored for particular sectors or circumstances, while still reflecting the fundamental values. Taken together, "The Hague Ethical Guidelines" provide the key elements that should be applied universally."

The following key elements from the ethical guidelines are extracted from (OPCW Organization for the Prohibition of Chemical Weapons):

The Key Elements include:
- *Core element.* Achievements in the field of chemistry should be used to benefit humankind and protect the environment.
- *Sustainability.* Chemistry practitioners have a special responsibility for promoting and achieving the UN Sustainable Development Goals of meeting the needs of the present without compromising the ability of future generations to meet their own needs.
- *Education.* Formal and informal educational providers, enterprise, industry and civil society should cooperate to equip anybody working in chemistry as well as others with the necessary knowledge and tools to take responsibility for the benefit of humankind, the protection of the environment and relevant and meaningful engagement with the general public.
- *Awareness and engagement.* Teachers, chemistry practitioners and policymakers should be aware of the multiple uses of chemicals, specifically their use as chemical weapons or their precursors. They should promote the peaceful applications of chemicals and work to prevent any misuse of chemicals, scientific knowledge, tools and technologies as well as any harmful

or unethical developments in research and innovation. They should disseminate relevant information about national and international laws, regulations, policies and practices.

- *Ethics.* To adequately respond to societal challenges, education, research and innovation must respect fundamental rights and apply the highest ethical standards. Ethics should be perceived as a way of ensuring high-quality results in scientific endeavors.
- *Safety and Security.* Chemistry practitioners should promote the beneficial applications, uses and development of science and technology while encouraging and maintaining a strong culture of safety, health and security.
- *Accountability.* Chemistry practitioners have a responsibility to ensure that chemicals, equipment and facilities are protected against theft and diversion and are not used for illegal, harmful or destructive purposes. These persons should be aware of applicable laws and regulations governing the manufacture and use of chemicals, and they should report any misuse of chemicals, scientific knowledge, equipment and facilities to the relevant authorities.
- *Oversight.* Chemistry practitioners who supervise others have the additional responsibility to ensure that chemicals, equipment and facilities are not used by those persons for illegal, harmful or destructive purposes.
- *Exchange of information.* Chemistry practitioners should promote the exchange of scientific and technical information relating to the development and application of chemistry for peaceful purposes.

Chemists appreciate the registration, evaluation, authorization and restriction of chemicals, known as REACH, which entered into force on June 1, 2007. It streamlines and improves the former legislative framework on chemicals developed by the European Union (EU). The main aims of REACH are to ensure a high level of protection of human health and the environment from the risks that can be posed by chemicals, the promotion of alternative test methods, the free circulation of substances on the internal market and enhancing competitiveness and innovation. REACH makes industry responsible for assessing and managing the risks posed by chemicals and providing appropriate safety information to their users. The EU can also take additional measures on highly dangerous substances where there is a need for complementing action at the EU level (Published by the EU).

Drawing upon my experience, I believe that the Chemical Industry is an excellent example of one which is able to "make living more lively." It serves, among others, the industries of Health, Nutrition, Energy, Communication, Transport, Clothing, Housing, Environmental Protection and Leisure. In this industry, Sustainable Environmental Responsibility means manufacturing with high standards, being informed about what customers are doing with the product that are sold, and supporting them in the production of goods which are of clear benefit to mankind.

What is Green Chemistry? What follows is a collection of design principles that various individuals and groups have proposed over time to answer that question, mostly in the form of examples of application of green chemistry.

Sustainable and green chemistry in very simple terms is just a different way of thinking about how chemistry and chemical engineering can be done. Over the years, different principles have been proposed that can be used when thinking about the design, development and implementation of chemical products and processes. These principles enable scientists and engineers to protect and benefit the economy, people and the planet by finding creative and innovative ways to reduce waste, conserve energy and discover replacements for hazardous substances.

It's important to note that the scope of these of green chemistry and engineering principles go beyond concerns over hazards from chemical toxicity and include energy conservation, waste reduction and life cycle considerations such as the use of more sustainable or renewable feedstocks and designing for the end of life or the final disposition of products.

Green chemistry can also be defined through the use of measureable effects. While a unified set of measurements has not been established, many ways to *quantify* greener processes and products have been proposed. These measurements include ones for mass, energy, hazardous substance reduction or elimination and life cycle environmental impacts.

The following is a statement from The ACS (American Society of Chemistry) concerning the importance of *Green Chemistry:*

Rachel Carson wrote the mainstream, scientific book, *Silent Spring* in 1962. It outlined the devastation that certain chemicals had on local ecosystems. The book served as a wake-up call for the public and scientists alike, and inspired the modern environmental movement... In 1969, Congress recognized the importance of the issue and passed the National Environmental Policy Act (NEPA). The law's goal was to "create and maintain conditions under which man and nature can exist in productive harmony," and called for a Presidential Council on Environmental Quality.

In the following years, a lot of initiatives were undertaken in the US and Europe. In 2001, the Green Chemistry Institute" became a part of the American Chemical Society, the largest professional scientific society and membership organization for chemists in the world ... The Nobel Prize in Chemistry was won for research in areas of chemistry that were largely seen as being green chemistry in both 2001 (Knowles, Noyori, Sharpless) and 2005 (Chauvin, Grubbs, Schrock). These Nobel Prizes helped solidify the importance of research in green chemistry and helped create a higher awareness among scientists that the future of chemistry should be greener.

Moving forward with Green Chemistry. After all of the research advancements in green chemistry and engineering, mainstream chemical businesses have not yet fully embraced the technology. Today, more than 98% of all organic chemicals are still derived from petroleum. Green chemists and engineers are working to take their research and innovations out of the lab and into the board room through the creation of viable industrial products that can be embraced by today's industry leaders ... The concept of greening chemistry is a relatively new idea which developed in the business and regulatory communities as a natural evolution of pollution prevention initiatives. In our efforts to improve crop protection, commercial products and medicines, we were also causing unintended harm to our planet and humans.

By the mid-20th century, some of the long-term negative effects of misguided practices could not be ignored. Pollution choked many of the world's waterways and acid rain deteriorated forest health. There were measurable holes in the Earth's ozone. Some chemicals in common use were suspected of causing, or at least directly linked, to human cancer and other adverse human and environmental health outcomes. Many governments began to regulate the generation and disposal of industrial wastes and emissions. The United States formed the Environmental Protection Agency (EPA) in 1970, which was charged with protecting human and environmental health through setting and enforcing environmental regulations.

Green chemistry takes the EPA's mandate a step further and creates a new reality for chemistry and engineering by asking chemists and engineers to design chemicals, chemical processes and commercial products in a way that, at the very least, avoids the creation of toxics and waste.

> Green Chemistry is not politics.
> Green Chemistry is not a public relations ploy.
> Green chemistry is not a pipe dream.

We are able to develop chemical processes and earth-friendly products that will prevent pollution in the first place. Through the practice of green chemistry, we can create alternatives to hazardous substances we use as our source materials. We can design chemical processes that reduce waste and reduce demand on diminishing resources. We can employ processes that use less energy. We can do all of this and still maintain economic growth and opportunities while providing affordable products and services to a growing world population.

This is a field that is ready and ripe for innovation, new ideas and revolutionary progress. This is the future of chemistry. This is green chemistry.

The US EPA and the ACS Green Chemistry Institute® have played a major role in promoting research and education in pollution prevention and the reduction of toxics over the past three decades. Governments and scientific communities throughout the world recognize that the practice of green chemistry and engineering not only leads to a cleaner and more sustainable Earth but also is economically beneficial with many positive social impacts. These benefits encourage businesses and governments to support the development of sustainable products and processes. The United States, desiring to reward and celebrate significant achievements in green chemistry, has presented the Presidential Green Chemistry Challenge Award annually since 1996.

Since the word "Green" first started being placed in front of chemistry, many people have argued about what the "right" definition of green chemistry is or isn't. And, more importantly, what can we actually do to make chemistry "green" or "greener"?

What follows is a collection of design principles that various individuals and groups have proposed over time to answer that question. The examples of green chemistry accomplishments listed below illustrate how green chemistry impacts a wide array of fields from pharmaceuticals to housewares, and offer a pathway to a better world.

In 2005, the Nobel Prize in chemistry was awarded for the discovery of a catalytic chemical process called *metathesis* – which has broad applicability in the chemical industry. It uses significantly less energy and has the potential to reduce greenhouse gas emissions for many key processes. The process is stable at normal temperatures and pressures, can be used in combination with greener solvents and is likely to produce less hazardous waste.

In 2012, Elevance Renewable Sciences won the Presidential Green Chemistry Challenge Award by using metathesis to break down natural oils and recombine the fragments into high-performance chemicals. The company makes specialty chemicals for many uses, such as highly concentrated cold water detergents that provide better cleaning with reduced energy costs.

Many chemicals along with large amounts of water and energy are required to manufacture computer chips. In a study conducted in 2003, the industrial estimate of chemicals and fossil fuels required to make a computer chip in the ratio of 630:1! That means it takes 630 times the weight of the chip in source materials just to make one chip! Compare that to the 2:1 ratio for the manufacture of an automobile. Since then:

– Scientists at the Los Alamos National Laboratory have developed a process that uses supercritical carbon dioxide in one of the steps of chip preparation which significantly reduces the quantities of chemicals, energy and water needed to produce chips.
– Richard Wool, former director of the Affordable Composites from Renewable Sources (ACRES) program at the University of Delaware, found a way to use chicken feathers to make computer chips. The protein, keratin, in the feathers was used to make a fiber form that is both light and tough enough to withstand mechanical and thermal stresses. The result is a feather-based printed circuit board that actually works at twice the speed of traditional circuit boards. Although this technology is still in the works for commercial purposes, the research has led to other uses of feathers as source material, including for biofuel.

The pharmaceutical industry is continually seeking processes that produce less toxic waste and the development of medicines with fewer harmful side effects.

Several companies have been working to develop plastics that are made from renewable, biodegradable sources.

Oil-based "alkyd" paints give off large amounts of volatile organic compounds (VOCs). These volatile compounds evaporate from the paint as it dries and cures and many have one or more environmental impacts. Better, more durable and environmentally friendly, nonoil-based paints are now prevalent in the market'.

What is the position of the GDCh (German Chemical Society) on the evolving themes in chemistry? The contribution of chemistry to sustainable development is becoming increasingly important and increasingly a key issue. Therefore, in March of 2007, the German Chemical Society established a Working Group on Sustainable Chemistry. The themes of sustainable chemistry are manifold and of particular importance for our future.

What is Sustainable Chemistry? Sustainability generally involves the recognition of the manifold merits of meeting the needs of those living today while at the same time keeping the development options of future generations open. Consideration of economic, environmental and socioeconomical objectives is a fundamental and crucial factor, as is a holistic approach toward products and processes over their entire lifecycle, from the "cradle to the grave.." Keeping in mind this general definition, sustainable chemistry explores the use and conversion of available physical resources in a manner which does not limit or harm future generations. During the next few decades, solving potential social and economic issues through new developments in the field of sustainable chemistry will become increasingly important. How can we achieve this goal?

Some examples are:
– through new catalytic processes in chemical production;
– by energy and raw material saving in chemical processes;
– through energy and feedstock use of biomass that does not compete with food production;
– by the use of CO_2, through research and development work on new energy sources;
– through solutions to mobility, nutrition, clothing and housing issues, among others, in which chemistry can play a role by contributing to all aspects of envi-

ronmental protection including soil, water and air, by creating sustainable solutions along the entire life cycle of any chemicals produced, sold and applied;
- by introducing the idea of sustainability into school curricula. Suggestions for the educational sector may include the following:
  - sustainable Chemistry in education
  - sustainable Energy
  - renewable Resources
  - catalysis
  - alternative reaction conditions
  - assessment of chemical processes and products
  - sustainable product"

To honor the work of Friedrich Wöhler (1800–1882), who was one of Germany's most important chemists, excelling in work in urea synthesis, and in the breaking down of barriers between inorganic and organic chemistry, the Chemical Society of the GDR established the Wöhler Prize for Sustainable Chemistry. Awards were donated in his name between 1960 and 1991. By a decision of the GDCh board, this former recognition of Wöhler by the Chemical Society resumed in 1997, and by 2011, they added an additional award for initiatives in interdisciplinary work in science which resulted in "resource-saving processes.." Awards are made to individuals who make innovative research contributions through forward looking work in the entire field of chemistry which may contribute to greater environmental friendliness as well as the responsible use of existing or new resources. Their innovations are also expected to lead to self-sustaining developments in chemistry, as well as toward basic research.

In 2012, the prize was renamed the Wöhler Prize for Sustainable Chemistry and has since been awarded for pioneering and outstanding contributions to the development and implementation of sustainable chemistry. Pioneering work by selected exemplary individuals is expected to contribute to innovative methods in all areas of chemistry, as well as leading to improved sustainable processes.

To further promote innovations in "Business Chemistry," particularly from the viewpoint of sustainability and the desire to promote the development of chemical products or processes with high societal value, I founded the "Meyer-Galow-Foundation for Business Chemistry" which annually awards the "Meyer-Galow-Prize for Business Chemistry." The Foundation exists in accordance with the Board of the German Chemical Society's decision of March 5, 2012 and is managed by the German Chemical Society.

The prize is awarded to someone who has successfully launched a current innovation in chemistry in the German-speaking world – either alone or with a team. It can be a product or a process. The innovation does not necessarily have to have originated exclusively from efforts of the recipient. However, the recipient must be the driving force for implementation in the marketplace.

The prizewinner proves to be worthy, in particular, if he or she:

- has introduced an innovation to the market that takes sustainability into account to a large extent;
- has introduced an innovation to the market that represents a special necessary value for society ("must have" not simply "nice to have");
- is a mature personality who enjoys a high degree of esteem among employees, colleagues, superiors and all business partners. The recipient's management style is characterized by a particularly high degree of empathy.

Laws and regulations are attempts to protect our environment through sustainable behavior. They are a necessary, progressive step for those leaders who have not yet embarked upon a journey of inner growth in so far as it will lead them toward decisions which are consistent with sustainability. But they will never be as effective as leaders who are on an inner growth journey; leaders who regardless of laws and regulations which they have helped to develop and enact, assume responsibility for protecting, and where possible *improving* the environment, as a result of their maturity, their realization of Self, and of their recognition of the interconnectedness of all of mankind and nature. Once fully realized, the Self cannot do otherwise.

Hans Peter Dürr *stated:*

> We must take care of our own sustainability and the future of our societies. Because nature will not force us to do so. In it, the rule is that "fools" who neglect their long term vital interests are simply dismissed from biological evolution. (Dürr 2011)

4.17 Intuition, Creativity, Innovation: Gifts from Within

> For me, intuition is that "something else" to which I am connected and which is behind everything which I experience every day. It is through surrendering to this "something else" that I am able to experience it, and the more I surrender the more access I have to it. I can draw upon its richness and wealth and receive a vision that is important to me if I really want to act in this world. (Dürr 2010)

In addition to what has so far been suggested as sources for greater ethical awareness and moral practices, intuition is another powerful resource at our disposal. However, a precondition for trusting our intuition is that we have achieved considerable inner maturity. Intuition, when tempered by maturity, is a formidable source of creativity.

Those in management positions have an obligation to take part in the creative process of answering important questions, both those of immediate relevance and those which will have a future impact. It is necessary, indeed essential, that we are on a path leading toward inner growth so as to be able to work in the "outside" world with creativity which is coupled with an ethical spirit. When as managers we undertake this transformation, the entire company benefits from our transformation. Leadership style is an essential component in the determination of a company's innovative potential. Are we open, receptive and trusting of ideas which arise intuitively, or are we crippled and limited by the simple reliance upon our intellect; our ego mind? Companies without a constant stream of innovations are destined to perish. Very often they are the last to come to this realization, even though it is abundantly evident to others. They cut costs and attempt one efficiency program after the other, but these egocentric actions do not help them to survive because their competitors are doing the same, and the competitive edge which is available by attending to our intuition is absent. Efficiency programs destroy creativity. They result in employees feeling vulnerable, fearful that their jobs will be eliminated in the next attempt at greater efficiency. *Employee anxiety is not fertile ground for creativity!*

For many companies which remain in the so-called old economy, innovations dry up over time. The focus then becomes cost cutting and hiring management consultants to introduce new programs designed to increase efficiency. A wiser and more ethical approach is to be proactive. Rather than waiting until the company is in trouble before taking action, it is wise to initiate the necessary changes which ensure that the *life* that is in the company is made *livelier* now! Inventions are dependent upon intuitions which derive from the Latin *intueri, to turn inward*. Meditation is an excellent method of accomplishing this. Meditative practices lead us inward, allowing intuition and inspiration to arise from the unconscious, often quickly and unexpectedly. Only in this way can we reasonably expect to progress forward in a sustainable manner.

Any problem which we wish to resolve must be considered in the form of a question. Then all of a sudden, not necessarily in the office or in the laboratory but perhaps in nature or in listening to music or during some other unrelated activity, an intuition flows into our consciousness. Many very famous scientists and Nobel Prize winners, such as Georges Köhler, Werner Heisenberg, Wolfgang Pauli, Alex Müller, Carl Friedrich Gauss, August Kekule, Justus von Liebig, Henri Poincare, Gerd Binnig and Rene Descartes, attribute their success to intuitive breakthroughs. A recent example is the Nobel Prize Winner for Chemistry in 2014, Stefan Hell, who stated: "I received the enlightenment as an intuition on the ferry boat to Finland."

Frank Wilczek, a professor at MIT and a Nobel Prize winner in 2004, achieved a scientific breakthrough with his doctoral thesis on quarks at the age of 22. He identified four forces of nature. Gravitational force and electromagnetic force were already known, but there are two other forces encountered by physicists when they study atomic nuclei. The strong force which holds together atomic nuclei and the weak force which is responsible for a number of decay processes. Along with David Gross, he attempted to formulate equations which would represent the strong force. He said: "We guessed it, because we were looking for intuitively particularly beautiful, symmetric equations." Experimentation has since confirmed his intuition.

Einstein stated: "Intuition is what really counts." Alexander von Humboldt tells us: "Very often the imagination is prior to the knowing," Sheldrake commented: "Especially in Europe and the USA many people were taught at an early age to ignore their intuition. In our society which over-values the mind there are prejudices against this form of information. It is called superstitious and irrational." Einstein also gave us the following gift: "The most beautiful of what we can experience is the mysterious. It is the real source of all art and science."

When we live compassionately in the moment, faithfully trusting in benevolent universal forces, we open ourselves to an unimaginably powerful source of previously untapped energy; energy of healing, of contentment and of success which is measured by growth. When we allow *our personal link with the universe*, our intuition, to direct our thoughts they become our most powerfully energetic gifts which, when resonating with a multitude of similar thoughts from others, are able to manifest as "events" which interact in accordance with the Laws of Nature, allowing us to "move mountains." The energetic dimension through which we are all connected, not only one with the other but also with all knowledge and all potential that exists, has been given various names by different authors, names which include the Divine Matrix, the Undifferentiated Reality, the Cooperative Background and the Ever Acting Process of Life.

I spoke a lot with Hans-Peter Dürr about the sources of intuition and he pointed out that everybody has intuitions, just a few and never enough. But we do not know from where they arise. Intuition means very simply that something is coming from somewhere. They come from the "Ever Acting Process" which has the potentiality to manifest as reality in each and every moment. Many people believe that they just think with their mind, but this doesn't lead to really new results. We will never know the extent of our potential resulting from intuitions when we are not able to enter the trans-rational space from which they arise.

According to my teacher Willigis Jäger, intuition flows out of stillness and silence. When we are silent in peace and quietness, spontaneous ideas, valuable insights and intuitions arise within us. All of a sudden we understand correlations which we have never known before. Intuition is emerging out of the unconscious, one layer deeper than the subconscious. As previously mentioned, in the *New Economy*, intuition is only possible in an organization in which mindfulness and compassion play an important role, open and fearless. Creativity is accessible only by holistically oriented organizations. This also demonstrates that the Depth Psychology approach not only benefits the new ethics but encourages creativity by opening the door to the unconscious.

What we are referring to as intuition and inspiration, Soren Gordhamer (Gordhamer 2013) calls "the creative mind." He comments that it experiences life freshly, thinks out of the box, finds new solutions to old problems and expresses itself in innovative ways. This wording is misleading, because *the creative force is not limited to our mind.* Hans-Peter Dürr sagely tells us that we experience much more than we think and know. It is the reality which we cannot describe but only experience. When we are building up the connection, for example by meditation, intuition can flow into us as inspiration which is then followed by our mind and our intellect putting it all together along with our knowledge into an innovation. It could be that Soren had the correct concept but simply used the incorrect terminology. He was quoting the co-founder of Google Larry Page (Gordhamer 2013, p. 5), who got the idea for what was to become Google's search algorithm in a dream one night, as well as drawing upon the revelation that Amazon CEO Jeff Bezos spent several days at the end of each fiscal quarter locked away so that he could visualize and let his mind focus. Soren Gordhamer (Gordhamer 2013, p. 5): "Without a connection to the inner world, to our own thoughts and body, the creative mind becomes inaccessible amid the mass of other content we digest."

I have found that our inner world is not only the unity and balance of body and mind, but the *experience* of the unity of body/mind, *soul and spirit*. And this experience unleashes the creative forces within us. Soren quotes Steve Jobs, who captures a powerful yet seldom recognized realization (Gordhamer 2013, p. 9):

> I began to realize that an intuitive understanding and consciousness was more significant than abstract thinking and logical analysis.

We are able to receive many intuitions encouraged by our spiritual life. Because they show up all of a sudden and they disappear all of a sudden, we need to "inhale" them immediately to make them part of our own. *Inspiration* comes from the Latin term *inspirare*, which means to take a deep breath. We must inhale the intuition so as to integrate it within ourselves and not lose it. Intuitions and inspirations are collected by our *intellect* and compared with our knowledge and inner images. Intellect is a combination of the Latin words *intra-legere* and *collectio*. With our *intellect* our ego mind assimilates and synthesizes within ourselves everything that is contained within, along with that which we know from the "outside." This is how creativity arises within us.

Unfortunately, most of us limit ourselves to mental activities, or if we include psychological sources at all, it is only to the limits of our psycho-mental capabilities. We don't use the *unlimited* resources of the entire cosmos to assist our intellect in creative endeavors. This is like living as fish in an aquarium where the limits of the aquarium are defined by a limited consciousness. The fish have never experienced, and thus do not yet know that their aquarium is in a greater "ocean." By linking our intuitions and inspirations with our knowledge, we allow ourselves to be creative. We can either accomplish this linkage by ourselves or approach it jointly by exploring and sharing possibilities and desires with others. A very good practice is Dürr's "Loving Dialogue" as presented previously. It opens us to the possibility of experiencing new dimensions. Empathy and compassion are essential conditions when wishing to share in the manifestations which arise from an honest give and take with others.

Many believe that great creativity *can* arise from the rational mind, in spite of its limitations. Often the first approach toward encouraging creativity is simply directed thinking. I adopted this approach before I initiated meditation. I attended seminars with Edward de Bono on *Lateral Thinking* and with Tony Buzan on "How to use your

Head." During these early years in business, it was a great experience. It served me well. It was better than idling, but not the ultimate solution. When psychology is added, the experience is enhanced over that of purely rational thought. But, trying to use our psycho-mental capacity to overcome our psycho-mental limitations is a logical inconsistency and as such can never succeed. Jack B. Soll and Katherine L. Milkman along with John W. Payne address this mental effort and present recommendations to "Outsmart Your Own Biases" (Soll et al. 2015): The authors used the word *intuition* seven times:

1) "You might trust your *intuition*, which has guided you well in the past, and send her on her way. That's what most executives say they'd do when we pose this scenario in our classes on managerial decision making
2) The problem is, unless you occasionally go against your gut, you haven't put your *intuition* to the test. You can't really know what's helping you make good choices if you've never seen what happens when you ignore it.
3) But as the psychologist Daniel Kahneman has shown, it's also a common source of bias that can result in poor decision making, because our *intuitions* frequently lead us astray.
4) In situations like this, we're far from being decision-ready, we're mentally, emotionally, and physically spent. We cope by relying even more heavily on *intuitive*, System 1 judgments and less on careful reasoning. Decision making becomes faster and simpler, but quality often suffers.
5) Much of the time though, delegation isn't appropriate, and it's all on you, the manager, to decide. When that's the case, you can outsmart your own biases. You start by understanding where they're coming from: excessive reliance on *intuition*, defective reasoning, or both. In this article, we describe some of the most stubborn biases out there: tunnel vision about future scenarios, about objectives, and about options. But awareness alone isn't enough, as Kahneman, reflecting on his own experiences has pointed out. So we also provide strategies for overcoming biases, gleaned from the latest research on the psychology of judgment and decision making.
6) We're cognitive misers – we don't like to spend our mental energy entertaining uncertainties. It's easier to seek closure, so we do. This hems in our thinking, leading us to focus on *one possible future* (in this case, an office that performs as projected), *one objective* (hiring someone who can manage it under those circumstances), and *one option in isolation* (the candidate in front of us). When this narrow thinking weaves a compelling story, System 1 kicks in: *Intuition* tells us, prematurely, that we're ready to decide, and we venture forth with great, unfounded confidence. To 'de-bias' our decisions, it's essential to broaden our perspective on all three fronts.
7) Although you need a critical mass of options to make sound decisions, you also need to find strong contenders – at least two but ideally three to five. Of course, it's easy to give in to the tug of System 1 thinking and generate a false choice to rationalize your *intuitively* favorite option (like a parent who asks an energetic toddler, 'Would you like one nap or two today?'). But then you're just duping yourself. A decision can be no better than the best option under consideration."

My interpretation of these extracts is that the authors are promoting an acceptable but limited way for "de-biasing," but they do not really know what "intuition" means, from where it arises, or how we may prepare ourselves for receiving more of them. Therefore they recommend mental options:

- thinking about the future
- making three estimates
- thinking twice
- taking an outside view
- thinking about objectives
- seeking advice
- cycling through your objectives
- thinking about options
- using joint evaluation
- trying the "vanishing options" test
- fighting motivated bias

By using these methods, we may clearly become more effective through the creation of more intellectual associations, but our great potential of intuition arising from the unconscious is not being utilized.

After having studied the success stories of astronauts, artists and scientists, the authors of the book *Intuition, Creativity and Holistic Thinking* come to the following conclusions:

- that at the base of "human consciousness" there is according to Brahms an un-manifested cosmic level of creativity and intelligence;
- that human consciousness is capable of experiencing this transcendent level of creation through inner self-reference, i.e. meditative immersion;
- that this Self-centered level is, so to speak, located in a Self-conscious state of consciousness between waking and sleeping;
- that this level lies beyond the 'usual' content of thought and therefore cannot be experienced through reflection;
- that the experience of this level leads to an unusual unfolding of creative, intuitive, intelligent and ethical values;
- that outstanding achievements are made possible by the 'holistic experience' of this level;
- that this level is to be regarded as the origin of human creativity and intuition and thus contains the actual basis of human existence and the associated subjective aspects (Volkamer et al. 1991).

Innovations are successfully introduced inventions in the marketplace which often result from the establishment of an open and honest dialogue with customers. Sales representatives, technical service people and marketing managers who have developed mindfulness and compassion are excellently prepared and positioned for successful innovations. Paving the way to successful innovations are intuition and creativity. Creativity in management is not limited to research and development activities. Numerous other management decisions may also be intuitively approached with great success. Many innovations fail simply because they are the products of our ego-centered mind, devoid of spiritual input. In excess of 50% of all mergers and acquisitions fail, Personal and organizational shortcomings, which are inevitable when mindfulness is lacking, result in strategies doomed to failure, encumbering entire companies.

4.18 Resilience: An Essential Quality

Resilience is a gift available to anyone who allows their inner growth to develop. If we follow the recommendations contained within this book, we will become more resilient to the myriad temptations for immoral actions. We will also become more resilient to burn out, depression and numerous psychological and physical diseases. The numerous and diverse publications on the market which address burnout and depression are evidence of the suffering the world is experiencing in our fast paced, impersonal, egocentric, high-tech society.

What is resilience? The term originates from the field of physics. It refers to the elasticity of a material (from Latin *resilire* – to recoil). Brigitte Dorst writes in her book *Resilience* (Dorst 2015, p. 13f.):

> The word resilience has become increasingly important in many areas of psychology, psychotherapy, counseling and coaching in recent years. We can understand resilience as a kind of psychological immune system, one which includes internal stabilization and healing powers. Resilience is the answer to the following questions:
> – How can people overcome difficult life crises and traumas without any lasting damage?
> – How can children and adults continue to grow despite the adverse conditions of life?
> – How can people maintain their mental and physical health and find joy in life?

A great deal of research is being conducted in this area because of its importance for our society. Currently, the world's most largest study, involving 4,700 participants, is being coordinated by Professor Clemens Kirschbaum at the Institute of Biological Psychology in the University of Dresden in Germany. In addition to the psychological symptoms, the utility of various medicines are also being studied. Strikingly often, people who are overweight and suffering from fatigue and insomnia experience burn out. Our resilience is related to genetics, epigenetics (inheriting our parent's weaknesses), neurobiology and environmental factors ... We can directly observe that those who have worked too hard for too long without taking some quality free time in which both the body **and the spirit** may recover are prone to burn out.

What is recommended? Scientists and therapists are now mostly of the opinion that we can deliberately build up our resilience. A break from work, changing the nature of our work or working less is recommended as a beginning. The program is accompanied by relaxation techniques, sports and healthy eating. This all sounds positive, but are we looking in the wrong places for the cause of burn out? Are we ignoring the underlying cause while only tinkering with the symptoms? Once again the causes are being sought in the outside world while the influence of the inner is being ignored. It is so much easier to ascribe blame to factors outside of ourselves than those within. Burn out may be initiated by outside factors, but the underlying reason that those factors result in a breakdown can be found within. This is entirely consistent with my personal experiences.

Burn out is the implosion of ego.

When the ego collapses due to increased pressure from the outside world, most of us have nothing within that can accommodate the collapsing ego. That is the problem. Personally undertaking internal growth is a necessary prerequisite for healing but it is most often never attempted or achieved. Undertaking psychological or spiritual training will radically increase our resilience to stress as a result of the consequent growth of inner maturity. Recall the testimony of C. G. Jung, who after an incredibly rich lifetime of experiences concluded that the separation from the Holy inner source, the Divine, is the cause of all psychological illnesses. Once the connection to the soul has been lost, we cast ourselves adrift in an ocean of despair.

The cure clearly lies in the restoration of our connection to our soul. This can be accomplished by the methods of Depth Psychology along with teachings of spiritual wisdom and a study of the relationship of quantum physics to our individual psyche. In this way, we address the heart of the problem rather than merely the symptoms. The result is lasting resilience.

Brigitte Dorst (Dorst 2015, p. 6) sees intuition, imagination and fantasy as the resonance forces of Depth Psychology. She recommends the strengthening of the soul with inner images and symbols. The table of contents of her book reads accordingly:
- Explore the streets of life
- Find protection and security
- Grow and find a solid base
- Cope with difficult tasks
- Elicit the inner light again
- Recover the sources of life
- Hope and begin again
- Arrive in your inner center
- Connect and hold together
- Trust the wisdom of the heart
- Follow proven sign posts
- Deepen self-awareness
- Meditation and self-reflection
- Emerge stronger out of difficult situations

When we follow the way of individuation or meditation, maintaining these exercises daily will strengthen our resilience such that the many external stressors experienced in our everyday life will be mitigated.

4.19 Summary of Current Studies on the Effect of Mindful Meditation

There has been a recent influx of interest in the neurocognitive and psychological effects of meditation, in particular mindfulness meditation and how it leads to greater resilience. A few examples from this scientific research, in addition to those presented in Chapter3, Section 3.2.2, follow as quotes from a number of publications

4.19.1 Brain and Immune Function

Alterations in brain and immune function produced by mindfulness meditation (Davidson et al. 2003.):

The *underlying changes in biological processes that are associated* with reported changes in mental and physical health in response to meditation have not been systematically explored...... We report for the first time significant increases in left-sided anterior activation, a pattern previously associated with positive affect, in the meditators compared with the non-meditators. We also found significant increases in antibody titers (a blood test) to influenza vaccine among subjects in the meditation compared with those in the wait-list control group. Finally, the magnitude of increase in left-sided activation predicted the magnitude of antibody titer rise to the vaccine.

Conclusion: These findings demonstrate that a short program in mindfulness meditation produces demonstrable effects on brain and immune function. These findings suggest that meditation may change brain and immune function in positive ways and underscore the need for additional research.

4.19.2 Anxiety and Depression

The Effect of Mindfulness-Based Therapy on Anxiety and Depression: A Meta-Analytic Review (Hofmann et al. 2010):

The search identified 39 studies totaling 1140 participants receiving mindfulness-based therapy for a range of conditions, including cancer, generalized anxiety disorder, depression, and other psychiatric or medical conditions.

Effect size estimates suggest that mindfulness-based therapy was moderately effective for improving anxiety (Hedges' $g = 0.63$) and mood symptoms (Hedges' $g = 0.59$) from pre to post-treatment in the overall sample. In patients with anxiety and mood disorders, this intervention was associated with effect sizes (Hedges' g) of 0.97 and 0.95 for improving anxiety and mood symptoms, respectively.

Conclusion: These results suggest that mindfulness-based therapy is a promising intervention for treating anxiety and mood problems in clinical populations.

4.19.3 Stress Reduction and Management

Mindfulness-based stress reduction for stress management in healthy people: a review and meta-analysis (Chiesa and Serretti 2009):

Mindfulness-based stress reduction (MBSR) is a clinically standardized meditation that has shown consistent efficacy for many mental and physical disorders. Less attention has been given to the possible benefits that it may have in healthy subjects.

MBSR showed a nonspecific effect on stress reduction in comparison to an inactive control, both in reducing stress and in enhancing spirituality values, and a possible specific effect compared to an intervention designed to be structurally equivalent to the meditation program. A direct comparison study between MBSR and standard relaxation training found that both treatments were equally able to reduce stress. Furthermore, MBSR was able to reduce ruminative thinking and trait anxiety, as well as to increase empathy and self-compassion.

Conclusion: MBSR is able to reduce stress levels in healthy people. However, important limitations of the included studies as well as the paucity of evidence about possible specific effects of MBSR in comparison to other nonspecific treatments underline the necessity of further research.

4.19.4 Coronary Heart Disease

Meditation and Coronary Heart Disease: A Review of the Current Clinical Evidence (Ray et al. 2014):

Chest pain from coronary heart disease (CHD) accounts for more than 8 million emergency department visits every year in the United States, emphasizing the need for cardiovascular (CV) interventions to help reduce this high number. Meditation – a state of contemplation, concentration, and reflection – has the potential to help decrease CV disease...

Conclusions: During the past few decades, multiple studies have demonstrated the beneficial effects of meditation on various CV risk factors. In addition to decreasing CV mortality, meditation has also been shown to improve conditions such as hypertension, type 2 diabetes mellitus, dyslipidemia, and high cortisol levels.

4.19.5 Pain and Quality of Life

Effectiveness of mindfulness meditation on pain and quality of life of patients with chronic low back pain (Banth and Ardebil 2015):

Recovery of patients with chronic low back pain (LBP) is dependent on several physical and psychological factors. Therefore, the authors aimed to examine the efficacy of mindfulness based stress reduction (MBSR) as a mind-body intervention on quality of life and pain severity of female patients with nonspecific chronic LBP (NSCLBP).

The findings showed MBSR was effective in reduction of pain severity with the patients who practiced 8 sessions of meditation reporting significantly lower pain than patients who only received usual medical care.

Conclusions: MBSR as a mind-body therapy including body scan, sitting and walking meditation was effective intervention on reduction of pain severity and improvement of physical and mental quality of life of female patients with NSCLBP.

4.19.6 Depression

Mindfulness-based cognitive therapy for depression: trends and developments (MacKenzie and Kocovski 2016):

Mindfulness-based cognitive therapy (MBCT) was developed as a psychological intervention for individuals at risk of depressive relapse. Possible mechanisms of change for this intervention are in line with its theoretical underpinnings, and include increases in mindfulness and/or decreases in negative repetitive thoughts. ....

There is consistent empirical evidence in support of using MBCT to decrease the risk of depressive relapse.

4.19.7 Mindfulness and Medical and Psychological Health

Relationships between mindfulness practice and levels of mindfulness, medical and psychological symptoms and well-being in a mindfulness-based stress reduction program (Carmody and Baer 2008):

Relationships were investigated between home practice of mindfulness meditation exercises and levels of mindfulness, medical and psychological symptoms, perceived stress, and psychological well-being in a sample of 174 adults in a clinical Mindfulness-Based Stress Reduction (MBSR) program. This is an 8-session group program for individuals dealing with stress-related problems, illness, anxiety, and chronic pain ...

Conclusions: Increases in mindfulness were found to mediate the relationships between formal mindfulness practice and improvements in psychological functioning, suggesting that the practice of mindfulness meditation leads to increases in mindfulness, which in turn leads to symptom reduction and improved well-being.

When we give ourselves the gift of meditation we connect ourselves directly to the blessings of the Cosmos.

Are these not enticing reasons for us undertaking inner growth, even if we do not wish to assume responsibility for a sustainable economy in the sense espoused by the new Integral Business Ethics 3.0? Creativity, resilience, increased health greater balance in our life and unprecedented satisfaction are guaranteed. Is that not enough? Who knows, perhaps in time a transformation of our inner awareness of the benefits of moral decisions and ethical practices will find a life in our external personal and professional lives. Truly a win/win situation!

5 Reflections by Richard Warrington

Mindful awareness. What is it? How do we achieve it? Is it important? Why? The answers to these questions form the content of this book. A necessarily bold, but compassionate and empathetic approach has been followed in the comprehensive unfolding of the mess we humans have made of our lives, as well as why after *thinking* ourselves into the mess we are in, it is unreasonable to expect that further *thought* is going to lift us out. Only through a greater understanding and acceptance of our innate intuitive ability to recognize right from wrong, by elevating our awareness of ourselves and embracing our spiritual nature so as to experience our inter-connectedness with all of life, may we hope to be blessed with the *essential* personal transformation which will lift us out of our self-centered *mind* set and position us as leaders who will, through being respectful, be respected.

We live in challenging times, societally and individually. Over millennia, civilizations have alternated between progressive evolution and troubling devolution. Dark periods fraught with disappointments and setbacks are no strangers to us, but neither are the emergence of enlightened individuals who, when times are darkest and we are ripe for guidance, rise to the challenge of illuminating a way forward. Any successful proposal for personal advancement, regardless of the unique context within which each historical period is enveloped, must resonate within us as being intuitively sound and sensible. Most proposals for personal/spiritual/moral growth are rooted in antiquity. Many have previously spawned diverse spiritual disciplines or psychoanalytic practices which vary in the degree to which they address our mind or our spirit. Along the way, in the Western world, our approach to exploring the nature of our reality found different expression from that of many Eastern societies, with the disastrous result that our ego mind and our intuitive awareness no longer played well together. We have severed the connection between the two.

What is at the root of our individuality? Does being an individual preclude a common unity of purpose, of desire, of respect and compassion? Is our apparent uniqueness really important? We are all incarnated onto this same Earth sphere in order to further our learning about ourselves and others and to experience the transforming power of love so as to become more fully actualized. But our most important lessons, to love one another and to extend charity, are too often the ones we neglect. Are we individually *really* so different, or is it rather that we have never bothered to discipline our childlike ego which insists that *we* are so special? Is our personal success as a human being as important as being a successful human being? As singer and songwriter, Elvis Costello asks us, what *is* so funny bout peace, love and understanding?

Professor Erhard Meyer-Galow has boldly, but gently interwoven offerings from Depth Psychology and Individuation along with observations gleaned from Quantum Physics which unequivocally establish the interaction between thought and matter,

https://doi.org/10.1515/9783110572292-005

into the ancient tapestry of spiritual traditions and practices, enticingly offering empirical evidence along with compassionate guidance toward practices which may encourage us toward greater mindful awareness. In so doing, he encourages us toward an individual intuitive revelation: the recognition that we are intimately interconnected and resonate with all of creation.

As someone who has for several decades undertaken inner maturation through actively seeking and critically examining knowledge, along with welcoming and embracing intuitive wisdom; someone who is able to fully experience both *doing* and *being*, Professor Meyer-Galow has undertaken, experienced and benefitted from most if not all of the approaches which he promotes in this book. His decision to deliberately use the all-inclusive "we" rather than the prescriptive "you"' is recognition that we are all in this together, and his acknowledgment that any real, lasting solution to our current world moral and ethical crisis must be undertaken by every one of us, regardless of our state of consciousness.

There is no substitute for authenticity. Knowing *about* something is a pale reflection of *knowing* something. No amount of study which may lead us to greater knowledge can favorably compare to a direct, personal experience. We have become disillusioned with spiritual guides who have never directly experienced God, and equally dismissive of business coaches and consultants who have never successfully managed an ethical enterprise. Professor Meyor-Galow has achieved an altered state of consciousness which has led him to directly experience a higher, unifying cosmic energetic force, one which many of us choose to call God. He has also had a long and illustrious career as the CEO of a number of both industrial and benevolent enterprises in which his lasting signature has been a progressive, productive and all-inclusive style of leadership. His knowledge, wisdom, empathy and respect for others encourage us to trust his guidance and excite us to apply his suggestions in both our professional and personal lives. There is nothing more credible than success. It adds authenticity to theory.

Our world is vastly diverse, defined by geography and culture as well as spiritual beliefs and religious rituals. But our differences need not divide or limit, indeed they can be a springboard to further personal growth by vaulting us toward a greater appreciation of the richness which accompanies diversity. An exploration of different ways in which those in other societies have learned to live in harmony with nature, of their interesting food choices and alternate ways of preparing foods similar to ours, along with their ceremonies celebrating coming of age, marriage and death rituals, can enrich and unite us. We may also avail ourselves of the opportunity to discover and investigate how others perceive the nature of a supreme organizing Entity or Deity, and how they pay homage to that greater energetic Presence.

Differences only become divisive when, as adults, we retain and allow ourselves to be dominated by our immature "me first" or "winner take all" ego mind, rather than fostering the greater emotional and spiritual maturity which recognizes that however we treat others is reflected back upon ourselves. When we treat employees as expensive liabilities instead of assets to be valued, fostered and promoted, we begin down a limiting, self-destructive path which ultimately can only lead to both personal and corporate failure. Our soul and our spirit hunger for the recognition which will allow them to serve us as they are meant to do, but our ego demands that it be fed first, and once satiated it ensures that we become self-limiting, no longer able to rise above our spiritual malnutrition.

Our ego may rationalize our self-centered attitudes by transferring responsibility for them to our parents, our teachers, our peers or our political, spiritual or religious leaders. But in fairness, more often than not those others and their teachings are *also* seduced and sabotaged by *their* ego mind. So, we must take responsibility for our own limitations, never allowing ourselves to be defined by the limitations of others. Ultimately, we must learn the often lonely and painful lesson of how to live in mature harmony with our ego, alone. The journey is difficult, often with disappointing discouragement from without, but once *we form the intention* and begin to open to our receptive, intuitive self, we are blessed with inspiration from within. As we begin to encourage our SELF toward the revelation of our cooperative and collective place in a world society, we find we are more fully peacefully present in the many realities which constitute our daily lives.

Perfection is a moving target. The best we can achieve is to relax into the acceptance that if we have the intention of approaching perfection gently, that we will arrive where we are best able to serve ourselves and others with a joyful heart.

We live in, and are an integral part of polarities. North and south, hot and cold, health and illness, light and dark. Let us be clear that polarities *are not* divisive, they do not divide. They are not *exclusive* as is duality, but rather *inclusive*, both essential polar components uniting diversity into a single unified whole. Nature promotes and encourages diversity in all of both material and sentient creation. Nurturing our awareness that diversity is *natural* helps us to recognize our unity with all else, to recognize that our perceived differences are simply struggles with and within ourselves. This recognition allows us to reach out to others with the same loving compassion as we ourselves would expect and value from others. It encourages us toward moral decisions and ethical actions. It completes us, and it is only through this process of becoming complete within ourselves that we can become complete with all of humanity. There are many routes up the mountain, but all paths lead to the summit.

Rejection, or even simple repression of our Dark side, regardless of the purity of our intentions, has "fatal" consequences for both ourselves and our entire sphere of influence. Religious doctrines which advocate this approach have failed to reduce the conflict, indeed have exacerbated the conflict between our Dark and Light polarities. Each aspect must be recognized, accommodated and allowed expression within the limitations which *we* must establish *ourselves*, otherwise our conflict is projected outward and becomes world conflict. We may take the same approach to our Dark and Light sides as Jung took to sexuality and spirituality, considering each to be the opposite side of the *same* coin, with each being equally important in its expression, and equally essential for the dynamic balance which underlies our holistic Self.

While assisting Erhard with the structuring of this book, I often found myself reflecting upon the myriad of different spiritual pathways and religious beliefs. This topic has been reflected upon by many authors, one of the most compelling being Eckhart Tolle in his book, *A New Earth: Awakening to Your Life*'s *Purpose*. My own extensive exposure to the metaphysical has resulted in many traditional Christian precepts being retained, but being repositioned such that the light they capture and reflect back emanates from a nontraditional part of the spectrum. How do the constructs underlying the spiritual and the religious differ? Why is an integrative approach which takes into account input from Depth Psychology and Individuation, along with intuitively arising realizations resulting from intensive "inner work," more likely to prepare us for a transformation of our state of consciousness than will acceptance of traditional religious interpretation of the scriptures?

First, let us recognize that it is *thoughts* arising from our ego mind consciousness that result in our limited awareness. This limited awareness in turn precludes us from *thinking* our way into an altered state of consciousness. Suspending our ego mind allows us to recognize that we *are not* our thoughts or experiences, it connects us to a universal intelligence which eases us into an awareness that we *are* something quite different from the sum of the trappings ... as difficult or as pleasant as they may be ... of our life. We cannot rise above a self-imposed, self-destructive condition by applying the same premises which caused the condition. It takes a shift in consciousness for us to break out of our dysfunctional state. Anything short of that shift is doomed to failure. Only when we become receptive can we awaken to enlightenment, which involves a break in the continuity of our normal thought patterns and conditioning, allowing us to *recognize* our un-awakened self. However, the information and suggestions contained in this book *can* help us to establish a personal foundation which is receptive to a shift in consciousness, enabling us to receive an Act of Grace, which is the only way that our consciousness is able to be transformed. As Erhard so aptly reminds us, once we *begin* to do the necessary "heavy lifting," we are forever changed, we begin to make moral decisions and follow ethical practices *because we cannot do otherwise*. Those changes, recognized by others, gain us the respect which allows us to become confident and competent leaders, a light, shining in the wilderness even while we wait, in faith, for an Act of Grace.

A basic tenet of Christian teachings is that we are born in sin and need to be saved. Heaven knows, we do need to be saved! But not from original sin. The *New Testament* was written in Greek in which *to sin* means to be misdirected so as to think or act incorrectly, generally resulting in a misunderstanding of our life's purpose. It has no inherently spiritual meaning, and as a focal point of Christianity it acts as a "red herring" which serves to misdirect our efforts toward preparing ourselves for a true transformation of consciousness. Even to devout Christians it is confusing, and when we are confused we suffer. The greater tragedy is that when we suffer, we generally ensure that we cause suffering in others as well. Any scheme which encourages evangelism, in which individuals who embrace a particular belief system attempt to convert "others" to their beliefs, promotes duality along with its inherently divisive nature. It speaks to an old, tired, failed and unreasonable belief that we can achieve unity by promoting division, by promoting an "us" versus "them" scenario. It can only fail. Giving our unbridled ego mind free rein ensures that we become our own worst enemy. We must "get out of our own way" in order to progress.

It is all about connections. Because of our historic refusal to see our interconnectedness with everything, our history is one of insanity, one in which we conscientiously work toward self-destruction. We are collectively dysfunctional. Our state of consciousness and the well-being of our planet are directly related to one another. Unaware of our connection to our environment, we are polluting our precious water and killing off the plants and animals that are necessary for the diversity in nature which gives it the strength and endurance to sustain our planet. As Earth dies, so do we; slowly, from the inside out. However, recognition of our own insanity ushers in the beginning of sanity, healing and a shift in consciousness. As more and more individuals embrace a new consciousness, our planet is compelled to change as well. Initially, with unprecedented, monumental, even catastrophic environmental events, such as are being realized world-wide at present.

Over the centuries, a few individuals were blessed with a recognition of basic truths to which all religions aspire. These truths were then conceptualized within the context of their own religious leanings. Early Christianity spawned mysticism and the Gnostics. Judaism recognized Hasidism and Kabbala and Islam embraced Sufism. Advaita Vedanta arose from Hinduism and Zen and Dzogchen from Buddhism. Established religious leaders felt threatened by these upstarts, which shunned dogmatic dictates in favor of counseling inner maturation as our route to intuitive awareness and subsequent enlightenment.

Over 2,500 years ago, both Buddha, in India, and Lao Tzu in China, who blessed us with the *Tao Te Ching*, recognized our dysfunctional state. They attempted to illustrate the way out of our suffering, but they were too far ahead of their time. Their teachings became modified by subsequent teachers with self-serving agendas which were themselves dysfunctional. Religions embarked upon the slippery slope of becoming exclusive rather than inclusive. Religious leaders began to act as if they *were* God, or at least had the exclusive right to speak on God's behalf. Divisions fostered intolerance and hatred, wars were fought and people became further divided *by* their religions, and even *within* their religions. It became "*my* God is better than *your* god." Meanwhile "*our* God" was abandoned.

Enlightened teachers like Buddha and Lao Tzu did leave a valuable legacy for those who are willing to look beyond the ensuing madness and embrace their simple, empowering message. Spirituality has little to do with an established set of beliefs. It is about recognition of our limited state of awareness, and how to *allow* it to expand within us. Our ego mind is preoccupied with our past, present and a probable future. This artificial, but very practical two-dimensional construct of time, imagined to be moving from left to right across a page, allows us to interact with others in our daily lives but it inhibits us from being fully present in each and every moment, so as to live it fully. A more useful construct of time for truly connecting with our Self in every moment is a three-dimensional one in which we imagine time to move from a single point on a page, inward. Mindful awareness is a blessing which results from being fully present with the wisdom of the universe.

Believing we have "arrived," have identified and accepted the "truth" is inconsistent with spirituality. The more we become our *beliefs*, the further we distance ourselves from real spirituality which exists as a dimension *within* us, a dimension inaccessible through thought alone. The fact that spirituality is gathering momentum in the Western world, where reliance upon the ego mind has traditionally been most prevalent, is quite remarkable. As a result, partially due to the "shrinking" of the world due to the digital revolution which allows us greater insight into Eastern practices, there is an emptying of the churches. We are turning away from externally established rituals and proclamations by those largely unqualified to establish them, and re-discovering the possibilities that lie within ourselves. This "spiritual awakening" is threatening to those who are more concerned with dogma than process, who in response are becoming even more enamored with their immature ego conscious state and becoming more radical in their insistence that it is the only way. Fortunately, as the tension between the two polarities increases, the ego mind *will* give way. The greater the rigidity, the more vulnerable it is to imploding.

I will leave the final word to D.H Lawrence, writing in England in the 1920s (From *Lady Chatterley's Lover* 2010, p. 39). He has the gamekeeper, who is Lady Chatterley's lover speak to Lady Chatterley:

... My God, the world needs criticizing today ... criticizing to death. Therefore let's live the mental life, and glory in our spite, and strip the rotten old show. But, mind you, it's like this: while you *live* your life, you are in some way an organic whole with all life. But once you start the mental life you pluck the apple. You've severed the connection between the apple and the tree: the organic connection. And if you've got nothing in your life *but* the mental life, then you yourself are a plucked apple ... you've fallen off the tree. And then it is a logical necessity to be spiteful, just as it's a natural necessity for a plucked apple to go bad.

6 Closing Remark from C.G Jung

It is equally a grave mistake to think that it is enough to gain some understanding of the images and that knowledge can here make a halt. Insight into them must be converted into *an ethical obligation. Not to do* so is to fall prey to the power principle, and this produces dangerous effects which are **destructive not only to others but even to the knower.**

(Jung and Jaffe 1989, pp. 192–193)

https://doi.org/10.1515/9783110572292-006

References

Ackermann, Andreas (2004) Easy zum Ziel (Easy to Target), Verlag Peter Erd, München/Germany.

Akerlof, George and Shiller, Robert (2009) Animal Spirits: How Human Psychology Drives the Economy, and Why It Matters for Global Capitalism, Princeton University Press, Princeton/USA.

Amann, Susanne (2015) Jung und Unfair (young and Unfair), Der Spiegel 14/2015, Hamburg/Germany.

American Psychological Society (2003) Psychologists Discuss Developing Corporate Ethics, Vol. 34, p. 5 http://www.apa.org/monitor/may03/corporate.aspx.

Banth, Sudha and Ardebil, Maryam Didehdar (2015) Effectiveness of Mindfulness Meditation on Pain and Quality of Life of Patients with Chronic Low Back Pain, Front Psychol. 2013; 4: 1020. Published online 2014 Jan 10. And International Journal of Yoga (July–December) Vol. 8, No. 2, pp. 128–133.

Berger, Wolfgang (2013) Business Reframing, Springer Gabler Verlag, Wiesbaden/Germany.

Bouckaert, Luc (2015) Spirituality: The Missing Link in Business Ethics, chapter in Zsolnai, Laszlo The Spiritual Dimension of Business Ethics and Sustainability, Springer International Publishing, Cham/Switzerland.

Brinkmann, Ralf (2008) Keine Faulen Kompromisse (No Minimalist Compromises), FAZ (*Frankfurter Allgemeine Zeitung*), May 8, 2008.

Brinkmann, Ralf and Stapf Kurt, H. (2005) Innere Kündigung (Inner Resignation), Beck Verlag, München/Germany quotes from http://ergonomie-am-arbeitsplatz.de/innere-kuendigung/.

Campbell, Thomas (2007) My Big Toe – Awakening-Discovery-Inner Workings, Lightning Strike Books LLC, Huntsville/USA.

Campbell, Thomas (2015) 15 Key Discoveries that Led to My Big, Interview with Donna Aveni, https://www.youtube.com/watch?v=5fcKezLW_Q&feature=youtu.be&t=38m18s.

Carmody, J. and Baer, RA. (2008) Relationships between Mindfulness Practice and Levels of Mindfulness, Medical and Psychological Symptoms and Well-being in a Mindfulness-based Stress Reduction Program, Journal of Behavioral Medicine February, Vol. 31, No. 1, pp. 23–33. Epub 2007 September 25.

Cernohorsky-Lücke (2015) Initiativen und Projekte zur Unterstützung einer bewussten Schulkultur: Lebenskunst – praktische Philosophie und Psychologie, Entwicklung von Gestaltungsbewusstsein (The Art of Living- Practical Philosophy, Psychology and the Development of the Consciousness to Create), Journal *Bewusstseinswissenschaften* (Consciousness Studies), Vol. 1/15, p. 11.

Chiesa, A. and Serretti, A. (2009) Mindfulness-based Stress Reduction for Stress Management in Healthy People: A Review and Meta-Analysis, Journal of Alternative and Complementary Medicine, May, Vol. 15, No. 5, pp. 593–600.

Clark, John Maurice (1916) The Changing Basis of Economic Responsibility, Journal of Political Economy, Vol. 24, No. 3, pp. 209–229.

Dalai Lama and Alt, Franz (2016) An Appeal by the Dalai Lama to the World – Ethics are More Important Than Religion, Red Bull Media House GmbH, Wals/Austria.

Davidson, R., Kabat-Zinn, J., Schumacher, J., Rosenkranz, M., Muller, D., Santorelli, SF., Urbanowski, F., Harrington, A., Bonus, K. and Sheridan, JF. (2003) Alterations in Brain and Immune Function Produced by Mindfulness Meditation, Psychosomatic Medicine July–August, Vol. 65, No. 4, pp. 564–570.

Dorji, Tashi (2015) Father of GNH, Bhutan 28, Publication by the Tourism Council of Bhutan.

Dorst, Brigitte (2015) Resilienz (Resilience), Patmos Verlag, Ostfildern/Germany.

Dorst, Brigitte and Vogel, Ralf, T. (2014) Aktive Imagination (Active Imagination), Kohlhammer Verlag, Stuttgart/Germany.

Dürckheim, Graf Karlfried (1976) Meditieren-wozu und wie: Die Wende zum Initiatischen (Meditation-what for and how: The turn to the Initiatic), Herder Verlag, Freiburg/Germany.

https://doi.org/10.1515/9783110572292-007

Dürckheim, Graf Karlfried (1986) Mein Weg zur Mitte (My Way into Inside), Herder Verlag, Freiburg/Germany.

Dürckheim, Graf Karlfried (1988) Durchbruch zum Wesen (Breakthrough to Essence), Verlag Hans Huber, Bern/Switzerland, Stuttgart/Germany, Toronto/Canada.

Dürr, Hans-Peter (2010) Was ist Intuition? https://www.youtube.com/watch?v=ddpO3NglzX8.

Dürr, Hans-Peter (2011) Das Lebende lebendiger werden lassen (Make the Living more Lively), Oekom Verlag, München/Germmany.

Dürr, Hans-Peter (2012) Was unsere Welt im Innersten zusammenhält (What Keeps Our World Together Inside), Scorpio Verlag, München/Germany.

Dürr, Hans-Peter and Panikkar, Raimon (2008) Liebe-Urquelle des Kosmos (Love-Main Source of Cosmos), Herder Verlag, Freiburg/Germany.

Edinger, Edward (1996) The Aion Lectures: Exploring the Self in C.G. Jung's Aion Studies in Jungian Psychology by Jungian Analysts, Inner City Books, Toronto/Canada.

Elkrief, Noah, https://www.youtube.com/user/NoahElkrief.

Enomiya-Lasalle, P. (1977) Einführung in die ZEN Meditation (Introduction to ZEN Meditation), Benziger Zurich/Switzerland. https://www.youtube.com/watch?v=-LG_WxOZ-V4.

Flyvberg, Bent (2001) Making Social Science Matter, Cambridge University Press Cambridge/UK.

Francis, Pope, Holy Father (2015) Encyclical Letter LAUDATO SI' on Care for Our Common Home 2013, www.liveinthemoment.org

Francis, Pope, Holy Father, European Parliament in Strasbourg, on November 25 2014, https://w2.vatican.va/content/francesco/en/speeches/2014/november/documents/papa-francesco_20141125_strasburgo-consiglio-europa.html.

Gaede, Friedrich (2012) Der Gegenlauf – Das Grausame Gesetz der Geschichte (The Counter-Course – The Cruel Law of History), Königshausen und Neumann, Würzburg/Germany.

Gaede, Friedrich (2013) Millions of Christian people murdered each other. What power prompted people to act in this way? Vortrag für die Museumsgesellschaft, Freiburg/Germany.

Gebser, Jean (1986) Gesamtausgabe (Collected Works), Novalis Verlag, Steinbergkirche/Germany.

Geissler, Pete and O'Rourke, Bill (2015) The Power of Ethics: The Thoughtful Leader's Model for Sustainable Competitive, The Expressive Press, Pittsburgh/USA.

Gill, David (2010) Business Ethics 2.0. Beyond Damage Control, Comment Cardus, Hamilton/Canada, https://www.cardus.ca/comment/article/1992/business-ethics-20-beyond-damage-control/.

GMI (2005) GMI Poll Finds Doing Good is Good for Business, viewed December 12, 2012 at http://www.gmi-mr.com/about-us/news/archive.php?p=20050919.

Gordhamer, Soren (2013) Wisdom 2.0 – The New Movement Toward Purposeful Engagement in Business and Life, Harper Collins, New York/USA.

Gorrell, Paul (2010) Business Ethics 2.0, Talent Management Magazine December 2010, pp 16–19, Chicago/USA.

Haase, Michaela (2017) Economic Responsibility – John Maurice Clark – A Classic on Economic Responsibility, Springer International Publishing, Cham/Switzerland.

Hayek, F.H. (1955) The Counter- Revolution of Science, Studies on the Abuse of Reason, The Free Press of Glencoe IL, Collier-Macmillan Limited, London/UK.

Henderson, David (2010) The Coincidence of the Opposites, Studies in Spirituality, Vol. 20, pp. 101–113. doi: 10.2143/SIS.20.0.2061145. http://www.aip.org.uk/docs/aippub_coincidenceofopposites_dh.pdf.

Herrigel, Eugen (1953) Zen and the Art of Archery, Pantheon Books, New York/USA.

Heese, Hermann (1928) Bilderbuch (Picture Book), Fischer Verlag, Berlin/Germany.

Hirata, Johannes (2003) Putting Gross National Happiness in the Service of Good Development, Journal of Bhutan Studies, 2003, pp 99–139. http://www.thlib.org/static/reprints/jbs/JBS_09_04.pdf.

Hofmann, Stefan G., Sawyer, Alice T., Witt, Ashley A. and Oh Diana (2010) The Effect of Mindfulness-Based Therapy on Anxiety and Depression: A Meta-Analytic Review, Journal of Consulting and Clinical Psychology, April, Vol. 78, No. 2, pp. 169–183.

Horstmann, Ulrich (2016) Das Untier. Konturen einer Philosophie der Menschenflucht (Bibliothek des skeptischen Denkens) (The Beast. Contours of a Philosophy of Human Flight (Library of Skeptical Thinking), Medusa Verlag, Berlin/Germany.

Hüther, Gerald (2015) Psychologie Heute (Psychology Today), Vol. 5, Beltz Verlag Weinheim/Germany.

Humphrey, K. (2011) The simple and the Good: Ethical Consumption as Anti-Consumerism, in Lewis and Potter (eds) Ethical Consumption: A Critical Introduction, Routledge, London/UK.

Husserl, Edmund (1935) Die Krise der Europäischen Wissenschaften (The Crisis of European Sciences), Felix Meiner Verlag, Hamburg/Germany.

Jäger, Willigis (2009) Über die Liebe (About Love), Kösel Verlag, München/Germany.

Johnson, Robert A. (1986) Inner Work: Using Dreams and Active Imagination for Personal Growth, Harper and Row, San Francisco/USA.

Jünger, Friedrich Georg (1944) Die Titanen (The Titans), Vittoria Klostermann Verlag, Frankfurt/M./Germany.

Jung, Carl Gustaf (1933–1941) ETH Lectures on Modern Psychology Zurich/Switzerland, Vol. 5, p. 214.

Jung, Carl Gustaf (1951) Good and Evil in Analytical Psychology, Collected Works Vol. 10, p. 886, Princeton University Press, Princeton/USA.

Jung, Carl Gustaf (1971) Psychologische Typen (Psychological Types), Collected Works Vol. 6, Princeton University Press, Princeton/USA.

Jung, Carl Gustaf (1967) Collected Works Vol. 8, Princeton University Press, Princeton/USA.

Jung, Carl Gustaf (1967) Collected Works Vol. 16, Princeton University Press, Princeton/USA (Jung 1967 Vol. 16, p. 352).

Jung, C.G. and Adler, Gerhard (1973) Jung Letters I, Princeton University Press, Princeton/USA, p. 146.

Jung, C.G. and Adler, Gerhard (1976) Jung Letters II, Princeton University Press, Princeton/USA, p. 146.

Jung, C.G. and Jaffe, Aniela (1989) Memories, Dreams, Reflections, Random House Inc., New York.

Jung, C.G. (2009a) The Red Book (Philemon) 1st Edition, Sonu Shjamdasani Editor, Norton, New York/USA.

Jung, C.G. (2009b) The Red Book Liber Novus A Readers Edition edited by Sonu Shamdasani, Norton, New York/USA.

Jung, C.G. A Matter of Heart, Distributed by Image Entertainment, Inc. Directed by Mark Whiteney & Written by Suzanne Wagner. https://www.youtube.com/watch?v=lxXyTrdgJKg&feature=youtu. be https://www.youtube.com/watch?v=oXWIQAiUZUo.

Jungian Center for Spiritual Sciences, (2017) http://jungiancenter.org/components-of-individuation-1-what-is-individuation/., Zurich/Switzerland.

Kiel, Fred (2015) Return on Character by Fred Kiel, Harvard Business Review Press. A version of this article appeared in the April 2015 issue (pp. 20–21) of Harvard Business Review, Harvard/USA.

Kinslow, Frank (2008) The Secret Instant of Healing, Hay House Inc., Carlsbad/USA.

Klebe Trevino, Linda (1992) Moral Reasoning and Business Ethics: Implications for Research, Education, and Management, Journal of Business Ethics, May, Vol. 11, No. 5–6, pp. 445–459.

Knauer, Peter (2002) Handlungsnetze (Action Networks) Books on Demand GmbH, ISBN 3-8311-0513-8, Frankfurt/M., Germany.

Küng, Hans, Leisinger, Klaus M. and Wieland, Josef (2010) Manifesto Global Economic Ethic, Deutscher Taschenbuchverlag DTV, München/Germany.

LaRosa, John U.S. (2008) Sleep Aids Market Grows to $23 bn as Americans Battle Insomnia, Sleep Disorders, PRWeb June 9, www.prweb.com.

Laveman, David A. and Bright, Bonnie (2013) From Seeing the Shadow – The Importance of Depth Psychology in Leadership: An Interview with David A. Laveman and Bonnie Bright for Depth Insights™ June 29, 2013 Bonnie Bright http://www.depthinsights.com.

Lawrence, D.H. (2010), Lady Chatterley's Lover, Arcturus Publishing Ltd., London/UK, p. 39.

Leibig, Bernd (2015) Der Archetyp der Resonanz (Archetype of Resonance) in Jung Journal, 33, Verlag Opus Magnum, Stuttgart/Germany.

Leitzmann, Albert (1910) Wilhelm von Humboldts Briefe an eine Freundin (Wilhelm von Humboldts Letters to a Friend), Insel Verlag Leipzig/Germany.

Lewis, Tanja (2012) Ethical Consumption, First published in P. James and N. Soguk (eds) Annual Review 2012: Global Cities. Global Cities Research Institute (RMIT University): Carlton/Australia, p. 67ff.

Lewis, Tanja and Potter, E. (eds) (2011) Ethical Consumption: A Critical Introduction, Routledge, London/UK.

Littler, J. (2011) Radical Consumption: Shopping for Change in Contemporary Culture, Open University Press, Berkshire (UK).

Malik, Fredmund (2005) Die Verlorene Generation (Lost Generation), ZEIT online December 1, 2005.

Manemann, Jürgen (2014) Kritik des Anthropozäns – Plädoyer für eine neue Humanökologie (*Critique of the Anthropocene*), Transcript Verlag, Bielefeld/Germany.

MacKenzie, Meagan B. and Kocovski, Nancy L. (2016) Mindfulness-based Cognitive Therapy for Depression: Trends and Developments, Psychology Research Behavior Management, Vol. 9, pp. 125–132. Dove Medical Press, Princeton/USA. Published online 2016 May 19.

McMurthy, John (1998) Unequal Freedoms: The Global Market as an Ethical System, Kumarian Press, Bloomfield CT/USA.

Meyer-Galow, Erhard (1999) The Leadership of the Person in Times of Change, VCH Nachrichten aus Chemie (News from Chemistry) August 3/99.

Meyer-Galow, Erhard (2011) Leben im Goldenen Wind, Frieling Verlag, Berlin/Germany.

Meyer-Galow, Erhard (2014) Living in the Golden Wind, Frieling Verlag, Berlin/Germany.

Milgram, Stanley (1974) Obedience to Authority: An Experimental View, HarperCollins, New York/USA.

Müller-Camen, Michael (2015) Management, New Physics and Spirituality, Spirituality and Creativity Congress, Esade, Barcelona.

Neumann, Erich (1990) Depth Psychology, Shambala Publications Inc., Boston, USA.

Nonaka, Ikujiro and Takeuchi, Hirotaka (2011) The Big Idea – The Wise Leader, Harvard Business Review, May 2011, Harvard/USA.

Owens, Lance (2012) Jung and the Red Book, MP3 download, www.gnosis.ord/redbook.

Patzel, Nikola (2003) Bodenwissenschaften und das Unbewusste. Ein Beitrag zur Tiefenpsychologie der Naturwissenschaften (Soil Science and the Unconscious. A Contribution to the Depth Psychology of the Natural Sciences) 2. Auflage 2015 Ökom Verlag Munich/Germany; s. auch Süddeutsche Zeitung 23. Oktober 2017 http://www.sueddeutsche.de/wissen/schlaffor-schung-koenige-der-nacht-1.3720348.

Peale, Norman Vincent and Blanchard, Kenneth (1988) The Power of Ethical Management, Random House Books, New York/USA.

Prantl, Herbert (2011) Wir sind Viele (We are Many), Süddeutsche Zeitung Edition, Stuttgart/Geramany.

Ray, Indranill Basu, Menezes, Arthur R., Malur, Pavan, Hiltbold, Aimee M., Reilly, John P., Lavie, Carl J. (2014) Meditation and Coronary Heart Disease: A Review of the Current Clinical Evidence, Ochsner Journal, Winter, Vol. 14, No. 4, pp. 696–703.

Reiser, Thomas und Schedler, Uta (2014) Francesco Colonna: Hypnerotomachia Poliphili: Interlinear-kommentarfassung (Theon Lykos), Thomas Reiser, Wunsiedel/Germany

Reynolds, F. and Piirto, J. (2009) Depth Psychology and Integrity. In: Cross, T. and Ambrose, D. (eds) Morality, Ethics, and Gifted Minds, Springer, Boston/USA.

Reynolds, Pamela (1991) https://www.near-death.com/science/evidence/people-have-ndes-while-brain-dead.html#a01.

Schiller, Friedrich (1793) Letter to Christian von Augustenburg 11.11.1793, NA (National Edition), 26, p. 299.

Schmidt, Barbara (2015) Erfolgreich führen mit Innerer Macht (How to Lead Successfuly with Using Inner Power), Springer Verlag, Heidelberg/Germany.

Schwägerl, Christian (2010), Menschenzeit (Human Time), Riemann Verlag, München/Germany.

Schwery, Walter (2008) Das Böse oder die Versöhnung mit dem Dunklen Bruder (The Evil or the Reconciliation with the Dark Brother), Königshausen und Neumann, Würzburg/Germany.

Schwery, Walter (2014) Das Rote Buch – Die Sprachlosigkeit von C.G. Jung (Speechlessness of C.G. Jung), https://www.youtube.com/watch?v=fmUnmJUOqI4 (German).

Schwery, Walter (2016) The Mandalas in the Red Book of C.G. Jung, https://www.youtube.com/watch?v=hkHK2gGyIN8 (English).

Silesius, Angelus (1675) Cherubinian Wanderer or Spirit-Realm Meaning and Concluding Rhymes to the Divine Tranquility, Verlag Schubarth, Glatz/Germany.

Singer,Tanja and Ricard, Mtthieu (2015) Mitgefühl in der Wirtschaft, Knaus Verlag, München/Germany.

Soll, Jack B., Milkman, Katherine L. and John, Payne (2015) Outsmart Your Own Biases, Harvard Business Review of May, Harvard/USA.

Solomon, Robert C. (1992) Ethics and Excellence: Cooperation and Integrity in Business, Oxford University Press, Oxford/UK.

Strauch, Inge (2006) Traum. Traumforschung in historischer Sicht (Dream. History of Dream Research), Fischer Verlag, Frankfurt/M./Germany.

Swailes, Stephen (2013) The Ethics of Talent Management. Business Ethics: A European Review, Vol. 22, No. 1, pp. 32–46. ISSN 1467-8608.

Targ, R. and Puthoff, H. (1977) Mind-Reach: Scientists Look at Psychic Ability,Delacorte Press, New York/USA.

Tolle, Eckhart (2006) A New Earth: Awakening to Your Life's Purpose, Published by Plume, a member of Penguin Group (USA) Inc.

Tibet Office (2010) Altruism and Compassion in Economic Systems, Kongresshaus, Zurich/Switzerland www.tibetoffice.ch/news/hhdl_visit_april_2010/index.htm.

Vaccaro, Antonio (2015) Was man von Sozialunternehmen lernen kann (What you can learn from social enterprises), Wirtschaftswoche (Weekly Economic Journal in Germany), https://www.wiwo.de/erfolg/beruf/management-was-man-von-sozialunternehmern-lernen-kann/11499956.html., Düsseldorf/Germany.

Volkamer, Klaus, Streicher, Christoph, Walton, Ken G. (1991), Intuition, Kreativität und ganzheitliches Denken (Intuition, Creativity and Holistic Thinking), Sauer Verlag, Heidelberg/Germany, p. 37.

Visser, Wayne (2010) The Age of Responsibility: CSR 2.0 and the New DNA of Business, The Journal of Business Systems, Governance and Ethics, Vol. 5, No. 3, p. 7, 2010.

Wilber, Ken (2013) The Future of Spirituality: Why It Must Be Integral, Original Recording Download.

Wilhelm, Richard and Jung, C.G.(1986) Das Geheimnis der Goldenen Blüte (The Secret of the Golden Flower), Diederichs Verlag, Düsseldorf/Germany.

Zsolnai, Laszlo (2015) The Spiritual Dimension of Business Ethics and Sustainability Management, Springer International Publishing, Cham/Switzerland.

Zuckerberg, Mark (2015) Sydney Morning Herald, July 2nd, 2015 (http://www.smh.com.au/digital-life/digital-life-news/mark-zuckerberg-thinks-telepathy-is-the-future-heres-how-it-could-actually-work-20150701-gi34sc.html.

www.ingramcontent.com/pod-product-compliance
Lightning Source LLC
Chambersburg PA
CBHW081101220326
41598CB00038B/7178